THE FORCE WAS WITH ME

John Pye

Order this book online at www.trafford.com/08-0477
or email orders@trafford.com

Most Trafford titles are also available at major online book retailers.

Note for Librarians: A cataloguing record for this book is available from Library
and Archives Canada at www.collectionscanada.ca/amicus/index-e.html

Edited by Jill Todd
Cover designed by Mark OLeary

Printed in Victoria, BC, Canada.

ISBN: 978-1-4251-7599-3

*We at Trafford believe that it is the responsibility of us all, as both individuals
and corporations, to make choices that are environmentally and socially sound.
You, in turn, are supporting this responsible conduct each time you purchase a
Trafford book, or make use of our publishing services. To find out how you are
helping, please visit www.trafford.com/responsiblepublishing.html*

*Our mission is to efficiently provide the world's finest, most comprehensive
book publishing service, enabling every author to experience success.
To find out how to publish your book, your way, and have it available
worldwide, visit us online at www.trafford.com/10510*

 www.trafford.com

North America & international
toll-free: 1 888 232 4444 (USA & Canada)
phone: 250 383 6864 ♦ fax: 250 383 6804 ♦ email: info@trafford.com

The United Kingdom & Europe
phone: +44 (0)1865 722 113 ♦ local rate: 0845 230 9601
facsimile: +44 (0)1865 722 868 ♦ email: info.uk@trafford.com

10 9 8 7 6 5 4 3

Acknowledgements

I would like to thank the following people for their help and assistance in the completion of this book:

Katey Goodwin of the Stoke-on-Trent City Museum, for her assistance in locating some of the photographs I have used, which were formerly part of the Staffordshire Police Museum.

Retired police inspector, Maureen Scollan, a former instructor at the Ryton-upon-Dunsmore Police Training Centre, and author of the book, *Ryton Revisited*.

Mark O Leary, whose artistic skills have provided the artwork for the cover and internal sketches.

My son, Adam, whose time and computer skills have eventually pointed me in the right direction.

Jill Todd, my editor, who finally set the record straight.

My wife, Gladys, and also my family, for putting up with the 'hermit in the other room' for so long.

All my ex-colleagues, and criminals alike, who made my time 'in the job' extremely interesting and often very humorous.

ONE

Q UIET PLEASE! EXAMINATION IN PROGRESS, read the notice on the door.

The notice was signed at the bottom in bold black fountain pen with the name, *A Guest*. Following the signature, in capital letters and brackets, was the word *(SERGEANT)*.

Sergeant Guest was the pleasant-sounding man I'd spoken to on the phone, who had invited me along to the police station for my Police Cadet's Entrance Exam, and now here I sat, actually inside a police station – waiting and nervously tapping my shoes against the thick khaki-coloured lino.

Most of my friends at school had been amazed that I hadn't been to a police station before - what with arranging that end-of-term riot and the prank that had left the school cleaner in hospital. Oh God, that letter of apology I had to write.

Dear Mrs Huxley

Following your recent stay in hospital, I wish to apologise for what happened and hope that your head is now better.

Suddenly a cold chill went through me. Perhaps Sergeant Guest had heard of my previous life, if so, I hadn't a chance of getting in.

There was something else written on the notice, just underneath Sergeant Guest's signature, in tiny spidery letters in blue biro. *Balls*, it said, *Balls*! QUIET PLEASE! *EXAMINATION IN PROGRESS, A Guest (SERGEANT) - Balls.*

It must have been a criminal, someone who'd been arrested. No policeman would write that. How did a criminal come to be up here on the second floor of Newcastle Police Station? It was only offices up here.

"Hello, young man, what are you waiting for?"

I sprang out of my seat to answer the policeman with the bold silver stripes on his sleeves.

"Er… Sergeant Guest, Sir… er… Sergeant, is that you, Sergeant… Sir?"

"Sarge'll do nicely, son," he said, laughing, "sit you down. No, I'm Sergeant Haywood. You're after Guesty, are you?" He smirked. "Still, it's not *your* fault."

Sergeant Haywood was a short, plump man who hardly seemed tall enough to be a policeman, let alone a sergeant; still I don't suppose you have to be any taller to be a sergeant, otherwise a superintendent would be enormous… I had to stop thinking stupid things, I had to be serious. Policemen *were* serious. Sergeant Haywood seemed to find everything funny though, so he wasn't being serious. He had an enormous grin and a great mouthful of brown teeth. Under his left arm was a large bundle of documents and, clipped between the fingers of his right hand, was a minute cigarette; many years of smoking had turned two of his fingers a similar shade of dark brown to that of his teeth. A line of coloured military ribbons adorned his left breast pocket, including the blue and white of the Police Long Service Medal. This was one of the tips my dad had found out for me to remember.

"You'll have to wait a few minutes for Guesty, son, he's downstairs practising his limbo dancing... You're here for the cadets, are you?"

"Yes, Sir... er... Sarge."

Limbo dancing? Why would a police sergeant be practising limbo dancing, and at ten thirty in the morning?

"How old are you, son?" Sergeant Haywood asked, tilting his head to one side and smiling.

"Sixteen and a half, Sergeant," I retorted in semi-military fashion.

"Hmm," he murmured, crinkling up around the eyes as if about to laugh.

I knew what he was thinking... I looked about twelve.

On top of the bundle of papers under Sergeant Haywood's arm I could see a handwritten note held securely with a rubber band - tiny spidery letters in blue biro. The word 'balls' immediately sprang to mind. The note was signed. I craned my neck slightly to one side, trying not to be too obvious, as I read the signature - H Haywood (Sergeant).

"Oh, he's here now, son... Alwen, a young man to see you for the cadet's."

Sergeant Guest appeared from the stairway, fresh-faced and not at all as I had imagined him. He didn't seem very old, in fact, quite young. He had the same stripes as

Sergeant Haywood, but no military ribbons, no long service medal, no cigarette, no documents and no brown teeth. He had his full uniform on, complete with peaked cap, and wasn't even sweating. How could he have been limbo dancing?

"Ah, Mr Hibbs is it?" said Sergeant Guest as he bounded forwards, right hand outstretched.

I sprang up from my chair again and shook his hand, trying to appear really serious and grown up.

"No, Sir, er... Sergeant, John Pye... that is, Mr John Pye not Sergeant John Pye…"

'Shut up, you fool', a voice inside my head shouted.

"Oh, Mr Pye, nice to meet you," said Sergeant Guest, smiling at this nervous boy.

This was immediately followed by a loud farting sound from the direction of the office where Sergeant Haywood had gone, and several people laughing. Sergeant Guest grimaced as though he had a horrible taste in his mouth. Using all my self-control my face remained straight.

"Right then, Mr Pye, come through to the examination room," Sergeant Guest said, placing his hand on the doorknob.

As the door swung open I imagined a large room with rows of desks each with a pad of paper and a pencil, but no - just two tables and two chairs. A large figure sat at one of the tables, his back to the door. The figure swung around as the door opened

"Oh reight?" the figure half-shouted, in a most emphatic Potteries' accent.

My God, it was Hibbo, who lived down the road from me.

"Hey up, Pye. Are you joining up too?" Hibbo asked, half-shouting again.

It was as though Sergeant Guest was not there. I felt embarrassed by Hibbo's stupidity.

"Mr. Hibbs, I presume?" said Sergeant Guest, frowning.

"Yes, mate. Another bloke showned me in," Hibbo said, without even standing up.

"Right. I gather you two know each other," said Sergeant Guest, his frown now even sterner than ever.

"Yes, Sergeant, we live around the corner from each other," I stated in my most precise and unemphatic Potteries' accent.

Had my dad paid Hibbo to come and make a fool of himself?

"Anyway, gentlemen," Sergeant Guest said, looking over at us with raised eyebrows, "let's make a start. This is an English test, turn the question papers over and start now. You've got thirty minutes."

No rows of desks, no queues of applicants, just Hibbo and me. We both turned over the papers and a brief scan made me think it wasn't too difficult, but I was still nervous. That was until Hibbo coughed, paused and in his best and broadest Potteries' accent asked:

"Er… Sarge. Does spellin caint?"

How much had my dad paid him?

"Well, young man," said Sergeant Guest with a slight shake of his head, "it is an English exam, so do your best..."

Hibbo didn't make it.

* * * *

Monday, 2nd January 1967 was a wet, dark, cold winter's morning; it was 7.30 a.m. and I was off into the unknown, going on a train to Stafford and then to police headquarters - all new things to me. Would the train be late? Would I get off at the wrong station? I'd never been on a train on my own before. I nervously picked up my suitcase at the sound of an approaching train, only to replace it as a goods train rumbled through.

"Hi, John, where are you off to?" asked a familiar voice.

I turned to see Ian, an old schoolmate, also complete with suitcase.

"Police cadets, a course at Stafford," I replied.

"Me too," said Ian.

Great! I had an ally - we could get lost together. We exchanged interview and exam stories throughout the half-hour journey, both puzzling at the limbo-dancing sergeant, and jokingly wondering if he had a grass skirt. We giggled about the graffiti-writing, brown-toothed farting sergeant, and tried to imagine Hibbo's English paper.

A short bus ride from the town centre took us up to the headquarters of the Staffordshire County Police, which was a couple of miles outside town on the main A34 Cannock Road. The police headquarters had a large imposing front to it. A one-way tarmac road encircled a huge, neatly trimmed grassed area directly in front of the main building. To the left of this was another rectangular grassed area on which I could see there were strange, white painted wooden structures; there were ramps, ladders and fence-type structures, some with large circular holes in them. These were the police dog training fixtures.

The Staffordshire Police Headquarters was also the home of a regional Police Dog Training School, and was recognised as being one of the foremost centres for this in the country. Police officers from Staffordshire would be joined on these courses by other officers, not just from different parts of Britain, but occasionally by colleagues from other countries. They would spend thirteen weeks at Stafford, training their police dogs and learning all the skills that went along with this branch of the service.

A policeman directed us to the cadets' hostel, which would be our home for the next sixteen weeks. Within fifteen minutes Ian and I had been ushered back outside where we met the other youngsters who had also made the life-changing decision to join the Police Cadets.

Left… left… left right left, twenty-one of us; fifteen boys, six girls. We'd only been here an hour and now we were marching. What a sight! No uniforms, but suits, jackets, overcoats - tall, short, plump, thin, but all with spots. Was it possible for everybody to be out of step? Yes, and Rita, who had more spots than anyone, couldn't get her arms and legs going properly; it was as if her left wrist was connected to her left leg and her right wrist to her right leg. Every time she raised an arm, up shot the leg beneath it.

"Left, right, left, right, get those arms higher, they should be in line with the shoulder," bawled the inspector.

Rita was now beginning to take on the appearance of a drunken Nazi soldier!

The cadets' hostel, which was just for the boys, was a dark old building with thick khaki-coloured lino everywhere, just the same as Newcastle Police Station. There was a TV room downstairs with a black and white set in the corner. No one was allowed to stand by the window because it made the picture go all fuzzy. Several tatty armchairs littered the room and a small threadbare rug lay on the floor. There was a kitchen with a kettle and, in the front room, a table tennis table.

The bedrooms upstairs were all different sizes; some had as many as four beds, but there was only one with just the one bed. There was one communal bathroom with four basins and a bath, so if you wanted a bath you'd have to share the room with people using the basins. As there were only two toilets it wasn't long before people started peeing in the basins. We had no say in what room we had - they'd already been allocated. Unfortunately, I got the only single room, which wouldn't have been so bad but for the fact that it was universally known as 'the wankers' room'.

During that initial week we paid our first of many visits to the headquarters' stores where we met the store's manager, Mr Ryan, who was a slim, middle-aged man with slick, Brylcreemed black hair. Mr Ryan wore a grey lab-type coat and had a tape measure permanently around his neck as he measured us all up for various items of uniform. Most of the stuff came 'off the peg' with a few alterations here and there.

We were all given two uniforms complete with a peaked cap with a bright blue band and half a dozen light blue coloured shirts; they didn't have collars and were 'grandad' style with just three buttons down from below the neck. We were each given a box of a dozen separate collars; the only things we had to buy were our boots and collar studs.

During those sixteen weeks at Stafford, I was enlightened to the niceties of apple-pie beds, beds thrown out of the window, drinking, peeing in washbasins, being sick in washbasins, the longest peeing record - 1967 champion, J Pye, two minutes ten seconds - pressing trousers, ironing shirts and bulling boots.

Boot bulling was to take up a large part of my off-duty time from now on, both while I was a cadet and later as a new recruit. If those big black boots weren't polished to a mirror finish then watch out! If, however, you really could see your face in them then you might even get a commendation.

The age-old accepted method of bulling up your boots was, of course, 'spit and polish'. No doubt this was from where the expression came. However, the method of the day was to wrap one of those soft orange dusters around the first two fingers of your right hand and, with the remainder of the duster clutched into a ball in your palm, you were ready for action.

With a tin of black shoe polish of whichever make was deemed best at that time, and the lid of the tin filled with water, you would then proceed meticulously to wipe polish onto your duster-covered fingertips and rub this monotonously in tiny circles onto the toecaps of your boots, interspersed with the occasional dipping into the water followed by more rubbing. The 'spit' had evolved over the years into simple water, which was universally deemed to produce the best result. After many hours of this mind-blowingly interesting pastime, as long as nothing had gone wrong, you could expect gleaming boots and two deeply stained and sore fingertips. Weekends at home seemed to be spent on more pressing and bulling, and then posing for various people my mum and dad had invited around to see, 'our John in uniform'.

We had to make our sheets and blankets into a neat box shape every morning in readiness for the shout of, 'Stand by your beds', as Inspector Gladstone - or 'Gladys' as he was better known - decided whom to pick on that particular day by probing the neat pile to destruction with his inspector's stick. It didn't take long before everyone was sleeping in sleeping bags and retrieving beautifully constructed blanket 'boxes' from their wardrobes, pristine and ready for inspection.

Quite often we would be awakened from our sleep by the trainee police dogs whose kennels were not far from the hostel - once one started then all the others would join in.

Our course was sixteen weeks of square-bashing, sport, law lectures and bollockings, but not necessarily in that order. We had 'drill' every morning without fail and this would take place on the parade ground just around the corner from the cadets' hostel at the back of Mr Ryan's stores and just up from the old Baswich House, which was the headquarters of the Police Driving School.

The drill started off as a frustrating tiresome task with an unruly bunch of disjointed gangling idiots dodging about in an unco-ordinated pack, but by the end of the first month we actually started to enjoy it and began to look so good that often passers-by would spend several minutes just watching us.

I remember around this time that one of the dog handlers, who was on a course, was a young black policeman from the Seychelles Islands. The poor chap had a badly deformed head with a big dent in his forehead. Apparently arrangements had been made for him to overlap his course whilst he had surgery in London to correct the dent. I saw him after the operation and he looked great. I often thought what an experience it must have been for him to come over here and go back to his island town with all these new skills, a wonderfully obedient police dog and a brand new head.

Back in the classroom we were all filling our brains with police procedures, police powers, criminal law, road traffic law, who you should salute, what a coroner was and what the police rank structure was. The list was endless.

The chairs in the classroom were made from a red metal frame with a moulded black plastic seat fitted to it. One afternoon, as I tried to concentrate on why it was an offence to shake a mat outside after 8 a.m., I suddenly found myself involuntarily and violently twitching both my arms into the air, and letting out a muffled 'grunt'. The rest of the class all whirled around to see what the hell I was up to. The visiting lecturer glared at me, no doubt thinking that I was either a troublemaker or that the doctor had let someone with a serious medical condition slip through the net. The truth of the matter, which even I at this stage hadn't realised, was that I had received quite a hefty electric shock generated by a build-up of static in the plastic chair.

At the end of the lecture as the speaker left, no doubt heading for Inspector Gladstone's office to express concerns about 'the young man in the back row', I was quizzed by my laughing colleagues as to what the devil I was playing at. It then transpired that several other people had also had similar shocks from the chairs, and later 'experiments' revealed that the more you shuffled about then touched the metal legs, the bigger shock you'd get. In between electric shocks and all the other things that we had to cram into our heads, most of our time was spent on learning and being tested on 'definitions'.

'Definitions' were the legally worded interpretation of a particular offence, power or piece of law that someone had decided you should know. Each definition had to be remembered absolutely word perfect and you would be frequently called upon to stand up in class and recite verbatim the definition for whatever subject was being discussed. If you got it wrong you would have to do press-ups at the front of the class (the girls would be punished with half measures).

At the end of the course I couldn't believe that my brain could hold so much stuff. We had all been given a little beige booklet, which contained all eighty-nine definitions, and by the end of the course most of us knew nearly all of them off by heart.

It was very annoying when, after spending many evenings on the course learning the extremely long and complicated definition of 'larceny', I was told that later on the next year the law would be changed and the new Theft Act would be introduced, complete with another load of definitions to learn, which would supersede the old Larceny Act. I just wished I could paste it all into my brain over the top of the old Larceny Act and not have to use up any more brain space.

Cadet Course, January to April 1967 (I'm middle row second right)

Passing out parade came. It was Saturday, 22nd of April 1967. I was seventeen years and three days old, and much wiser, fitter and stronger than I had been sixteen weeks earlier. The weeks of drill really had worked. We looked great, perfect, well, nearly perfect; Rita still hadn't quite got the hang of it, but her spots were nearly gone.

My mum and dad came along with all the other proud parents. We stood to attention as Councillor Ash inspected us and then we did our drill display - stunning. We had to do a march past and a salute, which was taken by the Chief Constable, Arthur Morgan Rees. We finished off with a physical training display in the gym.

We had all been given our postings now and most of us had hoped for a posting somewhere near our home. When I was told I was going to Wolstanton, on the outskirts of my hometown of Newcastle-under-Lyme, this wasn't too bad. It was, however, another very new experience.

TWO

"Right then, young Pye. It is Pye, isn't it?"

"Yes, Sir." (Three chrome star pips on shoulder... Chief Inspector.)

"I expect you to be smart, be punctual, be helpful and to learn. If you don't know... *ask*. We've already got one cadet here, and he's enough for anybody."

This was Chief Inspector Harry Selwyn Sturdee Philips, who was an ex-military man with seemingly even more military ribbons than Sgt Haywood.

Wolstanton was a small village with a small police station. It was part of the Newcastle Division where the larger police station was. A friendly PC named Alan showed me around. There was only one cell, and that seemed to be used as a storeroom for brushes and buckets. There was a small kitchen and canteen, a CID office and some offices upstairs. It was an old building and had the same thick khaki-coloured lino that seemed to be a feature of every police building that I had seen so far. I noticed that each room had an open coal fire.

"Who's this, Alan?" enquired the detective sergeant, looking over at me suspiciously.

"Cadet Pye, Sarge, just started today."

This was Detective Sergeant Arthur Pointon. He was in charge of our CID. A real detective, and just like on the TV, just like the French detective, Maigret; trilby hat and belted raincoat.

"Can you make tea, boy?" the detective asked, frowning, as though this was highly unlikely.

"Yes, Sarge, I think so," I replied, using my most intelligent of expressions.

"Right, first job then, and let's hope it's an improvement on Roy."

Roy, who is Roy? I thought to myself.

All the crockery in the little old-fashioned kitchen at the rear of the building had the Staffordshire Police emblem on it in blue. I had just finished pouring out the half-dozen cups of tea I had calculated were required when Alan's head came around the door.

"The CID's had to rush out, so keep their tea warm," he said.

I safely delivered the other four cups of tea, leaving the two remaining CID cups and puzzling as to how I could keep these warm... Brainwave... I lit the grill on the big old-fashioned gas cooker and placed the two cups on a plate under it. Mrs Shut, the cleaner, collared me in the passageway and gave me a great list of daily jobs, which included the dangerous-sounding job of lighting all the coal fires with inflammable lino polish.

"And don't take any advice from Roy, or you'll get into trouble," she said, finishing off her list of instructions.

There was that name again, *Roy*.

On seeing the old grey Austin CID van pull into the backyard, I retrieved the plate of two lightly-grilled teas and placed it on the kitchen table. I watched excitedly as Detective Sergeant Pointon and the giant detective, named Gordon, hauled a protesting man from the back of the van. I could see the man was handcuffed behind his back, and watched intently as they took him through to the cell. There was a crashing sound as the bucket and brushes were flung out.

"Who keeps putting this shit in here?" shouted someone, as the heavy steel door was slammed shut despite the protests of the irate occupant.

"Now then, where's that tea, son?" Gordon asked calmly, completely unruffled by his recent struggle.

"In the kitchen, Sir," I replied, impressed by his calm nature, thinking, That's how I'll do it.

Gordon disappeared into the kitchen... *Crash!*

"Baa-lluddy hell!"

The door burst open, closely followed by Gordon, now not calm at all, his right hand pinned underneath his left armpit.

"What the bloody hell have you done, had a bloody blowtorch on it?" he bellowed at me.

"I'm sorry, Sir, I put it under the grill to keep it warm," I said, backing away, in fear of being hit by this giant.

"Bloody Roy, and now *you*. Grilled tea, whoever heard of grilled tea? Clear it up and make some more."

Recognising the fear in my eyes and seeing the funny side, Gordon's angry face turned into a big grin as he strode into the CID office shaking his head and muttering.

"Grilled bloody tea."

I learned my way around and got to know the staff during the first couple of weeks. I got to grips with a great list of odd jobs as well as learning how to answer the telephone and operate the switchboard, fill in message forms and use the radio. I watched and learned the way some people did things, some good, some bad, and then I met Roy.

"Hello, I'm Roy, Roy Whitfield."

"Hi, John Pye," I replied, smiling.

This was Roy, in full cadet's uniform, but with a big piece of sticking plaster on his forehead, a black eye and his hand bandaged.

"Whatever happened to you?" I enquired.

"Come off me scooter, here in the backyard."

"And you did all that in the backyard?" I said in astonishment.

"Yes," said Roy, "I fell through the coal cellar door. Bike's okay though," he continued as he pointed through the window at a blue motor scooter, which was adorned with seemingly hundreds of mirrors and lights. "I've been off sick for three weeks."

During the next few weeks I began to realise why Roy had such a reputation. He trapped his fingers in the cell door and had to go to hospital, drove his scooter into the side of the CID van putting a big dent in it, smashed Chief Inspector Phillip's best mug, was sick on Mrs Leak's typewriter after having had too much to drink the night before, got bitten by a stray dog in the pound and nearly blew up the CID office by putting too much lino polish on the fire. Roy made me look like a true professional during those first three months. Was he on my dad's payroll, as well as Hibbo?

Gordon had completely forgiven me for his burnt hand - he'd had that many laughs telling people about 'grilled tea'.

"What did Guesty want with you last week?" he asked one morning.

"Oh, just a training day, some law homework, did you know he did limbo dancing?" I said.

"Oh, I wouldn't say that," Gordon replied, frowning. "He is your training sergeant, so I guess he has to go under the boss's door occasionally... but you shouldn't be saying things like that anyway." Gordon's disapproving look turned to one of puzzlement. "You don't know what a limbo dancer is, do you?"

I related the story of my encounter with Sergeant Haywood, and Gordon laughed until he almost choked at the thought of my suggestion of Sergeant Guest in a grass skirt.

It was during my first few months at Wolstanton that I even got my name in the local paper for the first time when I went with Sergeant Cyril Buxton in the big black Austin Westminster police car to a muddy pool on the old Brymbo pit site where a swan had got itself stuck. I waded in and freed the bird, which showed its thanks by nearly knocking me over when I released it. The *Evening Sentinel* newspaper did a little story on the incident, which gave my dad something to boast about at the pub.

During my stay at Wolstanton I went on the first of the many Outward Bound camps that I would have to endure during my cadet's service. This took place at the formidably named Blackshaw Moor Army Camp. Blackshaw Moor is situated up in the Staffordshire moors between the towns of Leek and Buxton, and I spent two weeks in October living in a building that was nothing more than a larger version of my dad's garage back home.

I met up at headquarters on that cold dark morning with all my old mates from my induction course, and we were whisked off to the outer reaches of Leek in Land Rovers and a personnel carrier. Our billet was a pre-war, single-storey brick building with a corrugated asbestos roof. There were rusting metal-framed windows set into the walls, and rows of old, red-painted iron bedsteads either side. On each bed lay a very old and dirty-looking, candy-striped straw-filled mattress with the shape of a person firmly and irremovably indented into it.

In the centre aisle of the building were two, rusty, cast iron pot stoves, each with a pipe leading directly up through the roof. At the side of each bed stood a battered, green-painted metal locker, and the floor was just bare dusty concrete.

The six girls on the course had similar accommodation and, as the fifteen of us boys trooped our way into this stark, cold and barren-looking prison, which was to be our home for the next two weeks, we must all have thought that this was set as an endurance test.

Our first few amateurish attempts to get the pot stoves lit had failed miserably. How I had wished for a few good dollops of Mrs Shut's lino polish! However, the will to live took over and we all fairly quickly became 'pot stove' lighting experts; it was truly amazing just how much heat those small 'dustbins' could generate.

We had to get up for PT at 6.30 a.m. every morning, whatever the weather, and all of us had to jump up and down in ridiculous navy blue shorts and white vests. We'd have breakfast in the canteen along with all the soldiers who were based there, and then go off on some trek across the moors with a compass and map. We'd have to take a big rucksack each and sometimes we had to camp out for the night.

After the first few days, whenever we got back to our hovel in a state of total exhaustion, we found it had now changed in our minds from a stark and barren prison cell into a haven of peace and comfort. The vile-looking torture device that was your bed was, in fact, a place of warmth and comfort; that old straw-filled mattress with sharp bits poking through the cover was, in fact, better than any 'Slumberland', and the sight of all those tired, but cheerful, young faces reflecting with a glow from the cherry-red pot stove made you feel that it wasn't that bad - strange how you make the best of things. At the end of the two-week endurance test we'd all survived and no one had 'gone over the wall'.

My stay at Wolstanton was punctuated with various courses and training days at headquarters, and 'attachments' to different departments. All that training had given me a real appetite for sport, and I found myself called upon for the cross-country and boxing teams, and regular weekend charity performances with the cadets' gymnastics team. The only cadets who could get out of boxing were the girls. Everybody had to box, everybody, that is, except Jim.

Jim was an experienced cadet. He'd done nearly eighteen months and was brimming over with self-confidence, flannel and how to dodge work whilst outwardly appearing conscientious and knowledgeable. He would come up with the most amazing excuses to get out of boxing, often right at the very last moment, just when we were sure we were about to witness his demise in the ring; a court appearance, a dental appointment, a sprained thumb, the dog had died at home and his mum was upset, there were numerous mysterious telephone calls enabling a last-second exit from the gymnasium. Jim used to make the odd appearance in the gym, but only when he was sure the boxing ring wasn't erected. He was six foot two of skin and bone, with thin, white hairless legs dangling from navy blue shorts. Then it happened... Jim couldn't escape. Trapped in the gym with the full boxing ring erected and canvas laid; something had gone sorely wrong with his plans!

Various sweating bodies in different corners of the gym battered punchballs and sandbags, and shadow-boxed. Others skipped furiously. Medicine balls were heaved about and two heavyweight cadets, Les Rowe and Jock Smart, professionally battered each other into a blood-spattered pulp in the ring - this was called sparring.

Overseeing all, and refereeing the so-called sparring, was our boxing Instructor, Mr Brown. He was a likeable former boxer and referee, painfully thin and wearing his usual grey woollen tracksuit with elasticated ankles and wrists.

Jim was hiding in the equipment store, pretending to stack rubber mats and clearly getting very worried; no dental appointment, no dead dog and the mystery telephone caller had let him down.

"Okay, Jim. Gloves on... Let's see what you can do," said Mr Brown with a wry smile.

Everything stopped, total silence, just the creaking of the punchbag swinging from side to side as everyone looked over open-mouthed... Could it be true? Was he going to have to get into the ring?

I dashed off to the canteen to round up any stray cadets who might wish to witness the best entertainment of the whole year. When I returned, followed by a jeering mob, Jim was actually standing in the ring - Mr. Brown lacing up a pair of enormous black boxing gloves, which were fixed to Jim's wrists. Jim looked like a cartoon figure; those incredibly long, thin, white hairless legs supporting a long thin, white hairless body separated by baggy navy blue shorts. His arms were like white strings with great conkers attached. Jim could actually be seen to be shaking, made all the worse by twenty-odd blood-lusting juveniles chanting:

"Jim... Jim... Jim, Jim, Jim."

The bell rang, big Les Rowe - perfect boxing stance, mean look - made his way confidently across the ring towards Jim, who was now already pressed into his corner so tightly that the ropes were cutting into his back. Jim covered up, giant boxing gloves in front of his face.

Thwack!

With one single punch into Jim's gloves, behind which hid his head, it was all over. Jim crumpled to the canvas like a pile of old clothes at a jumble sale. The place went wild, cheering, shouting and whooping. Les was carried out shoulder high, as though he had just won a fifteen-round grueller against all the odds. That was the beginning and end of Jim's boxing career.

Cadets on Parade at the Rear of Headquarters' Stores
(photograph courtesy The Potteries Museum)

THREE

One whole week at headquarters was dedicated to a first aid course on which we all spent hours wrapping each other in bandages, applying splints and tourniquets, learning the medicinal wonders of 'hot sweet tea' and trying to explode 'Resussi Anne' - the life-sized plastic practice doll for learning mouth-to-mouth resuscitation. Resussi Anne also had to endure numerous other indignities throughout the week.

The triangular bandage figured prominently throughout the whole week's course. This was obviously a great medical invention, which we would all be able to fall back on to save many lives in the years to come during our chosen profession.

We frequently went back to headquarters for various other courses and occasionally had to spend a week or two away on an Outward Bound camp or something similar.

Another schoolfriend of mine, Roger Joynson, had now also joined the cadets. Roger had been my best mate at school, we'd done everything together since about the age of eleven, so it was equally surprising that he too hadn't been 'found out' and had actually been allowed to join the Staffordshire Police.

"Another camp, you say, and anyway, where the hell is Oakamoor?" I said.

"Near Alton Towers, the other side of Cheadle," Roger replied.

"Who's going?" I quizzed.

"It's a mixture," said Roger, "quite a few from your course, I think. I went up there last week to help set the tents up. It's a dump; just a field of mud."

"But we've only just done one camp!" I exclaimed.

"Yes, but they're doing mountain rescue, cave rescue, river crossings and that stuff... all the things you'll need in the middle of Wolstanton."

Roger was right, a dump it was. Two minibuses and a Land Rover carted us down through the tiny village of Oakamoor and then whined in first gear up seemingly vertical hills to finally deposit us in a mud-choked, mist-shrouded farmer's field on a grey drizzling March morning. In the field, on a sloping sea of mud, had been pitched four large, but very basic and very off-white, canvas tents; three for the boys and the other one for the girls. There was another, larger, more modern and much more luxurious-looking tent, pitched in a flat dry-looking area. This was the instructors' tent. This field was to be our home for the next two weeks, where we would learn to be accomplished mountaineers, cavers, river crossing experts and much more.

Bob Edwards, one of our instructors, was a young PC who professed to be some sort of survival expert. We soon learned that Edwards had his favourites by who got the easy jobs, or who was allowed to sit in the front seat of the Land Rover. John Bowers, Ian and I were certainly not on his list of favourites.

"Pull these ropes, tighten them up, it's all got to be really tight," Edwards shouted.

We had got one strong thick rope tied to a tree trunk on either side of the river, with several other 'tension ropes' coming off tied to other trees, making the rope across the river so tight it was like a piece of wood. The River Dove belied its name. There was nothing peaceful about it. It had rained solidly the week before this two weeks' camp and it was still coming down. It was a deep, dark, cold raging torrent.

"Right, Jock," shouted Edwards, "you've done this before, show them how it's done."

Jock Smart, obviously a Scot, was a stocky athletic lad, who was always grinning. A big shout of 'ock aye the noo' and 'hoots mon' rang out as Jock removed his beret. We all had to wear stupid little blue berets! Jock folded the beret in half and shoved it down the front of his trousers. A torrent of cheers, jeers and rude remarks followed, including, 'don't get the berets mixed up' and 'Jock's is the brown one'.

Jock was hoisted up the tree trunk, which was some good way back from the riverbank, and after overcoming the tension ropes carefully, hooked his right leg around the main rope and let his left leg dangle down as a counterbalance. With both arms outstretched, he slowly started to inch out along the rope towards the riverbank, pushing with his right leg and pulling with his arms. There was a hushed silence as everyone, aware that their time would come, watched pensively, trying to master what was taking place and realising that one false move could be more than just unpleasant. Every time the rope started to sway, Jock had stopped perfectly still until regaining his balance. A huge cheer went up as Jock successfully made it over to the other side and, as others slowly, but surely, also made it across, the crowd on the other bank grew in number and the mood then changed from one of willing people across to willing people to fall in.

"Girl Cadet Price, off you go," snapped Edwards.

Poor Linda was the first girl to attempt it and received no sympathy from the baying mob. She carefully folded her beret and shoved it down into her jeans - even more disgusting remarks followed.

"You won't get that back."

"I want it when you've finished with it, Lyn."

A disapproving stare from Lyn was enough to silence the main culprits temporarily as she mounted the rope and bravely made a start. Lyn's bottom moved gingerly up and down as she deftly made her way across. This brought a further barrage of rude comments and jeers, including requests from the now accomplished river crossers on the other side, who wanted to come back via the nearby bridge for a better viewpoint.

"No, you stay where you are," Edwards bellowed, "stop being so childish. Right, Pye, your turn."

Beret down trousers, deep breath, dangling leg, and pull. God! Now I knew what the beret was for! This could ruin me forever. Pull and push, pull and push, I was beginning to get the hang of it, out over the water already, it looked terrifying.

The chant started…

"Pye – Pye - won't – be - dry."

Ignore them, I thought. In the middle now…

Twang!

What was that? My whole body vibrated.

Twang!

It didn't take me long to realise that Edwards was plucking the tension ropes like a giant guitar with his stick. Each time he did it my entire body vibrated and I started to sway, I felt as though I was shaking to pieces. I stopped dead and just concentrated on balancing with my dangling leg.

Twang, twang, twang!

Edwards was determined to kill me. Loud jeering started up from the crowd who had already crossed, total silence from the other bank

"Come on, Pye, keep moving," came Edwards' oily sarcastic voice.

"Bollocks," came my involuntary reply.

"What was that, Pye?"

Twang!

"Nothing, Mr Edwards," I vibrated back.

"Keep moving, Pye."

Twang!

There was no way I was moving whilst he was doing that. I decided that I was going to stay on the rope for the rest of my life rather than give him the pleasure of seeing me drown. In the end the twanging subsided and I inched my way to safety. A big cheer went up as I dropped down onto the muddy bank side followed by laughter as Edwards swung around not quite quickly enough to see the two handed V-sign I'd managed to change into a wave in his direction.

"Right then, Brown, let's have you," said Edwards.

Tim Brown wasn't really cut out for this; thin and gangling with about as much co-ordination as Rita's marching. Brownie looked even younger than me, and the worst swear word he was ever heard to have uttered was 'sausages'. He was wearing a thick green anorak that was enormously oversized, baggy canvas trousers and heavy hiking boots and, if he went in, he would never be seen again. Beret in trousers, Brownie shakily positioned himself onto the main rope, but was quivering so violently that he seemed in danger of falling off before he even got out over the water.

"Come on, Brown, don't muck about, get on with it," bawled Edwards.

Brownie was now some twenty feet out over the water, a small white face dragging along a gigantic green flapping body.

Twang, twang!

Brownie's features distorted as the masochistic Edwards plucked the tension ropes.

Twang, twang!

Brownie now appeared to have six eyes, each one wide with terror. He was right in the middle and the raging torrent roared along underneath him.

Twang, twang!

"No, no, please, no!" pleaded Brownie in a high-pitched, quivering vibrato voice.

Twang!

Brownie was now vibrating so much he was just a blur. His counterbalance leg waved crazily and suddenly something fell away from his trouser leg and flopped into the torrent beneath him. It was his beret. It must have worked its way down his trouser leg with the shaking. The beret was swept away into oblivion. Laughter broke out.

"I thought he'd shit himself!" someone shouted.

More laughter.

Twang, twang!

"Don't, *please* don't!"

Twang, twang, twang!

"Don't, don't, no, *no!*"

Twang, twang, twang!

In a desperate panic, Brownie decided to make a bolt for the riverbank. Back arching, right leg pushing, he shot along the rope like a steam-driven caterpillar. All caution and balance were now gone. Only the will to live remained.

Twang, twang!

"No, ahhhhh, bastard!"

Splash!

He just didn't quite make it. Brownie's green anorak welled up to the surface full of air. It looked as if he was wearing a huge dinghy. A small, white terrified face looked up from the centre of the dingy, arms flailing, trying desperately to grab at bank side roots.

"Did he say 'bastard'?" a nonchalant voice asked.

"Sounded like it… beats 'sausages'."

Brownie was excused beret for the rest of the camp.

Edwards seemed quite displeased that his day had only resulted in almost killing just the one of us, but the following day the gleam had returned to his eyes as he shepherded us to the top of a fifty-foot sandstone cliff to enlighten us to the niceties of mountain rescue. Admittedly, it wasn't much of a mountain, but easily sufficient to kill you.

"When am I going to need to use mountain rescue anyway?" I moaned, as I looked up from ground level at my tormentors, who were standing over me.

"Shut up and stop trying to move your arms," sniggered John Bowers. "You've got the easy job. We'll be doing all the grafting."

He pulled hard on the rope that snaked around my feet and around and around the old wooden and canvas stretcher on which my blanket-swathed body lay, pinning me so tightly to the stretcher that I could hardly breathe.

"Right!" said Edwards. "This has got to be really tight, so that he can't move at all."

"No, don't do it any tighter, please, I can't breathe," I croaked as John Bowers, like a true friend, increased the tension yet more.

"Don't want you falling out, do we?" he said, winking.

"Okay," commanded Edwards, "now, this rope must go through the D-rings, like this."

He demonstrated by passing a thick old brown and rather frayed-looking rope through two small D-shaped iron legs that were screwed onto the wooden poles of the stretcher.

I'd been picked on because I was the lightest of the group and because Edwards' previous attempt on my life had failed. I knew what my fate was - I was going to be lowered over a fifty-foot cliff face. I started to wonder how old the stretcher was, the wood might be rotten. Who had assembled it all those years ago? Did he use the right screws? There were only those screws holding the D-rings on, and that rope, it looked pretty old. The D-rings made a horrible grating sound cutting into the sandstone as I was pushed towards the edge. Eleven of the lads had the rope around a thick tree. I could see deep rope marks in the trunk, evidence of where other poor souls had been tortured just for the crime of 'being light'. I was on a slope inching towards the cliff edge, gravity had me, and I was now reliant upon the wood, the screws, the rope, the D-rings and eleven lads - so many factors.

"Lower and stop, and lower and stop!" chimed Edwards.

Each time the order was given, the D-rings grated into the sandstone. My feet were sticking out over the edge now; two of the lads who were roped to a tree eased me over the edge, and I was now upright with my head just popping up.

"Thanks very much," I said sarcastically to the two lads, who were kindly helping me on my way as I slowly descended to the increasingly distant sound of Edwards' chimes.

"Lower and stop, and lower and stop!"

It seemed to take several years to reach the bottom, but I was determined not to let anyone think I was in the slightest bit bothered, despite the horrible creaking sound coming from my right D-ring and the spinning one way and then the other. At least if I did fall they wouldn't have to put me on a stretcher. I recited the definition of heavy motor vehicle, moped, peddler and even larceny, which was the really long one. I was halfway through the *Lord's Prayer* when I finally touched down.

* * * *

It was back to Wolstanton after the camp. Roy had somehow managed to attain the age of nineteen without any really serious injury and had gone off to the Police Training Centre at Ryton-upon-Dunsmore near Coventry, as a PC.

We had a new inspector now, Albert Deeth, an ex-military man, who used to beat out a tattoo upon his filing cabinet upstairs. This was a signal for me to take him up his cup of tea or fetch him a Kit-Kat, depending upon which tune he was playing.

I was now boxing for the force at my weight of ten stone four pounds, which fitted into the welterweight category, and was off to tournaments most weekends and some evenings. Sometimes we'd have an overnight stay somewhere. I'd won quite an array of prizes, which were mostly useful things rather than cups or trophies. I'd often arrive back home late at night sporting a black eye and clutching a pair of binoculars, a tea set or a transistor radio to wake up my mum and dad with:

"I won!"

"What the hell sort of a state was the other bloke in?" was Dad's usual question.

Dad was really proud when I won, and used to boast about it in the pub. Mum didn't like it and used to say things like, 'Do they have to hit you in the face? Can't you have a word with the umpire? You're going to get hurt'.

"It's a *referee*, Mum."

I think Dad didn't go to see me box because he knew I wouldn't want him to see me lose. So when he told me he was going with his mate, Harry, to watch me box at the Victoria Hall in Hanley, I knew he'd finally decided I was invincible.

We were fighting an army team, and I was drawn against a lad called McIntyre. It sounded like a real boxer's name. Mr Brown, my trainer, was the ref. The bell clanged, I edged forwards and jabbed McIntyre a few times - easy! I caught him again and again. First round over and all was looking good. Second round, jab, jab then I caught him a right wallop, he staggered.

"Finish him!" roared the crowd.

Yes, I will, I thought, as I bludgeoned him again, throwing all caution to the wind, Got to win this one. He turned his back on me and covered his head.

"Give him a bike," someone shouted from the crowd.

I chased after him raining blows.

Thump!

Stars appeared - everything was now red - he'd caught me one! My nose had exploded - what a fool... I'd got to finish it, I couldn't see, I was now a raging windmill roaring around the ring hitting out at every blurred image, Mr Brown included.

"Stop, stop!" I heard someone shout through the bloodied fog as I flailed onwards.

You could almost feel the draught as I ferociously whirled around in ever decreasing circles chasing after my quarry. Suddenly I couldn't move my arms. They were pinned to my sides; someone was holding me from behind. Had McIntyre got some of his mates in the ring to help him? I struggled desperately to throw off my attacker.

"Stop! Stop, John!" It was Mr Brown. "Stop! Stop, John! I've got to look at you," he shouted from behind me.

I turned to look at the blurred image of Mr Brown, his white shirt quickly disappearing into a speckled red hue as I blew clouds of bloodied mist all over him.

"I've got to stop it, John, your nose has gone," said Mr Brown's blurred image.

"No, no, me dad's here with Harry Masters. You can't stop it now, I can win, let me carry on," I pleaded.

"No, John, I can't," spluttered Mr Brown, as I blasted him with mouthfuls of blood. "I'm sorry, John, it's over."

Why, tonight of all nights, when my dad had come?

The bleeding stopped after a visit to the hospital. My nose hadn't 'gone' as Mr Brown had said. It was still there, but now a different shape, sort of rugged looking, I quite liked it.

* * * *

One foggy morning in May, Ian picked me up from home. It was Open Day at headquarters and we both had our part to play. We were helping out setting up different stalls and equipment. We'd got to take part in a marching exhibition that we'd all been practising for ages, and I had to do some boxing in the gym - just a bit of sparring.

I'd had a right old time with my boots. I just couldn't seem to get them right. I seemed to have been bulling them up all the previous day. In the end I'd tried to cheat by spraying them with some plastic stuff that was supposed to help you start your car in the wet - well, they actually looked pretty good, but they were still a bit tacky. I carefully placed them in the rear footwell of Ian's newly acquired smart, two-tone, green Vauxhall Viva, put my boxing kit and best uniform on the back seat and off we went.

It was a bright morning, but we kept running into patches of fog as we travelled along the main A34 dual carriageway from Newcastle towards Stafford. We joked about everything and laughed at nothing. Suddenly everything disappeared, all perspective and sense of distance was lost as we were enveloped in the twilight world of a thick bank of fog. The car lurched to the left as

Ian hit the brakes, a keep-left bollard appeared like a ghost and shot past on our right... Green grass swept towards us out of the gloom.

"Roundabout!" I screamed, but I think Ian had already seen it.

There was a loud dull thump as the car hit the roundabout - I had never flown before. We touched down briefly as we crossed over the roundabout and were then airborne yet again as we flew back over part of the road and bounced up an embankment towards a brick wall. As we headed towards the wall, which was now only some twenty feet away, it was as if I had as much time as I needed to take in what was going on. I studied the wall seemingly in detail, and realised that the impending collision was likely to catapult me through the windscreen in the general direction of Stafford town centre.

What a great idea if cars were fitted with belts that you could clip on to stop you flying through the windscreen in the event of an occasion such as this, I thought to myself. I don't suppose it would catch on though, so back to reality, and I decided to half-turn my head and hang on to the back of my seat. As this was a two-door car with tip-up front seats, this strategy was of little use.

Aided by my tip-up seat, the eventual sickening jolting crash smashed me upwards into the roof of the car rather than through the windscreen, and then suddenly everything returned back to normal speed. The wall was, now no more, except for a few bricks on the car bonnet. I slumped back into my seat, mind racing on overtime.

"Quick, let's get out," I shouted, "before it catches fire."

Ian looked dazed and was still holding the now distorted steering wheel as he gazed out into the garden that had never been on view to the public before. He slowly turned towards me and gasped in horror. Ian's expression, coupled with the wet feeling on my face and the blinding headache, gave me the realisation that I was injured. We both kicked open our respective buckled and jammed doors, and exited from Ian's previously shining 'splendid little runner'.

It was a beautiful garden, complete with goldfish pond, dwarf conifer trees and hanging baskets. The back door of the house was suddenly flung open and out dashed the worried-looking male occupant, clad in a dressing gown. The ambulance had arrived before I had finished my hot sweet tea, and Ian hadn't even had time to triangulate his triangular bandage, which he intended fixing to my badly cut head.

We soon arrived at Stafford General Hospital and nine stitches later, through the eye-watering smell of iodine, I could clearly hear my dad's voice giving Ian his tenth telling off in only as many minutes.

"You stupid bastard, what do you think you were doing?"

"Sorry, Mr Pye, sorry," Ian repeated.

"Sorry, bloody, sorry," shouted my dad.

"Leave it out, Dad! It was the fog," I croaked from my hospital trolley, coming to Ian's aid.

Dad kept muttering for the rest of the morning and kept having a go at Ian at every opportunity. I was at the hospital for only a couple of hours and then the three of us went down to Stafford Police Station to fill in some more forms and collect my stuff, which had been recovered from Ian's completely ruined car.

"Come and sign for your belongings, young man," said the sergeant as I followed him through into an office. "No boxing for you for a while with that head," he said comfortingly, "and no marching," he added, with a big grin, as he handed me my boots, which were now no longer black and shiny, but white and hairy.

In the crash my towel must have fallen from the seat onto the still tacky boots and given them a perfect flock coating.

* * * *

In August 1968, I was chosen to go on a four-week driving course at headquarters along with two other cadets. It was a pilot scheme that the force was trying out. I had already passed my driving test, but after attending the course, it would mean that I would be immediately eligible to drive certain police cars after being appointed PC on my nineteenth birthday. The force held only a few of these cadets' driving courses and this was the second one. I think it resulted in some bad feeling from constables who had been in the job years and were still waiting to get a driving course, and this probably was the reason for these courses being phased out.

As can be seen from the photograph of the course, some of the constables who were also on this 'standard' driving course were really getting on in service, particularly old PC Ivor Sturley, who stands next to me sporting his military awards on his left breast pocket. Ivor was the 'most commended officer' in the force with eighteen commendations to his name, but even such a glowing record didn't enable him to get on a driving course very quickly.

It was whilst I was on this course that twenty-two-year-old PC Bob Potts was killed when his police motorcycle had been involved in a collision with a petrol tanker. Bob had been a great sportsman and was always involved in the force boxing. I vividly recall the horror at hearing the news of this tragedy and then seeing the police Land Rover and trailer bring the smashed and mangled remains of Bob's police motorcycle back into the yard by the Police Driving School as we cleaned our police cars during the first week of our course. Bob's parents donated a trophy in memory of their son, which was awarded each year for the best performance at the force boxing tournament.

Standard Driving Course Cadets and Constables, August 1968
Instructors front row. I am middle row second from right

Camps followed courses, first aid practice, more courses, drill sessions, physical training, more courses and then I learned that I was to spend three months at one of the

Leonard Cheshire homes at Penn, near Wolverhampton. Together with another cadet I would work as a helper attending to the very ill people who were resident there.

We lived in a caravan on some wasteland at the back of the main building. It was there at the Cheshire Home that I learned how to wipe noses and bottoms, clear up sick, spoon-feed people and try to make some very unhappy people feel a little happier. I probably grew up more in those three months than I had done in all my now eighteen and a half years.

Two of the residents had electric wheelchairs, which were then really 'state of the art technology', and, together with the staff, we'd regularly organise a race around the passageways inside the home and arrange for all the residents either to have their doors open or to be seated by their door, if they were up to it, to watch the two competitors hurtle by to the accompanying cheers.

I became friendly with a lovely man named Jack Gill, who was severely disabled with multiple sclerosis and other illnesses. Jack had a very broad Black Country accent and I would tell him jokes and funny stories and, despite him being very much older than me and being so poorly, he had the same warped sense of humour as I did. I'd often push him down to the pub in his wheelchair for a pint, and we'd be laughing all the way there and back, and sometimes he'd splutter in his Black Country accent:

"Stop, John, stop, yam killing may!"

Jack wrote a letter to me a couple of weeks after I left, thanking me for cheering him up, and saying how he missed my company. I wrote back to him and was arranging to go over to visit him when I heard that sadly he had died.

FOUR

My nineteenth birthday had now arrived. This was the big turning point in my life, for I was now officially 'PC Pye', which had a rather stupid ring to it. I had to be content with filing and making tea for a couple of weeks in the admin office at Newcastle nick until there was a course available for me at the Police Training Centre at Ryton-upon-Dunsmore. The only bonus seemed to be that I was allowed to answer the telephone with, 'PC Pye speaking, how may I help you?'. I always said this in the hope that no one asked me anything difficult, and would usually end up handing the phone to the civilian clerk, Rosemary, to sort out the caller whom I had managed to confuse so expertly.

Two weeks before starting at Ryton, I met up at headquarters with another three new recruits, all new faces to me and none of them former cadets. We were taken down to Stafford Magistrates' Court to swear our allegiance to our 'Sovereign Lady the Queen', and be sworn in officially to become police officers. My new colleagues were Graham Woodward, a former electrician, Eric Cartwright, who had been a motor mechanic and who would become my friend for many years and Terry

Locket, a former guardsman. We were all to spend the next two weeks on this 'pre-Ryton' course learning law, drill and getting kitted out. Yes, yet another course, but this time I would be handing in my old cadet's uniform and, in return, getting a proper PC's uniform complete with huge helmet.

The Staffordshire police helmet was well known for its bucket-like appearance and when placed atop my still very young, although by now rather battered, face, it looked utterly ridiculous. Inside the helmet was a brown leather band, which could be folded down so that packing in the form of a folded newspaper could be inserted in the hope of getting the helmet to fit better, thereby hopefully enabling the wearer to use his eyes.

Staffordshire Police had just amalgamated with the smaller Stoke-on-Trent City Police Force. Stoke had a really smart helmet with a cockscomb on top, a wide leather black band and a large silver star (as shown on front cover). They even had a night duty helmet complete with a black star.

"Can't I have one of those?" I pleaded with Mr Ryan, the stores' manager, as I pointed up to a Stoke helmet on the top shelf.

"No! All new recruits have to have a bucket. Those are for the 'Stokies'. Anyway they'll all be withdrawn eventually and everyone will have the same - probably a bucket, so get used to it."

Neither the Stoke nor the Staffordshire bobbies wanted the amalgamation and there was a lot of bad feeling at the start, each trying to outdo the other and suggest that their way was better.

So I got my bucket helmet and Mr Ryan showed all of us the method we had to use to ensure that the helmet was placed correctly on top of our heads.

"Bend your thumb," he explained, "and get the tip of your thumb to just touch the rim of your helmet whilst the joint of your thumb touches the end of your nose."

Thereafter for the rest of our police service we, together with probably every other constable and sergeant (the only ranks who wore helmets) in the country, would go through this universally accepted little procedure every time we put on our helmets, without even thinking about it.

Mr Ryan then piled us up further with boxes of trousers, jackets, white cotton gloves and a raincoat. I also got my truncheon or 'staff' as I knew everyone called it. It was a second-hand one, as was most of the kit with which we were issued. Some of the stuff we were given must have been used by Staffordshire bobbies in Victorian times. My staff was very dark brown, almost black, but with a new-looking leather strap attached.

"Lignum vitae!" Terry exclaimed.

"What?" I queried.

"Lignum vitae," Terry repeated, "the hardest wood known to man. That's what the truncheons are made from."

My staff had a big crack throughout its entire length.

"Cor! Someone must have had a headache, then," I said, laughing.

We were also each given a chrome-plated police whistle complete with chain, which had to be worn with the whistle inside the right breast pocket and the chain hanging out and attached to the top chrome uniform button - although every force seemed to do this differently.

"Cuffs," said Mr Ryan, giving out three pairs of shiny new ratchet-type handcuffs to the others.

"What about me?" I said.

"Oh, hang on!" said Mr Ryan, rummaging in a box. "Here you are."

He handed me a second-hand pair of heavy, dull-looking handcuffs with a large screw-type key on the side. They looked like something you'd see at Stafford Castle.

"What's this?" I enquired, half-laughing.

"That's all there is left, so you'll have to make do." Mr Ryan then turned to address all of us. "Right, that's your lot. If you don't get booted out, you'll get more kit when you finish Ryton."

"Can't I have a smaller helmet?" I whined.

"No, that one's perfect," snapped back Mr Ryan.

"Me mack's too big as well. You can't see me hands."

"Well! Roll your sleeves up then. Oh! Here's your numbers," said Mr Ryan, handing us all a large brown envelope.

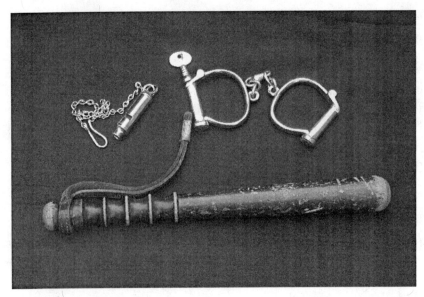

Staff, Whistle and those Ancient Handcuffs.

We peered inside our envelopes and saw they contained dozens of small chrome numbers. My envelope contained the numbers one, nought, nine and six, for I had now become PC 1096 Pye, a Constable of the Staffordshire Police.

Most of our evenings on the course were spent with the four of us huddled together in our dormitory room each using a fork (stolen, or borrowed, from the canteen) with one prong bent upwards for use as a hole bodger for poking through our various jackets, coats and shirt epaulettes hopefully in exactly the right place, so that each number could be fixed into place. Each number had two lugs on the back and a split pin, which was to hold it in place. This meant that each single numeral had to have two holes made, so it all took hours and hours, and if you didn't get the row of numbers straight you'd have to bodge more holes until you did. By the end of the week we had all contracted severe 'bodger's thumb'.

Collar Numbers and 'Bodging Fork'

The course was taken up with more of the familiar pressing and bulling, some square-bashing and plenty of classroom work; the weekend at home was taken up with 'our John in new uniform'.

So to Ryton - the Regional Police Training Centre, Ryton-upon-Dunsmore, near Coventry, May 1969.

I had my own car now, such as it was - a Ford Special. This had a red fibreglass sports car shaped body, underneath which lurked the innards of a 1953 Ford Popular, fitted with what resembled bicycle wheels and an ageing side-valve engine with a 0-57 mph acceleration time of several minutes - it couldn't quite reach sixty!

Arrival at Ryton was like nothing I had imagined. It closely resembled an army camp. An enormous parade square was visible from the road and, as I chugged along the outside of the camp heading for the entrance, a squad of some twenty constables, including some WPCs, marched backwards and forwards, turning left and right. Someone was badly out of step in the back row; I strained my eyes to see if it was Rita, but no! This was an enormous camp training hundreds of new bobbies from all parts of the country. Huge loudspeakers belted out a marching tune, but even above all this and the unhealthy clattering of my engine, could be heard the strident, raucous Scottish tones of the drill sergeant - William McIvor.

The black and white barrier pole was lifted as I proudly showed my brand new police officer's warrant card to the sergeant on the gate, who examined the card and laughed out loud as he showed the card to a colleague and then barked back at me:

"Pye J, Staffs, course 446B, classroom nine, room twenty-two, D Block."

The warrant card was the individual officer's official identification, proving that he really was a police officer. The Staffordshire Police version was a small flip open booklet covered in simulated brown leather with the wording 'Police Officer's Warrant Card' embossed in gold lettering. When opened, it revealed certification that John Pye was an officer of the Staffordshire Police. Mine also contained a photograph of a small boy with a basin haircut, broken nose and scarred face.

No, I Really was Nineteen!

Following the directions given, I drove my car along the concrete roadways that criss-crossed this vast area between seemingly dozens and dozens of single-storey buildings, in the hope of finding the car park. Everywhere I looked there were pipes, thick black metal pipes, some coming up out of the ground travelling along at the side of the road and then disappearing again into the ground. There were as many as four of these pipes in a row in some places. Some were as much as twelve inches in diameter and smaller ones of six inches. Some were covered in chicken wire and some shot up from the ground for ten feet or so and crossed over the road, only to disappear into the ground on the other side. Every so often there would be big, black, metal wheel valves fitted to the pipes. Steam could be seen venting out in some places, and sparrows flapped about in puddles of brown water beneath dripping pipes. After parking my car along with the rows of other wrecks, I made my way towards D Block, laden down with my two suitcases.

The complex had originally been built as a hostel for war workers employed in the nearby factory, which was engaged in the construction of military hardware and had opened its doors as such in May 1943. Consequently, it very closely resembled the Blackshaw Moor Camp where I had completed my two weeks 'endurance test' a couple of years previously. Each block or 'billet' had a letter in three-foot high red paint on the wall, this was 'D'. All the buildings were of the same weathered brick construction as Blackshaw Moor and Dad's garage back home, even down to the tongue and groove red painted entrance door and the corrugated asbestos roof. In fact, the whole building was once again like a larger version of my dad's garage and looked equally as inviting.

I opened the door, half-expecting to see Dad mixing some paint, but was met with a different and yet by now familiar sight, more of that khaki-coloured lino - it was everywhere. There was a toilet block and a room with a bath in it, but none of them were really rooms; they were just separated by red wooden partitions with a gap at the top and bottom. There was one, long narrow corridor leading down the centre of the building with bedrooms either side. It must have been sixty feet long. All the walls were painted with eggshell emulsion and the bedroom doors with yellow paint. Other figures started to appear; all with suitcases, rucksacks and uniforms draped over arms, helmets in carrier bags and biscuit tins containing goodies from home.

I lumbered up the corridor, which seemed hardly wide enough, carrying a suitcase in each hand, exchanging pleasantries with the new faces as I passed by the mostly open bedroom doors.

"Hi... Hi... Hello... Hi... How are you?"

Suddenly there was a familiar face.

"Eric, you made it then?" I said.

"Yes," Eric replied, "I've been here half an hour. Terry and Graham are in E Block. They'll be in different classes from us as well. What room have you got?"

"Twenty-two," I said, making a hopeful face.

I swung open the door to room 22 to reveal my home for the next thirteen weeks, apart from weekends at home. There was an iron-framed bed, an old brown wardrobe, a small set of drawers, a washbasin with a mirror above and, amazingly, green lino instead of brown - luxury! A small tea towel sized mat lay on the floor at the side of the bed and hanging on the wall, slightly askew, was a cardboard 'Inventory Notice', which spelled out the room contents in bold black type:

Bed: 1.

Wardrobe: 1.

Drawers (small): 1 set.

Mat: 1.

There was a signature at the bottom of the notice, *L Randall, Chief Superintendent, Camp Commandant.*

I mused at the term, 'Camp Commandant' and peered through the window at the distant parade square wondering if I might see a squad of goose-stepping SS Officers. I gave the inventory notice one last glance for the presence of any of Sergeant Haywood's graffiti and then moved on to the fire drill notice that hung on the door and was printed in red. It gave precise instructions of where to assemble in the event of a fire. A fire might not have been a bad idea!

The only communal room in the building was an ironing room, which was not much bigger than everyone's tiny bedroom and contained four ironing boards and irons.

It was now half past eleven and we all had to meet in our appointed classrooms at midday in full uniform, so I had some time to sort myself out. I put my things away as neatly as I could and decided to have a quick wash before getting into uniform. I turned on the hot tap. It coughed, gurgled, coughed again and then exploded into life with such terrifying violence that I felt sure it was about to break free from the basin and embed itself in the ceiling. I backed away in terror as a torrent of dark brown boiling water roared from the tap, splashing over onto the floor. Clouds of steam filled the eight by six room.

Protected by a bath towel and my floor mat, I turned off the tap and, after mopping the floor dry with my towel, I put on my uniform.

As Eric and I made our way down to classroom 9, together with other new recruits, we found out the brown boiling water was part of everyday life there at Ryton.

Sgt Neale, our class instructor, greeted us, assigned us each a desk and in his opening speech warned us against trying to bribe him with end-of-course gifts, but stated that if we did he would very much like a pair of spotlights for his Triumph Herald. We were given a timetable with meal times, class times, break times, a list of 'do's' and a very long list of 'don'ts'. There were twenty of us in class 446b, fifteen men and five women, and the same number in the two other classes on our course (446a and 446c). Sgt

Neale drummed it into us most days that 'A' stood for asses, 'B' for best and 'C' for clowns.

There were two other complete courses on the go at the same time, each with three classes; a junior course (us), an intermediate course and a senior course. There was a four-week gap in between each course. There were also other refresher courses on the go, which were for officers who'd already completed eighteen months' service. There must have been three hundred or more of us in total from all over the Midlands and, because of the shortage of spaces in other training camps, there were often some people from much farther afield.

The place seemed alive with dark-blue clockwork-helmeted figures marching in packs from classroom to drill square, from gym to canteen. Everywhere we went we had to march. There was always some shouting voice bellowing out instructions or telling off some poor soul.

The canteen was enormous, like an aircraft hangar. Meals were at 8 a.m., 1 p.m. and 5 p.m. After the silence of 'grace' the thunderous rumble of hundreds of chairs being dragged to one side, coupled with the clatter of knives and forks, and the chatter of three hundred youngsters all filled with new experiences, new problems and an eager ambition to do well, was deafening.

After breakfast it was drill every day for all three courses then one course would be picked for inspection; the two and a half years I'd spent as a cadet had benefited me no end. We were all issued with the same little definition book that I already had and knew off by heart, and I was already an accomplished presser, ironer, marcher and, to my mind, boot-buller, but even from the first day, no one on the camp could believe Terry's boots. They were incredible - gleaming, shining, glowing - words just could not describe. People from other courses would visit his bedroom just to look at them, and to try and extricate the secret from him. Terry, the ex-guardsman, would never fully disclose the secret of how he did it, even to his fellow Staffordshire officers. The problem was, no matter how good ours were, Terry's made it look as though we hadn't even tried, and he seemed to get a commendation at every inspection.

Eric and I, just like all the other students on the camp, spent hours sitting together trying different methods and different polish. It was always easy to spot a Ryton student, even when off duty in civilian clothes, because, apart from the basin haircut being a giveaway, everyone had two black stained fingertips, which would take several 'bulling-free' days to fade. This meant that you were stuck with this little trademark for at least three months.

"Cherry Blossom is the best," someone said.

"But Terry uses Kiwi, I've seen it in his room," said someone else.

The camp stores immediately sold out of Kiwi boot polish. I imagined someone from the Kiwi company coming to the camp to interview Terry for an advertisement and then posters going up everywhere with a picture of him pointing, in Lord Kitchener style, saying, 'Your Boots Need Kiwi'.

Eric had heard from someone that, instead of water or spit, we should use meths - no good! A heated spoon should be rubbed over the toecaps before applying the polish - disaster! Leave half an hour between layers of polish - no improvement! Someone got hold of some stuff for renovating patent leather shoes, you just painted it on. It looked quite good, but then McIvor rumbled it. It was deemed 'cheating' and anybody caught out was put on 7.30 a.m. staff tea duties for a week. Terry then slipped out a tip about 'candle wax'.

"Pour melted candle wax over the toecaps, rub it down until smooth and then just bull with polish and water."

The trouble was you could never be sure whether Terry's intention was to help or sabotage.

I spent several hours that weekend, melting, pouring, polishing and rubbing until I could contain my secret no longer and had to ring Eric.

"Is Eric there, please, Mrs Cartwright? It's John."

"Just a moment, love, I'll get him. *Eric… telephone!*"

"I've done it!" I said.

"Done what?" replied Eric.

"Me boots, you should see 'em, brilliant. I used the wax method and they're absolutely   amazing!"

Monday morning brought a   queue of inquisitive boot polishing fanatics to the door of room D22.

"Bloody hell!"

Most people gasped as they viewed a large pair of boot-shaped black diamonds nestling on my bed in a cardboard box, which was lined with tissue paper.

"Must have taken you years. That's got to be a commendation," someone commented.

Eventually D Block inmates formed up and we marched down to the parade ground for Monday inspection. I was almost tiptoe marching so as not to catch my boots on anyone's foot and cause damage to my masterpieces. We formed up in our now familiar fashion along with all the other classes as McIvor's distant figure, complete with polished wood and brass pace stick, could be seen strutting backwards and forwards, mouth opening as much as twelve inches as he shrieked abuse at late-comers and people whose turn it was to be shrieked at anyway.

"Paaaraaaade... shun!" bellowed McIvor's massive voice from his tiny distant figure, which was supporting his gigantic mouth.

With a form of proud violence I stamped my right foot down into the concrete, thrust my arms down by my sides and stuck out my chin. This was the first time I was actually looking forward to facing McIvor face to face as he desperately scanned his beady little eyes over me, delighting in the prospect of finding some minor fault that he could use to mentally torment me. As McIvor was still some good way off I decided it was safe to take one last admiring look down at the weekend's handiwork; with just the slightest movement of my head I glanced down.

My eyes must immediately have become as big and wide as McIvor's mouth. *'Oh no!'* I shouted inside my head, almost wanting to shout it out loud. My right toecap was now like a piece of crazed and broken pottery; almost the entire wax covering on the toecap had parted company with the boot and was lying rolling from side to side on the concrete like a piece of broken chocolate Easter egg.

"What's this, laddie?" roared McIvor directly into my face, as though he was communicating with someone half a mile away.

"An accident, Sergeant," was my feeble reply.

"Accident, laddie, accident," he bawled, as he crushed the Easter egg with his pace stick.

"Seven thirty tomorrow morning, laddie, staff tea duties."

"Yes, Sergeant."

I wanted to kill him, snatch his pace stick from him and chase him across the parade ground beating him around the head.

* * * *

Sport played a big part in our training and would often take up some part of most of our days or evenings. The summer was so hot - a really good summer in fact. We sometimes finished off the day with a five-mile cross-country run, and one particular day I'd done pretty well and had come fourth.

Sgt Neale was always there cheering on his class.

"Well done, Pye, I'll buy you a half in the bar tonight."

"Thanks, Sarge," I gasped, face like a beetroot.

I was now really looking forward to a long soak in a deep hot bath of dark brown water. I swilled a family of large spiders from the huge cast iron bath and went through the hot tap ritual, which all experienced Ryton dwellers knew well; 'turn on hot tap and retire to a safe distance'. The coughing and exploding was followed by a steady stream of steaming brown water interspersed with the occasional cough. I opened the ground floor window slightly to ventilate the steam-filled room to allow visibility, and then fished out the larger pieces of rust and a spider I had overlooked. After clambering over the side of this gigantic bath, I lowered my aching body into the mire - heaven - and smiled to myself as I recalled someone in class saying that the rust was 'therapeutic due to the iron content'. I closed my eyes and floated back home to Mum's cakes, clean water, ironed shirts and toilet paper that didn't give you a sore bottom.

A trickling sound caused me to jolt back to reality. Had I left the tap running? No! A hand had appeared through the open window and was just finishing emptying the contents of a large bottle of blue ink into the bath. I jerked upwards causing a tidal wave and shouted out at the villain, but he casually shook out the remaining few drops and disappeared as deftly as he had arrived.

The brown water was now black, and I had to start all over again with fresh brown water. This sort of prank was pretty commonplace and mostly taken in good part.

Quite often after our evening meal we'd all lie on our beds with our bedroom doors open, studying. Usually someone would wander in and a discussion over some point of law would ensue; six or more people would cram into the room sitting on the bed, the floor and the drawers, and we'd test each other on definitions.

As we approached the halfway mark on the course and were now 'intermediates', it was time for some practical work, both outside and inside. One of the buildings was very authentically fitted out as a magistrates' court. There was a bench, a dock, seats for the public, seats for the press and probation officers, and even a large coat of arms above the bench.

Outside Practical Exercise at Ryton (metal heating pipes in background!)
(Photograph courtesy of retired Sergeant Instructor Bob Duxbury)

Sergeant Neale had given us all an offence and we had to make up the circumstances, write up a report and then give evidence in the court, whilst he and other instructors would pretend to be solicitors for defence, prosecution, defendant and magistrates. All the students had to sit in the 'public gallery'.

He must have spent some time going through the law books trying to find the most obscure and ridiculous offences possible. I got the offence of a shopkeeper having a shop blind lower than eight feet. Hillary Margaret Timkins, who was always referred to for some reason by her full name, was given the offence of 'disturbing public worship' and Eric got 'selling or exposing for sale English hares out of season'.

We all wrote out our fictitious reports during the weekend prior to the event, some of us putting in daft sounding names and stupid circumstances for a bit of a lark.

"*Call PC Pye,*" a voice shouted.

I nervously strode into the 'court' as a titter came from the public gallery.

"*Silence in court,*" bellowed Sergeant Neale, who'd now also become the court usher.

I climbed into the witness box, gave the oath, announced myself and was duly coaxed through my evidence by the solicitor for the prosecution, Sergeant Neale.

Sergeant Stevenson, a huge, tall bald man, was now the defence solicitor.

"Thank you, Officer, and you measured this shop blind, did you, from its lowest point to the pavement?"

"Yes, Sir," I said with confidence.

"How did you come to receive this complaint, Officer?" quizzed Sergeant Stevenson.

"Several members of the public reported to me having banged their heads on the blind, Sir," was my reply.

"And what was the distance measured between pavement and blind?" Sergeant Stevenson asked as he rocked slowly back and forth on his heels whilst holding both his uniform jacket lapels between fingers and thumb – in true 'barrister' fashion.

"Seven feet, Sir," was my reply as another titter went up from the public gallery.

"Are they all giants in this locality?" pressed Sergeant Stevenson, covering his mouth with his hand.

"There are some very tall people, Sir," I replied firmly.

"Thank you, Officer. No further questions."

Other serious offences were found proved, including Eric's 'selling hares out of season', someone for shaking a mat outside a house at the wrong time of day, someone for being an 'incorrigible rogue' and someone else for having an 'uncovered meat wagon where offal and blood could be seen'.

Unfortunately, Hillary Margaret Timkins didn't manage to press charges for the person who 'disturbed public worship', as she went to pieces at the last moment and the case was adjourned indefinitely.

There was a good swimming pool at the camp, which was probably the only new facility to have been built since the war. We'd get an hour or so in the pool most weeks. Most people could swim already and some of us had done some life-saving. On the other hand, some were hopeless. One poor chap, whose home town was Rhyl, couldn't swim at all and, as he thrashed about in the pool with a rubber ring around him, Sergeant Willey, the swimming instructor, would shout in that echoing voice that you hear in swimming pools.

"Let's hope no one falls in the sea at Rhyl for the next thirty years."

One of the girls never used to make a proper job with the razor before swimming sessions and couldn't work out why her nickname was 'spider'.

We were taught self-defence holds and some judo throws. One of the holds we were taught was called 'the hammer lock and bar', which was a very effective way of restraining a person from behind. We were taught how to use our truncheon to best effect by striking at the shins or breaking the shoulder blade and, if things really got out of hand, by using the 'staff' as a sword to lunge at a person 'end on'.

We were given handcuff instruction and, as a matter of course, taught to restrain a prisoner by handcuffing him with hands behind back, or even in extreme circumstances with a violent prisoner, handcuffed bent over with the cuffs between the legs. These methods were banned in later years.

Everyone except me learned how to quickly snap their shiny modern handcuffs around a struggling prisoner's wrists, whilst I had to make do with being last to finish every time as I unscrewed the key from my museum piece cuffs.

We were taught that our cuffs should be stowed out of sight in the rear trouser pocket with one of the wrist loops buttoned in by the pocket flap. Even our truncheon strap had to be pushed out of sight into the truncheon pocket.

The students' bar, which was in the main admin part of the complex, was quite lively in the evenings. We weren't supposed to go off the camp to the only local pub, The Blacksmith's Arms, and it was quite common for someone to have very much more than his, or her, fair share of alcohol, especially if the definitions were proving too much.

There was always an instructor on duty in the bar, ready to pounce on anyone who looked like overstepping the mark. If anyone looked like making a fool of themselves by getting too drunk the other students would rally around and whisk the miscreant away to their room before they could be spotted by the instructor. On one occasion when it was Eric's turn to get blind drunk, after being safely delivered to his room, he made a verbal disclosure that, as he was about to die, he would leave me the brown wardrobe from his room in his will. By the end of the course I was also due his drawers, mat, bed, inventory and fire drill notice.

Back in D Block, as we now neared 'senior' status, everything was running like a well-oiled swatting and bulling machine, and there was always loud laughter coming from someone's room.

"What's this stuff, Stan?" I enquired, picking up a small canister from his sink.

"Shaving foam," Stan replied.

"What, in an aerosol can?"

"Yes, it's new, dead easy to use and saves a bit of time in the mornings too."

I squirted a small blob onto my hand.

"Hmm, it's good! I'll have to get some."

I spied my chance as Stan momentarily left his room, and proceeded to draw a three-foot long penis in shaving foam on his eggshell wall, carefully replacing the can and disappearing into Pete Hicken's room.

"You swine, Pye," Stan spluttered as he returned. "There's about six shaves there."

This was followed by howls of laughter, including Stan's, as the rest of the block visited his room for a look at my handiwork.

It was probably twenty minutes later, when Stan appeared in my room with an anguished expression.

"I can't get it off," he said.

"What?" I asked, looking up from my law notes.

"That knob on my wall - it won't go," Stan said, shaking his head.

"What d'you mean, 'it won't go'? It's only shaving soap," I said, puzzled.

"Yes, but the wall wasn't very clean and now I've wiped the soap off it's cleaned the wall underneath and left a perfect picture of the knob in clean eggshell."

I dashed up to Stan's room only to find I'd been beaten to it by the rest of the block, who were now all doubled up and screaming with laughter at the huge glowing eggshell penis that was picked out against the grubby background. It took Stan's entire can of shaving foam to clean the wall; it was the only way to remove his new mural. Stan had the last laugh, however, and beamed with pride a few days later when, following room inspection, he received a commendation for the pristine state of his room.

There was much to do on the senior course. We were still expected to attain the highest standards in appearance, so the pressing and bulling were just as intensive as ever, but there was now so much law to learn and so many practical exercises, and an end-of-course exam looming up. On top of all of this, we were spending even more time on the parade ground, learning our routines for our passing out parade.

We were now so good at drill that we enjoyed it. We looked good and we knew it, but the passing out parade involved much more than just being good at marching and doing drill on command. There were two main features. The first was a traffic signals exhibition lasting two minutes, which all three senior classes did together to a rousing marching tune. This entailed us all, in unison, carrying out all the different police officers' traffic direction signals including stop from the front (right arm raised), stop from the rear (left arm out in line with the waist), all the waving on signs including several elements of drill, such as marching on the spot, left and right turns, about-turns and saluting. All this was done by memorising the moves and doing them in time to the music. In 1976, twelve of the students from Ryton appeared on the television programme *The Generation Game* where they performed this routine, which the contestants had to copy. The results were judged by the then chief instructor from Ryton.

The second feature of the parade was a marching exhibition based on the same principle, but this time on the move and without any music or orders other than a starting command. We'd then count out in our heads the number of steps we had taken, before carrying out the next move, such as a left turn, right turn, about-turn, marching on the spot for so many steps and then quick march forwards for so many steps.

This was to last for two minutes, and to start with it was an utter shambles and really hilarious with even McIvor and the class instructors who were coaching us through it, occasionally finding themselves not able to contain their laughter as arms, legs, heads and bodies were all shooting off in different directions in total disarray. We all considered this exhibition to be impossible and started to learn it five weeks before our passing out parade, but come the day itself we had, without exception, got it, and it looked so good.

Most of us had to take our turn at night duty whilst on the senior course; just two nights was all that was asked of us - now it was the turn of Eric and myself. One of us would go out on patrol around the camp, whilst the other was at the reception desk to answer any late night telephone calls. We were to patrol the classrooms and admin blocks, and report back to the reception desk every so often using one of the various internal phones.

As I entered the ghostly gloom of the swimming pool, I looked over to the opposite wall and froze. There was another figure standing against the wall looking back at me. Was this my first encounter with a violent desperate criminal? I lifted my torch and started to stagger backwards, only to see the figure imitate me. It was a mirror. I was looking at myself. I phoned Eric and duly reported the incident; Eric laughed and told me the tea was ready.

It was a pretty uneventful night apart from that. There had been 'incidents' however. Someone from the previous seniors had chased and rugby tackled a suspicious figure seen leaving one of the female blocks at 3 a.m. one morning, only to discover it to be one of the instructors!

On another night the whole camp and surrounding residents were woken up to the sound of a loud marching tune being played over the parade square loudspeakers. Two figures were seen running away, last seen somewhere near G Block. There was hell to pay, what with complaints from the public as well, but the 'crime' was never solved.

* * * *

I would travel home at the weekends in my tatty old car. We usually had an early finish on Friday and, after spending a bit of leisure time in between 'bulling, pressing and swatting', I'd make my way back to Ryton on the Sunday evening.

The Americans had just landed on the moon. It had taken place during those last few weeks at Ryton on the evening of Sunday 20th July. I had travelled back that evening with clouds of exhaust smoke belching out of the back of my car, twiddling the knobs on the old valve-radio to try to get an update on the landing, and thinking, They've just landed on the moon and I can't even get the bloody Home Service.

The last week of the course was taken up with exams and practical exercises. Almost everyone had done okay. Eric, Stan and I had got joint top sportsman award in the camp sports, making B-class top dogs, so Sergeant Neale was chuffed to bits, even more so when he got the spotlights for his Triumph Herald.

The day of the passing out parade came at last. The weather was wonderful; the camp gates were opened up for the afternoon to all the proud parents, relatives, wives, girlfriends and some kids. My mum and dad came, together with my nan, and everyone seemed to be clutching a camera. The marching was spectacular – well, *we* thought so. The exhibition traffic signals and marching were faultless. I've never seen so many ear-to-ear grins.

Passing Out Parade Day at Ryton, complete with Staffordshire 'bucket'

There was a big dinner dance on the last night, for which we all had to hire dinner jackets. I don't think there was a sober person on camp that night. The next day, even without the help of the giant hangover, would have been a very sobering experience. It was time to say goodbye to so many good friends. Obviously Eric, Graham, Terry and I would be bumping into each other depending upon where we got posted in Staffordshire, -but as for all the other faces, this might be the last time we would see them.

I collected all my belongings and bits and pieces that I'd accumulated over the last thirteen weeks that had made D22 almost comfortable, and loaded up my car. I'd managed it in one go when I unloaded on the first day, but now it was going to take me three journeys back and forth from room to car park.

Class 446B, Ryton-upon-Dunsmore, June 1969. I'm, back row far left, Eric Cartwright next but one

We all said our goodbyes and Eric, Terry, Graham and I arranged to meet at reception at Stafford Headquarters on the Monday after our 'allowed' one week's leave. We would then spend a further week at Stafford on an, 'end of Ryton course'. During this week we'd be loaded down with even more uniform and equipment, and, most importantly, we would receive the one thing that we all knew could change our lives forever - our postings. We knew we could be posted anywhere in Staffordshire from Wombourne, near Wolverhampton, to Leek in the Staffordshire Moorlands, or Stoke-on-Trent, and this would be where we would begin our careers as 'real policemen'.

I spent a week at home with Mum and Dad, who were eagerly gathering boasting material, whilst I was wondering where I was going to be posted. I managed a night out with my old schoolmate, Roger, who was preparing for his own Ryton course, and was able to tip him off as to what to expect.

When the next Monday came I was glad to meet up with Eric, Terry and Graham again. There is little doubt that the thoughts of the three of us had been completely taken up with 'to where we would be posted', and now we would learn our fate.

A chief superintendent came into our classroom and the four of us stood up from our seats, me with my arms outstretched well away from the static electric chair legs, not wanting the sack at that late stage. Terry let out a small, but fortunately, unnoticed 'grunt'.

"Good morning, gentlemen," said the senior officer. "I've come to welcome you back to your force and give you your postings."

"Right, PC Pye, you're the ex-cadet?"

"Yes, Sir."

"You are going to Longton Division, part of the old Stoke-on-Trent force."

"Thank you, Sir." I said, but it could have been better.

Most of the people I knew were from Staffordshire and I didn't know much about Stokies, apart from their helmets being better than the Staffs' ones, and Longton was a hell of a place to get to every day - a traffic nightmare. It could have been much worse though; I could have gone to somewhere miles over the other side of county, meaning I would have had to live in digs.

"Yes, Pye," he continued, "Longton Division, but you'll actually be at Stoke, which is a sub-division."

This was much better, quite easy to get to; I just hoped that I would fit in.

As Eric's mum was a widow, they allowed him a posting in his hometown of Stafford, and Terry and Graham both received postings in the old Stoke force area. All very handy for where they lived, so we had all been very lucky, and as we marched over to the stores, I realised I would now be getting a Stoke helmet.

"There you are," said Mr Ryan. "You wanted one and now you've got one, and a night helmet with a black star. Make the most of 'em. There's no doubt they'll be withdrawn soon. They're planning to go over to buckets force-wide with a new badge for Staffs and Stoke."

"What about these handcuffs?" I asked. "They're bloody useless. By the time I've unlocked them to put them on a prisoner he'll probably have run off or died of starvation."

"No, I've no more new ones," said Mr Ryan. "You'll have to make do. Here you are; leggings, for when it's really pissing down - and one of these."

"What's this?" I asked, holding up the iridescent looking, quilted, armless jacket that Mr Ryan had handed me. "Looks like a bulletproof vest."

"No! It's Tropal lining," laughed Mr Ryan. "It goes under your coat when it's really cold. Here you are, a greatcoat."

I was now disappearing under a vast pile of blue serge.

"Cape," snapped Mr Ryan as he reached up to place yet another heavy blue item on top of the swaying tower of clothing behind which I had disappeared.

A cape. I wasn't expecting this and I wasn't really sure what it was. I hadn't seen one before. It looked really smart with two brass lions' heads and a chain where it closed around the neck.

A Gannex mack like the Prime Minister, Harold Wilson, wears, different colour though. One flat peaked cap, one pair of black leather gloves, four blue shirts, box of collars, one first aid book, which no doubt had even more uses for triangular bandages, one war-duties' manual, (just in case of any nuclear explosions), one six-foot steel measuring tape, one pocketbook cover, one stolen motor vehicle book, one wanted persons' book, one red accounts book, more trousers and two more jackets. All this was on top of what I'd had before I went to Ryton. I wondered if it would all fit into my car. Last on the list was another envelope bulging full of chrome numbers.

We had a few more lectures that week, local procedures, byelaws, got to know who our new bosses were to be and spent more hours making little holes in our various new jackets, coats and epaulettes, and fixing numbers.

We would be 'on probation' now for two years. The only thing considered lower than a probationer was a cadet. Even a police dog had a higher standing than a cadet, so I looked upon it as a promotion. When we got back we'd be 'attached' to an experienced constable (our tutor constable) for one month and then we were 'on your own'.

John Pye

FIVE

It was August 1969 and I'd got a couple of weeks' leave
and then it was into the real world. Stoke Police Station
was a faded, but beautiful, Victorian building, the bricks
the same as every other building in Stoke; grimy black
from years of pot-bank smoke.

There were half a dozen stone steps up to the front door,
each one worn with a dip in the centre through the
seventy years of feet walking, running and being dragged
up and down them. Above the doorway, carved into the
sandstone pediment in beautiful, stylised, two-feet high
characters, was the word 'POLICE', together with the
construction date of '1897'.

An archway, which looked more suitable for a coach and
horses than cars, led from the road into a cobblestone yard
at the back and separated the main part of the building
from an annex that was, I later learned, originally built as
the superintendent's house. This part of the building had
since been taken over as council offices.

"Hello, young man," said a friendly voice. "I'm Rodney,
but everyone calls me Bill."

I never did find out why.

"I'm your tutor constable for the next month," he added.

Bill was on a 9 a.m. to 5 p.m. shift just for this first day, so that he could show me around the offices and help me get to know the staff, but after that it was all shifts - earlies, noons and nights. Usually each shift would be eight hours in length. 'Earlies', therefore, would be 6 a.m. until 2 p.m., 'lates', or 'noons', as it was sometimes called, would be 2 p.m. until 10 p.m. and 'nights' would be from 10 p.m. until 6 a.m. The only way you'd get off shifts was for court appearances.

Bill reached over and unhooked a tatty looking sheaf of crumpled papers from a hook on the enquiry office wall.

"*This*," he said, as he placed the sheaf down onto the counter and patted it with the flat of his hand, "is the 'duty pad'. It gives the details of what duty you will be on, and should be checked by you every day. It doesn't matter what you *think* you should be on, it's always subject to change. You may be taken off your normal shift to appear at court, or for some other job, so keep your eye on it."

I nodded understandingly as I gazed at this small square of tattered hardboard with its large aluminium bulldog clip holding the ragged bunch of papers that was to dictate the 'life and times of PC 1096 Pye', for the next few years.

There was a newly built toilet block with a locker room, kitchen and canteen at the back of the old building, and on top of this fairly new extension stood the CID office. The canteen wasn't really a canteen as such because you had to bring your own food with you. Two cleaners worked at the station, Ethel and Elsie, and a janitor, Harry, and yes, there was khaki-coloured lino.

Stoke Police Station in Copeland Street, circa 1969 (just as I arrived)
(photograph courtesy Sentinel News & Media)

"Ethel or Elsie'll cook your breakfast on earlies except on Sundays," Bill explained, patting Elsie's extremely large bottom as she waddled into the kitchen.

"Cheeky monkey, keep your hands to yourself or you won't be getting any breakfast."

"All other meals on the different shifts you'll have to sort out yourself. Sandwiches, soup, chips, it's up to you," said Bill.

The front office was the nerve centre with an ageing telephone switchboard similar to the one at Wolstanton, and a newish looking radio for talking to patrols. The cell passage, which led from the front office, had six cells, each with a heavy steel door and crazed white tiled walls.

We were allowed to park in a yard that was across the road alongside the Copeland Arms pub and directly opposite the nick. We shared this yard with some of the council workers, and there was a makeshift green wire fence down the middle, which split our area from theirs.

The building seemed a maze of passages, steps and corridors. There was a parade room where Bill told me we assembled before each shift. There was a report writing room, which was just big enough for two people at a time, a chief inspector's office and an inspector's office.

Bill looked over at me as we stood outside the inspector's office waiting for a reply to my knock.

"Yes," came the rather sharp reply, eventually.

"Good morning, Sir, PC Pye to see you," Bill announced as he opened the door.

I marched in, helmet wobbling, crashed my right foot down onto the stone floor and flung up an arm-quivering salute. This was Inspector William Holdcroft, 'Wild Bill' as he was called just as long as he didn't hear you. Wild Bill, who was sitting on a frayed, old green armchair at a desk piled with papers, looked up at me over the top of his glasses.

"Right, you'll soon learn your way around. Stick with your tutor constable and you won't go far wrong. Smartness and punctuality. If you don't understand, *ask*..." (I'd heard similar words back at Wolstanton).

Upstairs in the old part of the building there was an admin office, and a snooker room complete with full-sized snooker table. It was only 2.30 p.m., but there was a game in progress. The curtains were drawn and the green baize was brightly lit by a heavy-looking wooden lighting system that hung by chains from the ceiling.

"These are some of the lads from our shift," Bill whispered, "they've just finished earlies."

I strained my eyes in the gloom, trying to focus on the two figures I could pick out, but then, yes! There was a third figure lying prostrate on one of the red leather bench seats apparently fast asleep. Familiar features began to emerge as my eyes became accustomed to the dark. There was no doubt it was definitely *Roy*. I thought I'd seen the last of him at Wolstanton, but here he was at Stoke, now a PC and on my shift.

My recent 'lecture' on the 'duty pad', had revealed that our shift for tomorrow was earlies.

"We parade at 5.40 a.m., so you'll need to be here for just after five thirty at the latest," Bill said.

I hated getting up early, but I had to create a good impression. I'd had a real battle with my mum, who wanted to get up and make me some breakfast.

"No, Mum, I'll only have a cup of tea and then I'll be gone," I said for the tenth time.

"No, no!" she said. "I don't mind… If I get up at half past four I can have a nice breakfast ready for you. You can't go around arresting people on an empty stomach."

"No, Mum, honestly!" I pleaded. "Just pack me something up - some bacon and stuff. I can get it cooked later on at my meal time - it's half past nine now, I'm going to bed."

"All right," Mum said, "now you're sure you don't want me to get up? Have you set your alarm and got all your uniform ready? What about that awful car? Will it start, do you want your father to get up and take you? Ron, you'll have to get up with him, he can't be late on his first day."

"Leave him alone, woman, and stop mithering," Dad mumbled from behind his newspaper.

I lay in bed trying so hard to go to sleep, but to no avail. I tried different positions. I read a bit - light on, light off - looked out of the window, wondered if my car would actually start, counted how many strips of wallpaper there were around the room, checked that both clocks were still working and made sure the alarms were set right. Suddenly there was a fire engine coming down the street with its bell clanging. I sat bolt upright... No, it was one of those stupid dreams where a noise is waking you from a deep sleep and you somehow instantly have a dream that involves the noise. I slammed my fist down onto the alarm clock and sent it crashing to the floor still ringing. I stumbled from bed and accidentally kicked the still spinning clock into the skirting board, silencing it.

I sat on the side of the bed scratching various parts of my anatomy for a short while, as I tried to come to terms with the fact that it really was four forty-five in the morning, and then dragged myself into the bathroom. I'd never realised what a loud noise the toilet flush made before. Oh, the other alarm clock was now going off. I could hear muffled voices from my parents' bedroom as I dashed back to my room to smash the other clock into silence. I then 'clumped' as quietly as possible downstairs in my gleaming size nines. After several more trips up and down the stairs for things I had forgotten, I now seemed all set. No! I'd left all the lights on upstairs; one more trip should do it. I collected the huge sack full of food that Mum had left me on the kitchen table and slammed the front door as quietly as it is possible to 'slam'. My car started okay and I was there in good time for parade. Everyone was there in good time, everyone that is, except Roy.

Vincent Turner was our sergeant and when he came into the parade room he seemed enormous; six foot three and heavily built, with an even broader Potteries' accent than Hibbo.

"Nar then troops, wane got a new un wi us this moanin, young constable Pye, fresh from Ryton and a berra time keeper than Roy. You'll naid a nickneem, theers too many Johns here, they't now answerable t' the neem o Porky, Porky Pye."

And so it was, despite my ten stone four pounds, I was now *Porky*, sometimes *Pork* for short!

Roy turned up at seven thirty with all sorts of daft stories about spark plug leads, punctures and the like. He was whisked off into an office with Sgt Turner. I couldn't hear properly, but part of it was something like, 'they't a bloody weest o' time, they't even late fer nights'.

Bill took me out on patrol, just around the town centre; almost everybody seemed to want to say 'hello' and 'good morning' to us. Every once in a while someone would just leer at us, or make some mumbled remark. Bill would usually tell me the person's full name and address, and add something like, 'You won't get a smile out of him. I had him in court the other week for drunkenness', or 'remember his face, he's a good cat burglar'. *Why would anyone want to steal a cat?* I wondered.

Bill showed me a few addresses that I would undoubtedly be visiting during my time at Stoke, and one or two short cuts through back alleys. We stopped a couple of cars and I had to give the drivers a form to make them produce their driving documents, and then it was time to go in for breakfast.

"Fried or boiled?" chirped Elsie.

"Pardon?"

"Fried or boiled, your eggs, how do you want them?" Elsie asked.

"Oh, fried, thanks."

"Are you really going to eat all this?" she said, looking at me, shaking her head.

I surveyed the large array of items Elsie had extracted from the bag my mum had packed up for me; four rashers of bacon, two eggs, a big lump of cheese, two sausages, a pile of mushrooms, a small tin of beans, two tomatoes and four North Staffordshire oatcakes.

"I'll do my best thanks, Elsie."

Elsie cooked the enormous feast to perfection on a white metal plate with a blue rim.

"Don't touch the plate, it'll burn you," she added as she placed the steaming plate in front of me.

Sgt Turner folded the top half of his *Daily Express* over and looked at the sizzling mountain I was about to devour.

"Dust know, Pork," he said, "I was held prisoner by the Germans and they'st got on that plate my rations fer a fortnight."

I ate the lot.

It had been an interesting day; nothing exciting had happened, but I'd made a start, and after my initiation into how not to play snooker I got home at about 3.30 p.m. I remember when Mum came in from work just after 4 p.m., she was rather quiet and looked a little tired, so I was a little puzzled when Dad came in after work later on and said:

"We'll be getting up with you tomorrow."

"No, don't be daft, I managed all right," I said.

"Yes," said Dad, "your mother and me, and Mr. and Mrs O'Neal from next door, Mr and Mrs Hancock from over the road, your Aunt Lily from around the corner, we'll all be there. We were all awake this morning, so we might as well make a regular thing of it."

"Did I make a noise then, Dad?"

Bill used to take every opportunity to remind me of the need for smartness and punctuality. It seemed that every new boss I met would be giving me the 'once-over', checking the sharpness of the crease in my trousers, my haircut, or how bulled my boots were.

Bill went further with this. He pointed out that your smartness gave you that look of authority and discipline, and that this alone could often give you a psychological advantage in a tricky situation.

"You've got to look the part, a scruffy bobby never gets anywhere," he would say.

We had to do regular point duty (traffic duty) each weekday on certain busy road junctions at peak traffic periods, usually 8.30 a.m. and 5 p.m. These were junctions that really should have had traffic lights. Some were quite easy when you got the hang of it, like the Copeland Street junction with Glebe Street near the nick, which was just a busy T-junction. Others were much worse, like Wheildon Road end, which was a real nightmare – a busy multi-junction; an hour on there and you were exhausted.

One day Bill pointed out a battered old Ford Anglia car to me.

"That's Fred Hales' car. Fred is the coroner of Stoke-on-Trent, a very important man, you'll have a lot to do with him over 'form 12s'."

"What's a form 12, Bill?" I enquired.

"A form 12 is the number of the form you use when you deal with a sudden death. Fred Hales is constantly in touch with the chief constable and what he says, goes." Bill went on. "You'll remember from Ryton that 'Her Majesty's Coroner' should be saluted by police officers, and if you don't salute him, and he's in a bad mood, he'll report you."

Considering the coroner's high status and his regular involvement in road safety, his car was astonishing. It was a complete wreck - a Ford Anglia with rust literally everywhere. Bill pointed out to me that on the radiator grille of the car a small plastic rose was fitted that had a light bulb fitted inside it, which was wired to light up every time he turned the ignition on. This device enabled any constable to spot the distant oncoming coroner and be ready with a quivering salute. Fred expected a salute in virtually any circumstances, and point duty was no exception.

"When you see the oncoming rose," explained Bill, "stop all traffic except the lane he's in, wave that lane on, come to attention and throw him up a smart salute as he drives by."

I got caught with Fred on most occasions on Copeland Street end and often used to think what a puzzling sight it must have been to other motorists as I brought the traffic to a standstill and rigidly saluted the elderly chain-smoking, monocle-wearing driver of the rust-encrusted deathtrap that they all must have presumed was en route to McGuiness's scrapyard.

* * * *

Winter was closing in fast now. I'd done my month with Bill and was now allowed out on my own, although he was always there on hand to help me out and give advice. I'd not been there long, but had been involved in quite a variety of incidents; thefts, burglaries, assaults and quite a few form 12s. Helped along by two and a half years in the cadets, I was now becoming fairly fluent in 'police jargon'. Certain phrases, abbreviations and ways of saying things that meant something to us, but nothing at all to other people, were commonplace.

'You've got to go and deal with a form 12', was a prime example, a 'RTA' was a 'road traffic accident', a 'domestic' was a family argument that was getting out of hand, a 'cough' was, of course, an admission of guilt.

The different types of 'assault' were usually referred to with a nickname derived from the section of the old Offences Against the Person's Act, which was most likely to apply to that particular assault. If you were told to 'come back into the nick, there's a Section 47 in here you've got to deal with', it meant that somebody had been injured in an assault. The more serious types of assault were nicknamed accordingly with the more serious section such as a 'Section 20' or a 'Section18'.

The victim in any crime was the IP or 'injured party', and if you arrested a *D&D*, it was a case of 'drunk and disorderly'.

Any offence that was classed as a crime had to be recorded on a form 34. These were blue foolscap-sized forms in triplicate with old-fashioned carbon paper in between, and which required endless and often seemingly unnecessary detail.

Each 'crime' had to be given a detailed MO, as it was called. This stood for 'modus operandi' (my only piece of Latin!) or 'method of operation'. It was supposed to be how the crime was carried out. Very often some of the rookies' descriptions for the MO were a source of laughter, and the MO was often followed by another police phrase, 'as opportunity arose'.

An amusing example would be, 'removed left-handed man's shoe from display, as opportunity arose'. This would often be followed by another overused police phrase, 'and made good escape'. Each crime had to be given a 'motive'; the motive for sexual offences would be 'lust'. Any description of an offender was never allowed to contain the word 'medium'. If you were daft enough to slip a 'medium' in anywhere you could expect to be called up to Detective Inspector Dodd's office for such questions as, 'what the bloody hell is medium height?' or 'what is medium hair?'.

I had arrested a man for theft one afternoon and was puzzled when the DI told me:

"You'll have to do a 'mippy' for him."

"Oh, right, Sir," I said as I wandered off thinking, What the hell is a mippy?

"Where can I get a mippy from, Jim," I had been foolish enough to ask the CID office mickey-taker.

"Oh, do you want a male or a female one?" was Jim's reply.

Being already used to Jim's sarcasm and immediately smelling a rat, I turned to Dave, the detective, and asked the same question. After an acceptable degree of laughter at my puzzled expression, Dave went on to explain that a mippy was in fact a nickname for the acronym MIPYW, which stood for, 'May it please Your Worships'.

At this point I was still none the wiser as Dave went on to explain that whenever we wanted to remand a prisoner in custody, either because of the seriousness of the offence or to make more enquiries, we had to present him before the court charged with an offence and apply to the court that he be remanded in custody.

Still none the wiser!

"But what's this bloody mippy thingy then, Dave?"

"That, Pork, is how the prosecuting solicitor starts off his appeal to the magistrates... 'May it please Your Worships, the defendant stands before you charged with blah, blah, blah', they don't really say it much any more, but that's where the term came from and it's stuck."

Another police phrase was the word 'cuffed'. Cuffed could mean 'handcuffed', but it was a term also used as a 'police adjective' for idleness or failing to deal with a job correctly. Certain officers were renowned for cuffing jobs to get out of having to do the paperwork, or so that they could finish duty on time.

Some people were such 'cuffers' that they frequently did *more* work by cuffing than they would have done had they dealt with the job correctly. The text in the 'action taken' column of a message form was sometimes a giveaway to a 'cuffed' job with phrases such as, 'advice given' or 'drivers exchanged names and addresses' and 'no injury apparent, advised re common assault'.

The phrase 'the job' was always used by police officers when talking about service in the police force. A conversation with a colleague could often include, 'how long have you been in the job?'. Even former serving officers would be referred to as 'ex-job' or 'retired job'.

One of the oddest things was the way we referred to individual criminals and troublemakers. They were always referred to in any conversation, even an off-duty casual conversation, by their full name, so Dave Woodward would never just be called Dave Woodward, he would always be David Ronald Woodward. If the person in question actually had a criminal record, he would be referred to with his full name, followed by the initials CRO. Dave Woodward would, therefore, become David Ronald Woodward CRO, the CRO bit standing for Criminal Records Office. The term CRO would often be used on its own to describe someone who had a criminal record. 'He's a CRO', would often come into a conversation when talking about a criminal.

It was strange how the worse the criminal was, the more names he seemed to have. Henry Kent CRO, for example, was just a drunk and petty thief, Melvin Edward Kenneth Cooper CRO on the other hand was a prolific safe breaker and burglar. This didn't always apply though, as some people deserved many, many more names than those with which they had been christened.

Often words that were very useful words to use on some official form or record would become a standard part of everyday police vocabulary. Again, even in general conversation, good examples would be, 'frequents' or 'associates', and even the word 'proceeding' was actually used in general conversation and in court, despite the fact that even in the early 1970s the use of such police phrases had already become something of a farce. I have actually heard a colleague giving evidence in court with, 'I was proceeding along North Street'. Why he wasn't just walking I do not know.

It must have been puzzling to any outsider listening in to a robotic conversation between police officers to hear something like, 'I saw David Ronald Woodward CRO the other day. I've heard he's been associating with Melvyn Edward Kenneth Cooper CRO and they've both been frequenting The Bridge Inn. Cooper got locked up for a Section 47 last week... Henry Kent CRO was the IP'.

Some of the police phrases could be quite ambiguous until you became accustomed to them. One good example in Stoke when dealing with a form 12 was the sentence, 'the body has been moved'. This actually meant that the body had been *removed* from the scene, and in those days this was done by the ambulance service.

Form 12s were a very regular feature of a PC's job in Stoke, certainly as a rookie you would find yourself dealing with probably two per week. There was a lot of paperwork involved and sometimes it could take up most of your eight-hour shift.

Fred Hales, as 'Her Majesty's Coroner' for the city of Stoke-on-Trent, was very thorough and was constantly on to the chief constable when things were not done in just the manner he liked. There is no doubt that the public benefited from his passion for detail in the way of compensation to relatives and the alteration of work practices.

One of the main causes of early death in these times would be from an industrial disease caused through working in the pottery and mining industries, which were, of course, the major forms of employment in Stoke-on-Trent. Some of the deaths were often quite gruesome affairs and a first consideration would always be if there were any suspicious circumstances. If there was the slightest suggestion of anything unusual then CID would have to attend and satisfy themselves that there was nothing untoward before 'muggins' could get the paperwork done.

Quite often, in the case of an elderly person dying alone at home, quantities of cash would be found in the house, which would have to be carefully collected, recorded and kept safely at the police station to be taken possession of by the next of kin, eventually.

Such was the case one summer Sunday morning. I had been on fatigues, which meant that I had to slop out the cells and cook everybody else's breakfast, as Ethel and Elsie didn't work on Sundays. I was just about getting the hang of cooking in the fashion that seemed to be required at Stoke, which was to fry the entire breakfast on the metal, white enamelled plate that it would be eaten off. I'd had only one complaint that morning, which was from Dennis, the senior shift PC, who seemed as old as my grandad…

"I don't remember my missus putting these black bits in for my snappin," Dennis had remarked.

Each and everyone's breakfast had to include North Staffordshire oatcakes and melted cheese. If it didn't then you were clearly a stranger.

I had just finished my own breakfast, when Sergeant Turner came in.

"Okay, Pork, there's a form 12 just come in, down at West End, an old lady dead in the bedroom, looked a bit dodgy first of all, but reasonably happy now. CID are down there now. I want you to deal."

"Okay, Sarge," I said, trying to be as non-plussed as possible whilst inside my head I was thinking, Why me again? This would mean working over again and we didn't get paid overtime, we just had to hope we'd get the time off another day.

I got to the house about 11.30 a.m. Dave the detective was there with the mickey-taking detective named Jim. The police surgeon, Dr Wood, was also there. Dr Wood was just an ordinary GP employed by the police to do various medical tasks such as certifying death, examining and patching up prisoners, taking blood samples for breathalysers and that kind of thing. Doc Wood only lived a couple of roads away in a street of huge, rambling Victorian houses, and always had a slight aroma of whisky about him. I climbed the stairs to the bedroom where I could hear the voices. Dave greeted me.

"Hi, Pork, you're dealing then?"

"Yes, Dave," I said, with a resigned expression.

"Another balls-up then, Porky," chimed in the sarcastic Jim - I'd already learned to ignore him.

The old lady lay fully clothed on her back on the bedroom floor. Dr Wood was bending down near her just shielding her head from my view.

"I'm happy," said the doctor, "obviously there will be a post-mortem, but I should say it will be a heart attack."

As the doctor moved away I was horrified to see the woman's face and throat coated in what seemed to be thick congealed blood. The doctor looked around at me and, seeing my expression, spoke calmly.

"Oh, don't worry about this, officer, there are no apparent injuries, this is the lady's stomach contents that have come up, which sometimes happens, and I think she's been eating beetroot."

My God, I thought, visualising the row of jars of beetroot my dad had put on the pantry shelf only the week before, I'm not sure I'll touch the stuff again.

"Right then, Pork," said Dave. "Doc's certified death at 11.05 a.m., we've had photos taken just in case and we've had to move the body about from its original position a bit for the doctor. All the doors and windows were secure," he continued, "and we're happy everything is okay, but there's a lot of money about and no relatives on hand, so PCs Banks and Mack are downstairs starting to make an inventory of the cash. The ambulance is on the way to collect the body, so we'll leave you to it."

"You can write, can't you, Porky?" came the usual expected sarcasm from Jim.

"Yes thanks, getting the hang of it now," I replied, as I followed the three downstairs.

I entered the front room where the other officers were searching for the cash as the doctor and detectives made their way out through the front door.

PC Dougie Banks, who was a senior PC, and PC Steve Mack, fresh from Ryton, were both rummaging through cupboards and drawers.

"There's a lot of cash about, Porky!" exclaimed Dougie. "It looks like she's been hoarding her pension money up; most of these haven't even been opened," he said, as he showed me a handful of little brown pension envelopes. "We're up to £230 already."

There hadn't been much happening that morning, so I wasn't surprised when another officer arrived at the scene to see if he could help out. It was Sam, the panda driver.

"Hey up, need anything doing?" he enquired.

"Well, there's cash everywhere, so we've got to search every room," I replied.

"Okay," said Sam, "I'll start upstairs then. Has the body been moved?"

Being engrossed in what I was doing and only thinking of Dave's information that they had disturbed the body slightly for the doctor, I unthinkingly answered:

"Yes."

I subconsciously heard Sam tramping up the stairs and a few seconds later dived towards the hallway as a terrifyingly piercing scream came from upstairs, followed by an almighty crashing sound as Sam leapt from top to bottom of the stairs, landing at the bottom by the front door and smashing a large jardinière that contained a huge cheese plant. As he lay on his back, his terrified face covered in soil and leaves, he spluttered:

"There's another one up there with its throat cut."

I had to buy Sam a pint next time on noons to make up for my misuse of police jargon.

On another Sunday morning, when still very new to the job, I was told to visit a house on Leek Road just within our boundary with Hanley. The house was in the middle of a row of other terraced houses and close to the railway line.

The chap who lived here hadn't been seen for a few days, and the milkman had called us, as no one had taken the milk in. The circumstances had a familiar ring to them. I tried the usual knocking on windows and doors, but to no avail, so eventually, on the second attempt, I shouldered open the rickety front door. The now familiar, sickly sweet smell of death met my nostrils as the door swung open revealing a tiny and gloomy hallway. Evidence of a lonely, elderly person was everywhere; faded family photographs, clutter, dead flowers. I pushed open the door to the darkened front room where the heavy dust-laden curtains were pulled together and switched on the light to reveal a horrifying scene.

The long-since dead man lay on the carpet, a thin and shrivelled excuse for a human being. Red spatters of blood covered most areas of the previously pale yellow wallpaper, and some splatters could even be seen on the lampshade. The body lay on its back staring wide-eyed and open-mouthed at the ceiling. Around the corpse was a black outline vaguely in the same shape of the body and stretching some two to three feet out around it. On the left wrist could be seen a blackened indentation.

As I moved a little closer my foot squelched down into a part of the black outline - this was blood, thick congealed blood. The only recognisable red blood was that which had been spattered around by the man in his death throes. A razor blade could be seen still pinched between the fingers of his right hand and a brief pencil written note stood helpfully on the mantle shelf against the clock explaining how he, 'could not go on any longer'. The black indentation in his wrist was, of course, the site where he had lacerated his veins and arteries, firstly starting with tentative cuts and building the courage to cut deeper. My radio report brought the attendance of the CID, Doc Wood, the police photographer, the sergeant and the inspector, and then, at last, I was left to get on with the paperwork.

It was fairly late on before the ambulance service arrived to take away the body to the city mortuary and, as we'd had some difficulty tracing a relative who was able to perform the identification for us, I was relieved to hear that a cousin had finally been found in the nearby town of Newcastle-under-Lyme, who was willing to come over and complete the task for us. I arrived back at the station to be told that, as it was a Sunday, there would be no mortuary staff on duty and it was, therefore, my job to collect the keys from Hanley Police Station, open up the mortuary and get the relative to identify the body.

It all sounded very daunting and so, in company with the relative, who was a middle-aged and rather nervous gentleman, and Policewoman Jacky, I made my way over to Hanley nick. Pulling up on the forecourt, I dashed inside and found the ageing station sergeant.

"Sarge, PC Pye from Stoke. I've got to do an ID at the mortuary, so I need the keys."

"Yes," said the sergeant, "I've been told to expect you. Have you done this before?" he asked, furrowing his brow.

"No, Sarge, I don't even know where it is."

"Right!" replied the sergeant. "Here's the keys," he said, handing me a huge bunch of large keys on a giant steel ring weighted down with a massive lump of shiny lead. "Each key is numbered and you just look for the corresponding number on the door. The rest of it is simple," he finished with a wry smile.

Following the directions and thankful of such intricate and helpful advice (I don't think!), I drove around the back of the police station and there, very thoughtfully positioned right next door to the abattoir, stood the dilapidated, crumbling Victorian building that served as the mortuary for the City of Stoke-on-Trent. Jacky asked the relative to sit tight in the car whilst we got things ready for him. Spying the number 'one' on the outside door, I rummaged through the bunch to find the right key. The tall, green painted door swung open easily and we found ourselves in a small porch with another locked door, this one with the number 'two' on it. After another four doors and keys, and a brief inspection of a couple of offices that were not what we were looking for, we found ourselves in a stark, white-tiled, lofty echoing room; four massive cream fridge-type doors, seven-feet high, stood against one wall, making a constant unnerving humming sound.

In the centre of the room stood a huge, white, crazed porcelain 'slab'. In a corner against a wall rested a heavy-duty looking, metal surgical trolley, a large metal table was in another corner and a galvanized metal bucket nearby with a wooden handled mop poking from it. Two pairs of white rubber wellingtons lay near the bucket.

"What do we do now, Jacky, any clues?" I asked.

"No," came Jacky's shaky reply. "I've not been here before either, and wish I wasn't here now."

"He's got to be here somewhere," I said as I pulled downwards on one of the chrome fridge handles.

The massive door swung silently, but heavily, open and was followed by a small cloud of cold air vapour, which tumbled out and down towards our feet. Inside the fridge were four sturdy looking tubular metal trays mounted one above the other, each one two feet or so apart. Lying on the top three trays was a human, corpse shaped, white linen swathed cocoon.

"Oh, God," I said, "which one's ours? I mean, how are we supposed to know?"

"I don't know," Jacky said with a slightly trembling voice, "but surely they're labelled?"

"Yes, they must be," I agreed, and peered down inside the fridge alongside one of the cocoons. "Yes, I think you're right, there's something tied around this one's feet." I tugged at the tray and it rolled out effortlessly with a metal castor sound similar to my old roller skates. The cocoon's head now stuck out of the fridge. "That's it!" I exclaimed, delighted at the fact that my discovery of how to pull a human body from a fridge appeared to be the nicest thing that had happened all day.

Confident that we would soon be able to complete our task, we stood either side of the tray and rolled it out. It rolled out with ease until just about three feet was left inside the fridge then suddenly, and without warning, crashed forwards and down. Both Jacky and I dived for our very lives as the immensely heavy metal tray, on which lay a twelve or thirteen-stone body, crashed to the ground. We both looked at each other open-mouthed, wide-eyed, in total disbelief and despair. It was a full minute before we started to pull ourselves from the suspended animation in which we seemed to be trapped. The reality was dawning. We should have wheeled the metal trolley under the tray and then jacked it up to the right height with the little hydraulic arm on the side, and then pulled the tray out onto the trolley. Too late for that now though, the body of who knows who lay on the floor and had partially parted company with his metal tray.

The only thing that was now just barely humanly possible for the two of us was to load the body back onto the tray and slot it back into the remaining lower empty slot, and after a huge effort this is what we managed to do. After all our efforts, when we opened the fridge next to the one where we had been playing 'musical bodies' we discovered that our suicide victim was just lying there without a cocoon and was instantly recognisable. It was only the bodies that had had a post-mortem carried out that had been 'cocooned'. As our man had been delivered by the ambulance on a Sunday when there were no mortuary staff he had simply been put into the fridge to await attention the following day.

We completed our task in a rather unsatisfactory way by merely pulling the front of the tray partially out of the fridge and asking the relative to come in and complete the identification, a task that the poor man duly carried out.

It wasn't until we got back to Stoke nick that we discovered that we should have used the trolley to roll the tray through a small aperture in the wall into another special room where we should have covered the corpse in a dignified manner with the purple robe provided and then invited the relative in. We both spent a few anguished days wondering if any of the mortuary staff would notice that someone had been moving bodies around.

* * * *

Once in a while I would hear from my old schoolfriend, Roger; whilst I had been lucky with my posting to Stoke, allowing me to live at home with my parents, poor Roger had drawn the short straw and had been posted to work at Burton-on-Trent, which was over forty miles from Newcastle. This had completely changed his life around. He had to live in digs in Burton and his landlady was really horrible to him.

Roger told me that on his first morning he should have been at the police station for 5.40 a.m. and he had overslept. He got dressed in his full uniform in a rush, and then ran out of the house into the street in a panic and suddenly realised he didn't know where the police station was. Imagine the dumbfounded look on the face of the passer-by when a uniformed policeman ran up to him asking for directions to the police station.

I'd got the hang of getting up quietly for earlies now and so far I'd always been in good time. Poor old Roy, on the other hand, was just hopeless; he really was late every day. He'd moved out of his parents' home and was living with a big fat girl over Longton way. There were all sorts of jokes as to why he was late, like him being trapped beneath her. As he had no telephone, we'd sometimes have to ring Longton Police to go and knock him up.

It was just after 5.30 a.m. one frosty winter's morning as I pulled into the car park, manoeuvring right up to the green wire fence. It was a bitterly cold morning and still very dark. A council gritting wagon trundled past, amber light flashing, spraying rock salt everywhere except on the road. I waved to the driver and made my way up the front steps and into the nick. I couldn't believe my eyes - there was Roy! Not only was he not late, he was actually early!

"What are you doing here, Roy? Have you changed shift? Are you on nights?" I joked.

"Very funny," Roy said, sneering a little with annoyance. "No, actually I made a special effort, I hitched a lift on the gritting wagon, so I was here for twenty-five past five."

Sergeant Turner strode into the parade room holding the duty pad in his hand. He staggered against the wall in emphasised sarcastic astonishment clutching his heart as he saw Roy.

"It's a bloody mirage, I dunner beleeeve it," he said.

"Special effort, Sarge, got a lift on the gritting wagon!" Roy proudly exclaimed.

Sergeant Turner flipped the pages of the duty pad back and forth squinting over the top of his glasses and furrowing his brow.

"Well, Roy, special effort it certainly is, because you are three and a half hours early, you shouldn't be here till nine-they't in court."

Roy went up to the snooker room for a sleep until he was due to start at nine, but I think the laughter probably kept him awake.

The meals on the noon shift would often be fish and chips from one of the local chippies, but watch out if Wild Bill caught you openly carrying your goodies in uniform. You could even get put on a charge for something as simple as this.

I soon realised how we overcame this problem when PC Dougie Banks returned to the station for his meal break with steam issuing from the two small vent holes in his helmet. Dougie removed his helmet to reveal a newspaper package of fish, chips and mushy peas.

There was a large wet-fish wholesaler in Welch Street in the town centre and we'd often have dealings with the owners and employees. We used to buy fish from them really cheaply, so it wasn't unusual to see someone unloading a helmet full of wet fish to take home.

I recall seeing the giant Sergeant Turner walking back towards the nick along Glebe Street one evening just before Christmas. He was wearing his helmet and cape, and I thought that he looked even more rotund than usual. As he drew closer I could clearly see two legs of a large turkey poking through the front of his cape. After unloading his cape he then emptied his helmet of four large pieces of finny haddock.

* * * *

I was now getting into the swing of things with the shifts. I really enjoyed nights; there was always the chance that something interesting might happen. I got on well with the rest of the shift and had had quite a few arrests by now, mostly for everyday stuff like drunkenness and fighting.

We were in the depths of a really cold winter. I'd never realised just how cold it could be in winter at night and now I really appreciated all that cold weather uniform that Mr Ryan, the stores' manager, had heaped upon me.

I was on a town centre patrol. There could be as many as six constables patrolling the town centre on nights, each with a different beat to look after. I was on 'number one' beat and my radio call sign was 'Sierra One', the police station call sign being 'Lima Alpha'. Correct radio procedure had to be followed at all times. This meant that you must always use your full call sign and always refer to the police station by its full call sign. At the end of each transmission you had to use the word 'over', indicating you had finished speaking.

It had been a really quiet night. I'd had to turf someone out of the Talbot pub, and I'd been sent off my beat to deal with a domestic in Water Street just outside the town centre. A bloke had been having a right argument with his missus over him coming in drunk, and the neighbours had called the police. So there I was, not yet twenty and looking about fifteen, advising these people who were the same age as my mum and dad how to behave, and telling the bloke that it was about time he grew up. Anyway, 'all quiet on departure' and back to the town centre.

As I came out of the house I spotted Bill waiting in the shadows across the road. He was still keeping an eye on me.

"Okay, Pork, you seemed to handle that all right," he said.

We strolled back towards the town centre together chatting and it was apparent that Bill must have been listening outside the window, as he seemed to know everything that had gone on. We separated on to our different beats as we neared Church Street and it must have been just after four thirty as I strolled alone along South Wolfe Street.

There was a big post office there, a beautiful old building entitled 'Majestic Chambers', which was carved into the stonework over the main door. All the windows, which were of the small mullion type, were opaque, apart from one. This, Bill had pointed out to me, was a special window designed for no other reason than for the night duty policeman to look through. The windowpane was the same as the others, but the centre of it was specially polished in a circle, so that we could look through. It was of course known as, 'the policeman's window'.

The window gave you direct line of sight to a small mirror on the ceiling through which you could see the big safe. It was supposed to be checked several times on nights. Each time I approached the policeman's window my imagination would race, wondering what I would do if I saw a shadowy figure sticking the gelignite onto the safe, ready to 'blow it'. It never did happen.

It was so cold that night that I must have been wearing nearly all my uniform. Two pairs of socks, boots, trousers, a vest, shirt, pullover, jacket, the Tropal lining that I had thought was a bullet-proof vest, greatcoat, helmet, gloves and a pair of long johns. Everybody wore long johns on nights in winter, but nobody ever admitted to it - they were really warm!

I was further laden down with my big rubber torch, my staff, handcuffs and my two radios. One of the radios was for receiving messages and you would wear this clipped to your lapel; the other was for transmitting, which you'd keep in your pocket. It had a button on the side, which you pressed when you wanted to speak, and a little spring-loaded aerial would shoot up, which you'd push back in when you'd finished. I was only ten stone four pounds wet through, but now must have weighed in at the very least at thirteen stones. I could barely shuffle along, but I was warm.

As I passed by the darkened back entry to Woolworths and tested my bravery by going into the gloom to check all the rear doors, I saw that the fruit and veg man had been and made his delivery. He just used to pile the boxes up outside the rear entrance. It was asking to be pinched, so it came as no surprise when Sergeant Turner had told us at the beginning of the week that someone had been helping themselves on a regular basis. As I shuffled into Kingsway, I caught a glimpse of a distant figure. It was the first person I had seen for ages, and I slid into a doorway and watched as he drew closer. It was a young man, early twenties; he was wearing the familiar white overalls of a pottery worker and carried a small knapsack over his shoulder.

A cigarette machine was fitted to the outside wall of Preedys tobacconists opposite my hiding place. The man stopped by the machine, fiddled with the knob, looked up inside the slot and then started to pull at the top of the machine. He didn't try very hard and stopped short of doing enough for me to arrest him, but he was definitely up to no good. Should I nab him now and at least find out who he was?

As I considered my dilemma, the youth crossed the road and started to walk away up South Wolfe Street, furtively looking over his shoulder, but totally unaware of my presence. I crossed the road and slithered into a doorway, now certain that I was about to witness the commission of some heinous crime. As the youth drew farther away I spied my chance to gain further ground and tiptoed, helmet under arm, into yet another doorway. I peered carefully around the doorframe; I could see he was at the back of Woolworths and yes, he was rummaging through the wooden crates. This was the Woolworths fruit thief actually in the act.

"Sierra One to Lima Alpha control – over," I whispered into my transmitter, clumsily fumbling with my gloves, trying to turn down the volume control on my receiver, so that any answering voice would not alert my quarry.

"Yes, Pork, what's up?" crackled back Sergeant Turner's voice, barely audible.

In my whispered voice I hastily outlined the situation and then decided to move in closer; fit as I was, I wouldn't be able to run fast with all this clothing on. As I moved up another ten feet or so and moulded my bulbous blue serge into another recess, I could clearly see the shapes of apples and bananas being stuffed into the knapsack. I still had some fifty feet to go before I was within grabbing distance, and the evil deed now appeared to be finished, as the youth had slung his bag over his shoulder and had started to walk nonchalantly away in the direction of Minton's pottery.

I now commenced a running, tiptoeing, darting into doorways strategy. This lasted about five seconds before the youth turned and spotted me in full tiptoe without a suitable refuge in which to dart. I was caught, seen, spotted right in the middle of the pavement. I stopped dead, one foot still off the ground, one arm outstretched holding my radio. He stopped too, mouth open, arms in the air. I almost expected him to point at me and send me back to the end of the street as he'd seen me move, like in that game we used to play as kids, but in one movement he had turned and was in full flight.

As I slowly started to gain traction with the pavement I blurted some garbled message over my radio. I just could not seem to get going, I was so laden down with clothing and other cumbersome items. In its special trouser pocket, my staff was clonking against my right knee; I could hardly lift my legs up with my greatcoat buttoned. I threw away my helmet and caught a glimpse of it bouncing away across the road as I started to pick up speed, then a glove went. I was now nearing the end of South Wolfe Street and the swiftly disappearing figure had turned right.

I was now travelling at an alarming rate and seemed to have to bank over as I negotiated the corner, when suddenly a familiar looking figure could be seen; dark blue uniform, peaked cap. Great, one of the lads, I thought, he's bound to gather what's happening and cut the thief off, but no, as the fruit thief sped away from me the figure just stopped and watched him hurtle past.

"You prat," I gasped, as I steamed along, "why didn't..."

It wasn't a policeman at all. It was a bus conductor. It was time to lighten my load a little more. As I closed in on the completely bemused bus conductor I threw my heavy rubber torch in his general direction.

"Look after that," I spluttered.

The long black torch flew from my hand with the velocity and accuracy of a heat-seeking missile and homed in on the bus conductor's testicles. I clearly heard the dull thud as it embedded itself between his legs, and saw him crumple to the ground as I sped by like a runaway train. The Woolworths' fruit thief had escaped. I gave up the chase about two hundred yards away in Spark Street. It took me another two hundred to come to a stop, and he'd vanished.

When I returned to collect my belongings from various locations, I found the conductor sitting on the pavement still hunched over with both hands buried down his trousers.

"You bloody well hurt me," he said, looking up at me and grimacing.

"Sorry, mate," I said.

* * * *

Roy hadn't been too well of late. He'd been trying really hard to get to work on time, as he'd had several warnings and could end up with the sack, but he looked really pale and was making a bigger botch of things than normal. We reckoned that the fat girl wasn't feeding him properly, or was wearing him out.

"You look like death warmed up, Roy," I commented as I made my way up the station steps looking forward to the pile of chips that were burning the top of my head.

It was noon shift on a Wednesday, and Roy was just going back out on his town centre patrol after his meal break.

"Yes, I feel a bit off, something I ate," was Roy's reply.

I scoffed my chips and, after potting two reds, a yellow and the white during an attempted game of snooker, made my way down to the front office to see if there were any jobs for me.

"Yes, Pork, a death message in Bath Street, details are on the pad," instructed Sergeant Turner.

He'd hardly finished his sentence when Roy's voice came over the radio.

"Sierra Two to Lima Alpha - over."

"Yes, Roy, go ahead - over," returned Sergeant Turner.

"Sierra Two to Lima Alpha, can you send me a car down to Campbell Place, please, Sarge - over."

"Yes. What's the problem, Roy? Over."

"I, I, I wonder if you could send me a car down to Campbell Place, please, Sarge – over."

"Yes, Roy, I got that bit, but what's the problem? Over."

"Sierra Two to Lima Alpha, I just wondered if you could send me a car down to Campbell Place, please, Sarge - over."

"*Yes, Roy,* but *what* is the problem? *Over.*"

"I could do with a lift into the station, please, Sarge. Could you send me a car down? Over."

"For the final time, Roy, *what* is the problem? Over.

"I've shit meself, Sarge… Over."

It took several days for the laughter to die down. Roy's plight was made even worse when Sam the panda driver pulled up alongside him in Campbell Place unaware of Roy's difficulty.

"What's up, Roy?"

"Shit meself, Sam."

"Well, you're not getting in here then," Sam shouted, and drove off leaving Roy to waddle over to the taxi rank and cadge a lift back to the police station.

Poor old Roy, he really wasn't cut out for the job. It must have been pretty embarrassing for him when everything was made even worse with his new nickname, 'Shitty Witty'.

He managed to turn in early the next day, but without thinking someone said to him:

"What's up, Roy, shit the bed?"

It wasn't too long after this when Roy decided that the police wasn't for him and packed it in. I don't know what happened to him after that; someone said he'd got a job on the council working on the gritting wagons.

"He probably gets to work on time now," someone quipped.

* * * *

In May 1970 one of the country's first open air pop concerts had been arranged. It was to take place in a farmer's field near the village of Madeley, which was a few miles outside my hometown of Newcastle-under-Lyme.

The venue, which took place on Saturday 23rd and Sunday 24th May, attracted forty-five thousand people, and some famous names were on the bill including Mungo Jerry,

Jose Feliciano, Keith Moon, Spencer Davis, Black Sabbath, Grateful Dead, Eric Clapton and many more.

I was ordered to do a 'special duty' (paid overtime!) on one of the days, and spent a very pleasant afternoon strolling around chatting to students and lots of very hippie types, most of whom had long hair and wore psychedelic clothing. There was very little trouble and not much for us to do except wander about chatting to people and enjoying the entertainment.

I can remember seeing a young student girl sitting in front of her tiny little tent playing a guitar during a lull in the real entertainment. She sung a bluesy soulful version of Gershwin's 'Summertime'. She was brilliant and got a well-deserved round of applause from me and two other uniformed constables; I always think about it every time I hear the song… maybe she became famous.

It was truly amazing how little trouble there was throughout the two-day event, with only a couple of minor theft reports and just two suspected drug overdoses.

SIX

Having now served almost twelve months, I was overdue for my one-month attachment to the Criminal Investigation Department. I had got to know most of the detectives, who were a real mixed bunch, but mostly long serving and experienced.

Detective Inspector Tommy Dodd was the man in charge of Stoke CID, and chain-smoked small cigars; he seemed to know all the personal details of every crook on the patch and was obsessed with detail.

I'd had a suit from Burtons especially for this month, as all the detectives wore suits, and, of course, I was really looking forward to answering the phone with, 'CID; PC Pye speaking'.

My first job was, predictably, making a large pot of tea and, as by now I'd had plenty of practise and the grilled tea story from Wolstanton had not reached Stoke, this went without a hitch. We had huge metal teapots and it was the ritual that the milk was poured into the teapot rather than individually into the cups.

I was given my very own desk complete with wire in and out trays. I noticed that the in tray was already distorted by the huge amount of papers, documents and brown folders that were stuffed into it. As I started to sift through the great wad, I quickly realised that this was all the time-consuming, boring and mostly very mundane work that no one else in the office wanted.

"Yes, it's not all robberies and burglaries, there's tons of that rubbish," commented Dave the detective, whose desk was opposite mine.

"Hmm," I said, "it's going to take me the whole month just to get through this lot."

"Well, no time for that now," Dave said, "I've had some info. Davis's Bottling Stores is going to get screwed this evening by Edward William Ray CRO and, with a bit of luck, we're going to catch him in the act."

It was almost 10.30 p.m. as Dave drove the battered Ford Anglia CID van onto the waste land at the side of Davis's Bottling Stores in Leese Street. For some unknown reason our CID van had no gear knob, just a gear stick with a sharp end on it, which gave you a sore left palm. The whole area was littered with derelict and partly demolished buildings. Davis's was no exception; two tall, heavy, wooden blue gates hung at a slant between large crumbling brick pillars that formed part of the high brick perimeter wall. Crazily tilted skyscrapers of wooden beer crates were silhouetted above the wall; Davis's was a drinks supplier to pubs and clubs.

"Let's get in here," Dave whispered, pushing me into the yard of a derelict house.

As I peered over the wall, I could pick out the gates in the dim light of a street lamp.

"When's it going to happen, Dave?" I asked, expecting a long wait.

Dave checked his watch with a quick flash of his torch.

"Well, it's just gone closing time, so any time now."

The words had barely left his lips when a figure rounded the corner at the top of the deserted street and slid into a doorway.

"Right on time," whispered Dave.

A silhouetted head peered around the doorway, looked one way then the other, and then crept unsteadily along against the wall in the shadows. My heart was now pounding with excitement. The figure stopped by the gates, lurched one way then the other, and then fell against the gates and slumped to the ground. One of the beer crate skyscrapers behind the gates swayed as though made of rubber and then toppled over the gates, sending two of the wooden crates of empty bottles smashing into the pavement inches from the drunken prostrate burglar-in-waiting.

"He's pissed as usual," sniggered Dave.

"I don't suppose he'll do it now, will he, Dave, what with all that noise and everything?" I asked.

"Oh, that won't put him off," said Dave.

The figure staggered to his feet crunching the broken glass underfoot, and then piled the two beer crates against the gate and, with one last look over his shoulder, clambered onto the crates and hoisted himself over the gates. There was a sickening dull thump as he landed on the other side, followed by all manner of crashing as several of the skyscrapers disappeared from view.

After about twenty minutes the gates started to shake and rattle.

"Right, Pork, get ready to nab him," said Dave.

Two hands appeared over the top of the gate, followed by a head quivering under the strain of pulling up the weight of a drunken body laden down by pockets full of bottles. A leg swung up to join the hands and head, followed by a low moaning as the sensation of pain started to filter through the anaesthetic of several pints of beer.

"Is that him, Dave?" I whispered excitedly.

"What?"

"Is that him, Edward William Ray CRO?" I said, trying out my newly acquired police vernacular.

Dave shook his head at me in puzzlement and made no reply. The figure was now astride the top of the gate, perfectly silhouetted against the night sky, both hands pushing down onto the gate trying to alleviate the obvious pain caused by the twelve or thirteen stones pressing down onto his genitals. The moans turned to a high-pitched squeal as the figure started to fall in the direction of the street.

"Right, Pork, go get him."

I shot out of my hiding place like a sprinter from the starting blocks and virtually caught Ray before he'd hit the ground. He didn't struggle - not with twenty half-pint bottles of Bass and three bottles of Babycham in his pockets. Edward William Ray CRO denied everything, which he always did apparently, even when caught red-handed.

I visited Davis's the next day in my Burtons suit and took a witness statement from Mr Morley, the warehouse manager. I carefully included all the required detail in it about what time he had left the premises the night before, and he then went on to say how he had returned much later that night following a call from the police, to find that the property had been broken into and how numerous bottles of drink had been stolen. I also detailed that he had noticed that a large pile of excrement had been deposited on the office floor. I recall being quite pleased with my wording in Mr Morley's statement...

I discovered a pile of excrement on the office floor, which appeared to be human and of recent origin.

True to form, Ray pleaded not guilty, and the court broke out into stifled laughter as the brilliant defence solicitor, George Slater, who was noted for his awkward questions, quizzed poor Mr Morley about his 'expert' knowledge on human excrement. Edward William Ray received three months' imprisonment.

* * * *

Lenny Fowler CRO wasn't much of a crook and if it was possible for a CRO not to warrant even one Christian name then this would be Lenny's position. Lenny was more of a pain in the neck, pinching people's lead waste pipes from outside their kitchens by bending them back and forth until they snapped, stealing two left shoes from the display outside the shoe shop, drunkenness and that sort of thing. Consequently, Lenny's all-time big heist wasn't too well planned.

The lead he had decided to steal from a house in Shepherd Street would have been easy money for him to weigh in at the local scrapyard, but his capture was inevitable. His plan had included carrying out the theft on a Sunday afternoon whilst the occupants were at home watching television in the front room beneath the bay window up onto which Lenny had climbed in order to hack away with a small hand axe.

As the police arrived to see the annoyed homeowner standing inside his front door and an anguished Lenny looking down at the approaching police car, no doubt thinking, 'I wonder if they've seen me?', Lenny's 'getaway vehicle', a large wooden wheelbarrow, was spotted on the pavement right outside the door to the house.

Lenny duly received a small custodial sentence. A few months later, it was realised that his wheelbarrow still stood taking up space in the CID property store. A bemused and nervous Lenny was shown up to the CID office to be met with a fanfare, which was hummed by half a dozen detectives to the theme tune of the 'This Is Your Life' programme.

DC Geoff Virgo stood in the centre of the room holding the large red leather bound property register in both hands and welcomed Lenny into the gathering with a superb rendition of the Irish brogue of 'This Is Your Life' host, Eamonn Andrews.

"Lenny Fowler," twanged Geoff, "you thought you'd come here tonight to collect a wooden wheelbarrow, but tonight - Lenny Fowler - ace lead thief, drunkard and general everyday pain in the arse - this is your life."

The fanfare continued as Lenny was requested to sign for his wheelbarrow.

The CID did not do the same shifts that we did in uniform. The shifts were mostly 'days' (9 a.m. until 5 p.m.) and noons. Someone would also have to come at 8 a.m. to start work on any prisoners who had been arrested during the night and there was always a CID officer working on nights, but he would be covering the entire division, and would find himself called back and forth to jobs anywhere in the Longton or Stoke areas during his shift.

We didn't get paid overtime in those days and, as detectives were very often called upon to carry on working on a particular job because of its seriousness, or for some other reason, they were paid a small addition to their pay titled 'detective duty allowance'.

There was always a variety of new jobs to do on each shift on top of all the enquiries that you already had. Each day would bring another few thefts, burglaries, assaults and so on, and there was all that really boring stuff that weighed you down, such as the reports that came in every day by post from the gas and electricity board about meters in people's home being broken into.

One of the perks was that we were allowed - in fact 'expected' - to visit pubs and drink beer, and we could claim some small recompense at the end of each month. This would be covered under the official guise of 'cultivating informants' or 'making enquiries re burglary'.

Dave was a good detective and always had some juicy info that he'd picked up in some pub. When he came in on an afternoon shift one day with a broad grin and said, 'Right, Pork, job on, this afternoon', I knew we were in for something similar to the Davis's bottling store episode, or hopefully even better.

"You know All Saints Church down West End?" said Dave.

"Yes," I replied, "it's derelict, going to be pulled down."

"Correct," said Dave, "but there's a lot of lead on that church roof, or there *was*. Somebody's been systematically stripping it off and I know who that someone is - Gerrard Derek Bedson CRO. Apparently he's at it every afternoon and he's weighing it in at Moore's scrapyard."

Dave decided he'd use his own car for this job, as Bedson was a seasoned criminal and knew all the CID vehicles (both) off by heart.

It was about 2 p.m., on a bright sunny afternoon as Dave parked his car a short way up Vinebank Street looking down onto London Road, from where we had a pretty good view of All Saints Road and the church. We didn't have to wait long before Dave chuckled to himself.

"He's here, the cheeky bastard, he looks like he's going mountain climbing."

Bedson was a swarthy, well-built, fair-haired thirty year old who'd been in trouble for everything from parking on the pavement to house burglaries and serious assaults. Here he was on a bright sunny afternoon in a busy built-up area striding along with a very large coil of rope slung around his neck and intent on casually clambering the great height of this huge crumbling edifice to strip away its last remaining valuables.

"I could think of a better use for that rope," Dave snarled through his teeth, "and we wouldn't even have to take it off his neck."

Bedson casually strolled in through the church gateway and disappeared from view.

"Okay," said Dave, "we'll leave him to it for a while, we've got to get him bang to rights or it's a waste of time."

After ten minutes or so we could hear a distant, repetitive, dull banging sound.

"Right, we'll leave him a bit longer to cut some more and then we'll take a look and see what to do next," said Dave.

After another ten minutes we left the car and walked over towards the church, looking up towards the towering roof. There was no sign of Bedson anywhere, but the dull 'thump, thump, thump' of his hammer and chisel could still be heard coming from somewhere up on high. There was no sign of the rope or any clue as to how he had got up there, but from where the noise seemed to be coming, it was clear that he was high up in the valley between two steeply-pitched tiled roofs just below where the church tower rose up from the main building. Dave explained that the lead would be in this valley between the two roofs. The church had been a beautiful building, but its sandstone block walls were now completely black due to its lifetime in the Potteries, the stained glass windows had become victims to stones and the graveyard was waist high in grass.

"Okay, Pork, a bit of initiative here, see if you can borrow those ladders," said Dave, pointing towards a large, green GPO lorry parked just down the road.

Two other detectives, Jim and Derek, had arrived by now.

"Hope you don't mind heights, Porky," said Jim, in his usual sarcastic manner.

It was amazing that Bedson couldn't hear this going on, but the distant repetitive banging continued. I had no problem commandeering the enormous, three-storey wooden ladders, and the GPO team even came and set them up for us, making a tremendous noise as they reversed into the church gateway and clattered the ladders up against the wall of the building. The dull thumping carried on relentlessly, interrupted only when Bedson presumably had a little rest or piled up his booty. The ladders were positioned just below the level of the valley between the two roofs, so that Bedson would not be able to see them, but also because they were at their absolute limit.

"Okay, Pork, up you go then, go nick him," said Dave, grinning.

Oh no, I thought to myself as I started off up the ladder. Normally I'm okay with heights, but this was a 'church'; it was enormous, really high and the ladders were bending and shaking quite badly. Visions of the mountain rescue escapade flashed into my mind as I neared the halfway mark. If I was to fall off even at this point I would surely die, so there was no point in showing my fear from now on.

Jim had been positioned at the base of the ladder and gave it a little shake.

"Mind you don't fall, Pork," he called out.

"Cut it out," I replied, "because if I do, I'll make sure I fall on *you*."

Suddenly the thumping stopped, everybody froze. Had we pushed our luck too far with the noise? No, it started again, Bedson still hadn't a clue and was no doubt having another rest.

It was really scary when my hands were on the top rung of the ladder. The slightest movement seemed to make the ladder move in and out, and I had visions of it snapping. I now had to take hold of the edge of the building and climb farther up. As I did, my head was now above the floor of the roof valley I looked along. It was an immense building. The flat lead covering the floor of the valley was some four feet wide and stretched along for about thirty-five feet to where it joined the tower and there, at the far end, was Bedson, with his back to me kneeling down, banging away with a hammer and chisel. Three or four large pieces of lead were piled up on the tiles next to him. I took a deep breath; I was now shaking with fear, but did not want anyone to know.

"*Oy!*" I shouted.

Bedson swirled around, still on his knees, dropping his hammer and chisel and with a look of total disbelief shouted:

"F***ing hell, you're tall."

"Police, you're nicked," I shouted back in a quavering voice.

I wasn't even going to attempt to give him the police caution until I was on safe ground. I was shaking so much I would have got the words all mixed up.

Bedson walked over to me and looked down casually.

"Want a hand up?"

I really hoped that he hadn't decided to kill me, as I desperately wanted to get off this ladder, so I took hold of his outstretched hand and he hauled me up onto the roof.

"Thanks," I said, "you know I've got to caution you... you are not obliged to say-"

"Yes, yes," Bedson interrupted, "I know all that crap backwards, mate, no need to bother."

"But how did you get up here?" I asked.

"Through the window then up the steps in the tower," Bedson explained, "then out onto the roof through that little door there," he continued, pointing towards a small hatch door in the side of the tower.

How pleased I was to hear this, as there would be no way in this world I could have got back onto the ladder. I had resigned myself to living out the rest of my life on top of a derelict church. Bedson was directed down by way of his own, much safer, route and was then rather unnecessarily handcuffed and taken away, whilst I remained on the roof under Dave's instructions, to throw down some of the lead that had been cut off, as evidence.

I went back to the pile of lead and selected the smallest of the huge pieces. It was a tremendous weight and I had to drag it the full length of the valley, so that I could tip it over the edge. Jim was standing below right in the line of fire, but I thought better of it and shouted a warning before heaving the mass over, which landed with a dull sort of 'flop' as it hit the concrete. I was never as pleased as when I made my way back down to the ground, following Bedson's safe route, without anyone even suspecting how terrified I had been.

At the court hearing several weeks later, the stipendiary magistrate, Mr Geoffrey Smallwood, was visibly seen to stifle a laugh as I related from my pocketbook Bedson's reply to me of, 'F***ing hell, you're tall'.

* * * *

One of the enquiries I was given during this first brief brush with CID was to investigate a series of indecent exposures that had been happening in and around the Hancock Street area. The 'flasher' always wore an imitation sheepskin coat, and descriptions seemed to suggest that one fellow had been responsible for all five incidents. He had become known in the CID as the 'Hand Cock Flasher' and he usually chose between 7.30 a.m. and 8 a.m. on weekdays, when he could be sure of catching the attention of some of the pottery girls on their way to work. His last offence had gone a step further, as he had caught hold of a girl by the arm, and there was concern as to what might happen next.

I'd made an early start that morning to do 'observations', hoping to catch the culprit, and was wandering along Lytton Street for the third time. It was just after 7.30 a.m. as I tried to look inconspicuous in my 'duffel coat disguise', underneath which was hiding my Burtons suit.

I nonchalantly strolled up Hancock Street and slipped in under one of the Seven Arches railway viaduct alcoves with my snapping bag over my shoulder, hoping to look like someone on his way to work. I suddenly spotted him - mid-thirties, five feet seven, receding fair hair, overweight and wearing that all-important imitation sheepskin coat. It all fitted, this was the man. I radioed in, alerted the station to what was happening and heard a flurry of radio activity as other patrols were warned. I didn't really want to allow him to go as far as upsetting another girl, but would have liked additional evidence. I was certain this was the man, and was going to nick him anyway.

Suddenly the suspect bobbed out of view into an alleyway at the side of the houses. My God, I thought to myself, this is exactly what he has done before. He'd always flashed at a girl from an alleyway as she'd walked past, and there, on her own, heading in his direction, was his quarry; a pretty, twenty-year-old blonde, carrying a shopping bag.

To my horror, on the other side of the road, and clearly in full view from the alleyway, had suddenly appeared a policeman in full uniform and strolling along without a care in the world with a clipboard under his arm. It was PC Hawley from D shift. I was dumbfounded at this, as the earlies shift had been explicitly told to keep away from the area as I was on 'obs' for the flasher.

The flasher had seen PC Hawley and, as predicted, darted out from the alley back into the street clutching at his now unbuttoned trousers, and started to run full pelt away from the uniformed policeman and straight in my direction. I lurched from one side of the pavement to the other, both arms outstretched as he stumbled towards me, jacket and shirt flap billowing out behind him and trousers ever dropping. PC Hawley was now also chasing the man, but didn't know why.

"*Police! Stop!*" I shouted, as the flapping stumbling figure crashed to the ground in front of me with trousers now below his knees and backside on full view.

"I was only having a piss, Officer," the man gasped in desperation as he looked up at me.

PC Hawley arrived, also panting, but with trousers intact.

"What the hell's going on, Porky?" he shouted.

I explained the situation to the bemused officer, who had been told nothing of the operation to catch 'The Hand Cock Flasher' and had been busily taking a statement over another matter whilst I was patrolling in 'disguise'.

The flasher was reunited with his trousers, and a panda car arrived to take us all to the police station. It turned out that the flasher had a string of previous convictions for sexual offences and was in fact a true CRO, but it wasn't all sewn up yet, as he was sticking to his story that he had gone to the alleyway to relieve himself, and denied anything to do with all the other incidents. I now had to prove that he was 'our man'.

"Right then, Pork, now the work starts," said Dave, "we're going to have to put him on an ID parade."

This was something new for me. I'd learnt about identification parades at Ryton, but not in great detail as they were really a CID matter; what I had learned from anyone who had been involved with ID parades was that they were the biggest pains in the neck ever.

"Okay then, Dave, what do we do next?" I quizzed.

"*You*," said Dave, "have got to go out on the town and anywhere else that looks likely, and find at least twelve 'stooges' to stand in on the parade. I am going to organise the room and the paperwork. I want you to get the stooges all to report here for say, 1 p.m., and remember they've got to look a bit like him."

A 'stooge' was, of course, the police jargon for the people who would stand in on the parade alongside the suspect. The regulations stated that the stooges had to be of a similar description and position in life, and wearing similar clothing. I was now tasked with the job of finding twelve or so fortyish, five feet sevenish, fairish, balding, plumpish men with sheepskinish coats, who would all be paid the princely sum of 2/6d, (25p), which was to be paid for what would more than likely take up several hours of their day.

This wasn't going to be easy. It would be hard enough just getting twelve similar looking blokes from Stoke football ground on a Saturday, never mind at 10 a.m. on a dull wet morning in the middle of the week, and when they were told how much they'd receive, they were more than likely to give me a blunt, 'No!'.

"I suggest," said Dave, handing me an orange-coloured folder, "that you start with some of these, but you're probably going to have to use the Sally Army as well."

The 'Sally Army' was the Salvation Army hostel in Lovatt Street and was, unfortunately, the main reason why the town of Stoke itself was the gathering place for such a large number of vagrants.

Any new visitor to Stoke would have been surprised, when driving or walking through the town, to see so many drunks and down-and-outs in one small town centre. It was a sad fact that most of them had long criminal records or were hopeless alcoholics who were 'on the road', walking between one town and another with a preference for anywhere that had a Salvation Army hostel. Very few of the chaps were local to the area. Many of them would drink surgical spirit because it was cheap, but you could always tell who had been at it for any length of time as it caused blindness.

Inside the folder that Dave had given me were details of other possible 'stooge sources' - Minton's Pottery, Carlton

Ware Pottery, Bilton's Pottery, some offices, the fish warehouse in Welch Street and a few more places which were likely to let us borrow some of their employees for a while. I duly telephoned through the list, but my persuasive powers mustn't have been too good, as I ended up with only three possibles, and that would only be if their descriptions were anything like.

I trawled the town centre with a uniformed PC, but between us we had still managed only a total of six possibles, and even these men would require quite a vivid imagination to think that they were vaguely similar to the flasher.

The captain of the Salvation Army hostel was waiting at the door as we arrived outside.

"I've assembled all the men who wish to help out," he said, as he showed us through to the canteen, where I saw that about a dozen men were sitting at tables or standing about.

This really was a mixture of the most bizarre specimens of the human race. Each one seemed to be a different species, but things were now getting desperate and I simply had to get the stooges together at the nick. It was almost 1 p.m. Dave had already postponed the parade until 2 p.m., so I picked out seven of the men who, it has to be admitted, bore no resemblance to the flasher, and arranged transport for them. You would have thought that the 'chosen ones' had won the pools; they were so elated at the thought of earning the 2/6d. The remaining downhearted few wandered away.

Back at the nick things were getting busy as various people and stooges started to arrive, were given their instructions and had their details logged by the uniform inspector whose job it was to actually 'run' the parade. All the stooges were instructed to line up in the locker room, whilst Detective Sergeant Mellor arranged his large and complicated brass and wooden tripod and camera, which had big glass slides that he had to slot into the front before taking any photographs. The regulations stated that photographs had to be taken of the stooges, and then the suspect would be allowed to select his own position in the line-up. He was also allowed to object to any of the stooges.

As the stooges assembled in the line-up, the faces of the detectives and other officers assisting could be seen to be fighting back uncontrollable laughter. This was a bizarre scene; not a single one of the men vaguely resembled each other, let alone looked like the suspect. Detective Sergeant Mellor, the photographer, had to leave the room supposedly to fetch some more equipment, but could be heard laughing loudly in the corridor.

The flasher was shown into the room and he selected a place in the line-up in between two of the totally dissimilar Sally Army men. Amazingly he did not object to anyone, which was fortunate, as I had managed to get only eleven men together and, therefore, had no spares.

DS Mellor took the final photo, trying his best to control his laughter. All the men in the line-up blinked and rubbed their eyes as the camera flashed, even the flasher himself.

The five young ladies were shown in, in turn, and all picked out the flasher without hesitation.

After the parade, statements were taken and each 2/6d was paid out to the delighted Sally Army men and also to the other pottery workers, who had no doubt lost money on the deal. The flasher decided to make a full confession and even admitted to other 'flashings' and indecent assaults he had perpetrated in other parts of the city. I gave a sigh of relief because if he had contested the parade I'm pretty sure it would have been thrown out of court.

The photographs of the parade arrived a few days later, so that they could be submitted together with the file of evidence. DS Mellor had even been 'thoughtful enough' to put in several 'spares', which were immediately posted on the office noticeboard and became a great source of laughter for months to come.

The photograph showed that the line-up consisted of two very tall men, one of whom was bald, a short fat man aged about sixty-five, a young man with a Beatle haircut, a fifty year old with a gaping mouth of bad teeth, a bus driver in full uniform (apart from hat), a man wearing a polo-necked sweater, who had a deformed leg that made him stand at an odd angle, and the flasher himself (minus imitation sheepskin). The other stooges varied in height, weight and clothing, and two of the Salvation Army men were so suntanned from a 'life outdoors' that they appeared to be of a different race. Right in the middle of the parade was a huge fat man wearing a white boiler suit; to cap it all, it was later noticed that the flasher had chosen to stand in front of the only locker on the photograph that had a policeman's helmet perched on top of it. It was like 'X' marks the spot.

It was rumoured that the training department used the photograph for years to come as an example of 'how not to conduct an ID Parade'.

SEVEN

My month's attachment to the CID was extended to six weeks, as I'd been involved in quite a few cases and needed the extra time to clear everything up, but now it was over, so it was back to uniform and the regular nights, noons and earlies. I'd really enjoyed my short stay on CID and felt that that was what I wanted to do eventually.

I was still involved with boxing and represented the division at the Force Boxing Tournament held at The Borough Hall, Stafford, on Wednesday, 18th November 1970, when I fought two hard matches on the one night to become force welterweight champion. I arrived back home in the early hours clutching my trophy and sporting two black eyes to the usual comment from my dad:

"What the hell sort of state was the other bloke like if you won?"

The next day the chief inspector told me I was not allowed to go out on patrol until my black eyes had gone, 'as it didn't look very good', so I managed to catch up with some of my reports for a few days.

I still enjoyed doing the uniform work, despite there being a lot of mundane jobs attached to it. There were so many forms, books and booklets, each one with its own identifying number. A lot of these documents had to be revised following the introduction of decimal coinage in February 1971 (including the payment to ID parade stooges, from 2/6d to 25p!).

Great importance was still placed on some things that in the modern world may seem of little significance, such as swearing and dropping litter. If anyone was foolish enough to swear in the street within earshot of a constable they could expect at best the most fearsome and public humiliation possible and at worst - arrest. A similar line would be taken with anyone seen dropping litter.

Many of the jobs that we were expected to do were time-consuming and boring. We even had to check on people's houses when they were away on holiday, or if the property was empty for some reason or other.

People would come into the police station in droves as the potters' holidays approached, and fill in the small blue cards that were used for this purpose and predictably called 'void premises forms'. On the back of the forms were printed columns in which we were supposed to record our visits and which the sergeant would examine and initial to ensure that the premises were being inspected.

We had to try to get a few visits listed before the people were due back home, but with the pressure of other things I must admit that there were often a few imaginary visits, particularly so during the holiday period, as you could start out on your shift with dozens of them to do. The card, of course, had a number, but this one escapes me.

One of the things about these menial jobs was that you were always out and about, lurking in the shadows, or in some back alleyway, using some unknown short cut, getting to know all sorts of people and often seeing things that might otherwise have escaped you.

I was using up some spare time one evening whilst on foot patrol and getting as many void premises forms as I could, marked up. It was 7.30 p.m. and already dark. I had just checked the rear of an empty shop on London Road and as I emerged from the alley at the back of the shop into Penkhull New Road, I started to walk down towards London Road and was surprised to see a figure in Club Street on the other side of London Road. I could make out the silhouette of a man lifting something down from the concrete loading bay shelf at the back of Minton's pottery. I walked over London Road and down Club Street, keeping in the shadows and trying to walk quietly. As I came up behind the bending figure I could see he was shuffling a heavy-looking cardboard box along the ground against the wall.

"What are you doing?" I demanded.

I don't know if it was the sudden fright of looking up from almost ground level to see this seemingly seven-foot tall helmeted policeman (who was really only five feet ten), or the way I demanded an explanation, maybe it was a bit of both, but as the man swirled around and dropped even closer to the ground he immediately, and without any hesitation, shouted out in full voice.

"It's tiles, I've pinched 'em, I'm guilty. I'm pleading guilty."

This must have been the quickest cough any policeman ever had.

Suddenly another figure appeared out of a darkened doorway; a tall, well-built man, who clicked on a powerful torch as he strode towards us. I took a step backwards and reached for my radio as the thought went through my head that I had interrupted an international gang of tile thieves, who were now about to 'do me over'.

"Where in hell did you spring from?" the man shouted towards me, as he drew closer.

"Who are you, is more to the point?" I quizzed.

"I'm the security man for Minton's," he went on, "I've been after this feller for weeks, I reckon he's stolen enough tiles to do Stoke Baths. I've spent hours trying to catch him in the act and just when I've got him bang to rights, you suddenly materialise in front of me and nick him. I might as well have stayed at home."

Later, a search of the man's house revealed a veritable tile warehouse and a nice little sideline in kitchens and bathrooms, which subsidised his job as kiln man in the pottery factory.

The security man became a good friend and the security lodge became a regular tea stop. The tile thief lost his job, but after a short prison sentence went into business full-time as a tiler.

The void premises forms were kept in the sergeant's office, which doubled as the parade room where we all had to assemble before each shift to be given our duty for the day. Numerous other files were also kept there, mostly in the cardboard 'lever-arch files'. One contained the forms numbered '121' or 'complaint forms'. These were for everyday minor, but regular, ongoing problems that members of the public were experiencing.

Footballing in the street was a regular problem and, on many occasions, I've used my police whistle to blow 'full-time' to signal the end of a full 'eleven-a-side' street match. Pretty well anything that wasn't actually a crime could go down on a 121; noisy neighbours, thoughtless parking, prowlers and peeping Toms were all regular items.

Prowlers and peeping Toms could be a problem and would usually get more attention than other 121s because, nine times out of ten, the complainant would be a young lady and the prowler had 'located' a good vantage point to peer. Several interesting stories would often filter back from visiting officers, not all of which were written up on the 121, and there is no doubt that on occasions the complainant would ring in to report 'the prowler back again', when it was actually a visiting policeman taking advantage of a good viewpoint.

The year 1972 saw the arrival in Staffordshire of the motorists' scourge – the 'fixed penalty ticket'. We were all issued with a booklet containing twenty-five of the tickets, which could be issued to motorists or attached to cars when certain minor traffic offences had been committed. A bundle of little plastic bags would also be handed out to us for fixing the ticket to the windscreen of the offending vehicle. The tickets when they first came out were for a £2.00 penalty, and I guess this must give some insight into inflation and how the cost of living has changed over the years.

All copy tickets issued during the day had to be handed in at the police station before midnight each night. One little 'perk' on a cold wet evening would be to issue a ticket just before midnight, thereby enabling you to stroll into the nick as the church clock struck twelve and join the office staff for the 'twelve o clock brew' as you handed in the copy ticket.

* * * *

The enquiry office at Stoke Police Station was the first room that any visiting member of the public would see. This was the control room for the sub-division, the 'nerve centre'.

Once a visitor had climbed the few stone steps from the street and entered the building through the big, heavy wooden door, he would find himself in a corridor, which was used as a waiting room complete with a heavy wooden bench. Upon entering the enquiry office on the left, the visitor would be met with a scene of antiquated chaos. The walls were not plastered, but just brick, which had been transformed into a lumpy smoothness through countless layers of paint. The current colour scheme was then a very pale matt blue. The counter was very high, as it doubled as a stand-up writing desk. There were dozens of devices and structures bolted to or leaning up against the walls.

A big window looked out onto Copeland Street, beneath which was an old, brown wooden table, which supported the radio equipment for speaking to and receiving messages from officers out on patrol. The transmitter proudly sported its manufacturer's name: 'PYE'. The handset was similar to a telephone handset, but with a button in the centre, which was to be pressed when transmitting. Also on the table next to the radio was a strange-looking, two-tone grey, metal square-shaped device with a loudspeaker grille at the front and an on/off volume switch. The device was entitled WD400 and when switched on would just emit a constant, 'pip,pip,pip'. If a wailing noise followed by a voice should suddenly come from the speaker then you'd have to take notice, as this was the nuclear attack early-warning system; the fact that I am writing this book indicates that the device never went off apart from tests.

Screwed to the wall near the radio were four rows of battery chargers for the radios, each of which would take about twenty batteries; small yellow ones for the receivers and long red ones for the transmitters.

On another wall near the doorway to the cells was a huge wooden board that had dozens of metal boxes fixed to it. Each box was covered with switches, lights and numbers. This was the burglar alarm system; all the banks, clubs, many shops and warehouses, and dozens more properties in the area had their own burglar alarms connected directly to this board. Books were stored at the side, which kept records of activations, false alarms and problems with different alarms. Each alarm had to be tested every morning by flipping the test switch, which caused a buzzer to sound.

Each buzzer had a slightly different tone, so with a little musical skill, 'Jingle Bells' or 'Happy Birthday' could be played, and frequently were.

Burglar alarm calls on nights were always enthusiastically attended by patrols and, although a lot were false alarms, there would often be 'hits' resulting in arrests. When a radio call went out to a patrol to go to a burglar alarm call, it would not be unusual for several other cars and even foot patrols to also make their way without even being instructed. This was particularly the case if the alarm was at a pub or club, as it would not be unheard of for the licensee to switch the pumps on and serve up a half for everyone.

Burglar Alarm System like the one at Stoke
(photograph courtesy The Potteries Museum)

London Road Sports and Social Club in Shepherd Street had regular alarm activations, and Bill Cope, the secretary and keyholder, lived in a terraced house next door to the club. Bill liked a drink very much indeed and was often the worse for wear when it came to shutting up in the early hours. He was an expert at one-liner jokes and instant summaries on any situation. On many occasions he would press the wrong button on the alarm panel at the club, or leave a door open, and in no time at all several keen policemen looking forward to a free half would surround the place.

At 2 a.m. one Saturday morning the call went over the radio of the burglar alarm going off at the club and as I was only a one-minute 'run' away, I shouted back that I was on my way. To my amazement as I reached the club, even I had been beaten to it by a panda car and another foot patrol.

Silhouetted in the midst of the blue flashing light of the police car, and holding his left hand to his ear against the deafening ringing of the bell, stood a swaying Bill Cope, at the door to the club. He'd obviously mis-set the alarm in his drunken state, but had heard the alarm bell going off before he'd got in through his own front door. Bill had the keys in his right hand, but was swaying backwards and forwards with the key pointing in the general direction of the keyhole, but never getting any closer than about two feet.

"Slorry lads, done it again," Bill slurred, as his long-range tactics eventually paid off and he managed to open the door.

We entered the foyer of the club to the sound of an internal siren, which was wailing so loudly that it felt as though your ears would burst. We all followed Bill as he lurched through to the bottle store where we knew from previous visits that the alarm panel was to be found. We closed the foyer door behind us as we entered the bottle store, to keep some of the painful sound out, and instinctively looked up at the wall where the panel was fixed. This was a metal box complete with pulsating red lights and a small chrome keyhole. The box was fixed quite high up on the wall and was also issuing yet another, but not so painful, wailing sound.

Bill, who was only a short man, started to climb up onto a strategically placed metal beer keg, which was just below the alarm. On his second attempt he managed to mount the keg and shuffled about, arms waving for balance in his inebriated state. He now had to get the right key into the tiny silver keyhole on the panel and he started to carry out a similar performance to that used on the front door of taking a distant lunge at the keyhole. This additional strain on his drunken sense of balance increased the arm waving and leg wobbling tenfold. He seemed close to taking to the air like a humming bird, when the empty beer keg beneath him also joined in the vibrations and started to tip back and forth.

All this additional co-ordination and balance was far too much for the brain of a drunken man and, predictably, Bill shot forwards towards the wall, grabbing at any handhold available. The three of us nearest instinctively leapt forwards to try to break Bill's fall, but to no avail; the beer keg shot out from beneath him leaving his legs momentarily kicking in the air as he grabbed hold of the alarm box in desperation.

Bill crashed to the floor, legs still kicking, with the entire alarm box ripped from the wall and now clutched tightly to his chest. A silence came over the room as we all looked down at Bill lying on his back apparently uninjured, but still holding the box to his chest with dozens of broken wires poking out of the back. The box was now emitting a feeble distorted peeping sound.

Bill looked up at us from the floor and summed up the situation with his best one-liner to date:

"That's f***ed it."

Anyway, we all managed a free half pint, but there was a note in the burglar alarm book the next night saying, *London Road Club alarm out of action until further notice.*

Saturday, February 12th 1972 had been a bitterly cold day. I pulled my cape around my shoulders for a bit more warmth as I trudged my town centre beat on night duty. The thought had passed through my mind that it had been fairly quiet for a Saturday night and, as a distant church clock chimed midnight signalling the arrival of Sunday, I thought I was in for another pretty boring six hours until my shift ended; there was simply nobody about. That was until a group of middle-aged men came walking along Church Street towards me on the opposite side of the road; they were all wrapped up well against the cold and were chatting with each other.

The strange thing about this was that they all seemed respectable, well behaved and stone cold sober. Most certainly not normal behaviour for a Saturday night, but it would have seemed a little odd to have stopped and checked them out for being well behaved, so I carried on with my beat as the men wandered off, only to see another similar group come into view heading in the same direction. The quietness was disturbed even further as vans, cars, motorbikes and pushbikes appeared, and more and more people started to emerge from every alleyway and side street. Within a matter of half an hour there were crowds of people and cars.

"What the hell's going on?" I said to one group, with genuine puzzlement, and found myself briskly walking alongside in the hope of an answer - there was no way they were going to stop or even slow down to give me a reply.

They were all on a mission.

"League Cup Final, application forms for tickets, on sale this morning," one of the men shouted back at me with a puzzled expression as though I should already have known.

Of course, I thought to myself. Stoke FC had got through to the final of the League Cup and, as they'd never really won anything before, this was a big thing for Stoke-on-Trent. For some reason, the powers that be had overlooked making any arrangements to cover the policing of the thousands of people who were now eagerly en route to the car park at the rear of Stoke City FC's Victoria Ground, and all intent on getting their hands on the application forms for tickets.

I radioed the situation in, and after a moment the radio clicked back on with the despairing voice of Sergeant Turner.

"Just what we need. Right, Pork, get around to the car park and I'll start organising more troops."

As I arrived on the large black ash car park at the back of the Victoria Ground, the sight was amazing, for there were already thousands of people queuing up, all wrapped up warmly with coats, scarves and gloves; some had flasks of hot tea, some had sleeping bags and blankets. Two braziers had already been lit by some of the more enterprising fans, who had apparently been there since the Stoke match against Ipswich the previous afternoon.

In no time at all police officers from different stations started to appear, and an inspector took charge of the impromptu crowd control situation. All the traffic patrols had been called in and their crews turned out of the warmth of their patrol cars. By the time the sales started, the crowd had swelled to twenty thousand and every single ticket was spoken for. We were all told that we would have to work overtime until the sales had finished and, as we were there anyway, we considered it only fair that we should join the queues and buy tickets for ourselves - and that's what we did.

Temporary lighting had been set up by the traffic boys and it was an amusing sight to see these long snaking queues of overcoat-clad people that would be interspersed every so often with a uniformed policeman. I finished duty at 10 a.m. that morning, tired, cold and hungry, but happy in the thought that I would get my two tickets and, as a real bonus, we were all going to be paid overtime for the extra four hours - a very rare thing! I made it down to Wembley with my fiancée, Gladys, on Saturday 4th March that year to watch Stoke win the League Cup 2-1 against Chelsea. What a day!

I was even called in for a special duty the very next day, when I had to stand outside Stoke Town Hall in Kingsway when the team arrived in a red and white bus. They'd got off their train at Barlaston Station, a few miles outside Stoke, and had slowly made the journey in, showing the trophy as they went to the thousands of people who lined every foot of the way. There were fifty thousand in Kingsway alone, and I even got paid for being there.

That same night, officials from Stoke FC contacted the police station and asked if they could leave the League Cup trophy 'in safe custody' with us overnight whilst better arrangements were made at the club.

The cup was duly bought around from the ground and placed under lock and key in one of the empty cells. It was placed on top of a cardboard box on the floor in cell number one with the big steel door locked and the viewing hatch in the door down, so that it could be checked on every so often.

PCs Ken Hallam, Alan Stevenson and Alan Steele in 'Cell Number One' at the old Stoke Nick with The League Cup (photograph courtesy of Ken Hallam)

Later that night when there were no bosses about, the cup was given temporary police bail whilst some of the lads posed for a photograph with it.

At the 2 a.m. meal break the lads had a brew of tea ceremoniously poured from the League Cup, which was returned to the ground the following day with none of the officials at the club any the wiser as to its recent use - safe custody!

* * * *

Woodhouse Street, Stoke, was the home of Stoke-on-Trent's motor taxation authority offices. There were numerous similar such offices throughout the country whose job it was to keep all the records of motor vehicles registered to owners living in their own particular areas. Each authority was allocated certain (usually) two-letter codes, which would form a part of the registration number of the vehicle. By checking the lists, you could tell from which part of the country the car you were interested in 'should' be registered at. Stoke-on-Trent, for example, had VT and EH as two of its codes. There were others, of course, for the rest of Staffordshire, R, RE, RF and BF, so if a crime or something happened anywhere in the country involving a vehicle, the police who were investigating the matter would have to telephone the motor tax office where it *should* have been registered to find out the owner's address. In the case of a car that was registered, for example, with the number, OVT 123, they would have to start with Stoke-on-Trent motor tax office.

It was a very long-winded system because if the owner had moved to another area or lived in another area and had bought the car from someone in Stoke, then its records wouldn't be at the Stoke office any more, but they'd be able to tell you which motor tax office it had 'moved to'.

It could take several days and sometimes even weeks just to find who the supposed registered owner was and, of course, if something serious had happened and someone 'needed to know' after 5 p.m. or at weekends, then we would have to call around at the home of the 'on call' motor tax man and take him down to the office to look through the files.

This happened almost every night, and as far as I remember it was always the same chap who was on call. He didn't even have a telephone or a car, so it became a regular job for the Panda Six or Seven constable to drive to the chap's house in The Avenue, Harpfields, and knock on his door until he finally came down looking very weary. He would then be driven down to Woodhouse Street where he'd pull open metal filing cabinet drawers and sift through little coloured cards until he had the information that someone in some part of the county, or even another part of the country, needed. He did get paid a call-out fee and did eventually manage to afford a telephone.

* * * *

In June 1972, I went on an intermediate driving course at headquarters, which was the step in between the standard driving course that I had completed as a cadet and the coveted 'advanced course', which I hoped to complete eventually.

The course was four weeks in length with just weekends off. We lived in the old Baswich House accommodation block; a very old and historic building within the grounds of headquarters at Stafford. The building was reputed to be 'haunted'.

Downstairs there were the driving school classrooms and the most incredible permanent exhibition of 'How the Motor Car Works', which included an old Sunbeam car dating back to the 1930s, which was completely cut in half, so you could see all the insides of it. There were nine of us on the intermediate course; three, and an instructor in each car. There was also a standard course for learners, and an advanced course. All these courses were running at the same time, each with the same number of people per course, making twenty-seven students in total in nine cars. There would also be motorcyclist courses on the go at the same time, so the place was always very busy.

There was a lot of classroom work to do as well as driving, and we were given a thick blue book with the old Staffordshire County Police emblem on the front entitled, *The System Of Car Control*. The book was full of definitions and diagrams that we had to learn off by heart just like at Ryton.

On my first day in class I realised there were a few familiar faces whom I hadn't seen in a while, one being PC John Cornes, a former Stoke City cadet, whom I knew well from my cadet days. He had an amazingly wide, slightly toothy grin and always had a joke to tell. He spoke with an extremely broad Potteries' accent and called everybody 'youth'. Another old mate was Scottish former cadet, Jock Smart, who had been the first to demonstrate 'river crossing' and the importance of pushing your beret down your jeans.

Staffordshire was one of the few forces that had its own driving school, and many other forces used to send their own officers there to be taught, so there were also several constables from other forces on the course whom we all got to know over the next four weeks.

The course was interesting and exciting, although mentally and physically taxing. At the end of each day's driving, we would all have to take part in the cleaning and polishing of our car, and would have to go through an inspection and a form of drill with our three car doors open for inspection, and then on the command, *'close doors'* would all have to attempt to close twenty-seven doors with one bang.

The course had gone well for almost everyone, and during the last week we were subjected to several written exams as well as two very strict and testing practical driving exams. The formula for each of the three courses during this final week was the same - written and practical testing, but, of course, in greatly varying degrees of expertise. When 4.30 p.m. on the final Thursday (20th July) was heralded with the banging shut of twenty-seven car doors and a final wash and polish, we all knew that the evening would be a night for celebration and a sleepless one as we all awaited our results the following day.

As I drove back towards headquarters just after midnight with colleague, Alan, a constable from Lichfield, after spending our last evening together on the course, we were puzzled as to why the main A34 through to Cannock was closed off. Traffic officers were positioned just up from the front of headquarters and were directing traffic around the back of HQ towards Milford; we drove around and in through the rear entrance wondering what had happened.

"Must be something pretty serious, Alan," I said. "I mean to close off the main A34."

As we entered the old Baswich House and started to climb the stairs, a feeling of gloom descended upon us. There was the sound of muffled voices and sobbing. A terrible accident had happened; John Cornes, Jock Smart and PC Daniel Burnside from Nuneaton, all from the advanced course, had been killed in a head-on collision with a disqualified driver, who was driving a stolen car. He too had been killed. The news was devastating. These were young fit men with everything to look forward to, good friends who had so much to offer. I was close to tears myself as I thought how this would affect their parents, and I knew that John, just twenty-two years old, had only recently married. Several colleagues wept openly, including a young PC who was on one of the courses and was later to become a Deputy Chief Constable.

The following day, which should have been such a happy one, as almost everyone had passed, was reduced to a deeply depressing sorrowful few hours that were used to do nothing more than inform us officially of our course results and send us all home to grieve for our lost friends and to try to put these tragic circumstances behind us.

So with this awful memory it was back to Stoke and to a little more driving rather than walking, as I was now authorised to drive more categories of police vehicles, including the personnel carriers or 'Black Marias' as the public used to call them.

* * * *

The yard opposite the nick in Copeland Street, where we all used to park our cars, was often a cause of friction between ourselves and the council workers, who were also allowed to park there. It was most important that both groups kept to their own side of the green wire fence that separated *us* from *them*. The fencing was held up by wooden posts, which were just banged into the ground in the cobblestone yard, where a cobblestone had been removed. The fence was a pretty flimsy affair and swayed about in the slightest breeze, but had the power of the Iron Curtain, and there would be instant complaints if one of us strayed onto *their* property or vice versa.

Inspector Wild Bill Holdcroft was a man who, as his nickname suggested, had a temper. He didn't suffer fools gladly, but was always very fair and helpful after he'd firstly boiled over. Inspector Holdcroft was, in point of fact, one of the most atrocious drivers I have ever known. He would, for reasons unknown, rev to near destruction the engine of his old black Morris 1000 at each and every opportunity before letting out the clutch in one swift flick of the ankle just as the screaming engine was about to explode. He is the only person I've ever seen make a 'Moggy 1000' burn rubber.

It was a surreal sight that met my eyes as I pulled into the yard one morning to see a wide-open expanse of car park. Not a sign of any green fencing or posts to be seen anywhere. Was the cold war over; had the 'iron curtain' been removed? No! The reason was found to be that some mischievous constable, whose identity was never officially disclosed, had hooked the green wire fencing onto Wild Bill's rear bumper, 'as opportunity arose, and made good his escape'!

Apparently Wild Bill had got into his car to make the journey home the previous evening, started up, revved up to maximum and burnt rubber out of the car park and away down Copeland Street, dragging the entire fifty feet of green wire fencing and eight five-foot-high wooden posts with him all the way down Copeland Street and halfway to Burslem. Apparently oblivious to the horn-sounding drivers and arm-waving pedestrians, he was eventually flagged down by a puzzled and hysterical traffic officer, who was astounded to see the identity of the driver. The traffic officer managed to contain any further amusement until his meal break at Hanley Police Station later that evening, whereupon the story spread county-wide within a few minutes.

* * * *

In December 1972, a new addition arrived on the shift, fresh from Ryton, young PC John Moss, who was from the nearby town of Biddulph.

The wages at this time were really appalling. We were much worse off than most factory workers, and people were leaving the job in droves. Both new recruits and experienced officers were packing it in and taking up anything that was on offer to try to pay the bills. Staffordshire Police lost a lot of officers, who went to work at the Stoke branch of the Michelin Tyre Company. A lot of us tried to subsidise our meagre wages by secretly working. There were lots of ex-tradesmen in the job, who would be out on their days off earning a few extra quid. We had an ex-plumber at Stoke who did central heating and plumbing jobs for almost everybody in the division, there was another PC who repaired everyone's TV and radio. There were decorators, electricians and another constable who made a few extra pounds selling cut-price Durex. The comedian, Pete Conway, who is the father of singer, Robbie Williams, had been a PC at nearby Hanley and apparently used to find it difficult to make it in time for earlies after secretly performing until the early hours at some club far enough away from Stoke-on-Trent for him not to be recognised. You had to be really careful, as working like this was considered a disciplinary offence and you could get the sack.

I tried to make a few extra pounds by repairing cars and, together with Mossy, rented a garage out at the back of some old houses in Stoke, where we would spend some time on our days off covered in oil, messing about with some tatty old banger. It didn't last long, and we were soon back to just trying to make ends meet and getting as many 'special duties' as we could. Special duties were extra duties in addition to our ordinary shifts, for which we would get paid overtime. Normally we wouldn't get any overtime pay at all if we had to work over on a job, which was very frequent, and we would just be given time off for it.

Everyone was clamouring for special duties, such as Stoke and Port Vale football matches, or dances at the Kings Hall in Glebe Street and other 'specials' that would occasionally crop up, which would enable us to earn a few extra quid.

On one occasion Mossy and I had been given special duty to work at the outdoor swimming pool in the huge leisure complex of Trentham Gardens on the outskirts of the city. A local entrepreneur had organised the event. The Tremeloes were playing, there was a barbecue and people could use the pool if they wished. It was a red-hot summer evening and the place was absolutely packed with youngsters, all not much younger than we were.

The organiser had told us that it was a condition of the licence granted to him for the event that he must have 'special duty bobbies'. He didn't, however, really want us 'on display', as he thought it might spoil the atmosphere, so he shut us in a little shed with a couple of bottles of beer to keep us quiet. It wasn't long, however, before some idiots started throwing fully clothed people into the pool. It was really dangerous, as the deep end was well over twelve feet deep, so we emerged from our hut to the obvious astonishment of the group of idiots and went closer to the pool to lay down the law a bit without trying to spoil everyone's fun.

I was just in the middle of telling this group that they would get chucked out, when I caught sight of Mossy's face as he attempted to warn me of approaching danger. He managed to half-raise his arm and started shout something, but it was enough for me to brace myself, as I knew I was about to be launched. The lad seemed to come from nowhere and hit me in the back like an express train. I shot forwards, arms waving for balance, feet trying to get some purchase on the slippery tiles, and in the microseconds that this took, I imagined the embarrassment of wallowing about in the pool with all my dignity and authority diminished to zero as a huge cheer went up. I stopped right on the very edge of the pool with my arms whirling in a hummingbird style blur, as I desperately tried to grab hold of thin air to stop going in. The momentum jerked the helmet completely off my head, and it flew through the air and landed several yards out into the pool as I continued my attempts at unpowered flight and eventually overcame the forces inflicted upon me. I sat down with a bump on my backside in a puddle at the pool edge.

I sprang to my feet, as adrenalin took over, combined with anger. I was determined to get my attacker. The young man was away like a jackrabbit as a game of 'water polo' started to develop in the pool, with my helmet.

I brought him to the ground in a tangle of writhing arms and legs, and a sickening thud as his head hit the concrete. Got him! I thought, as I fumbled for my ageing old-fashioned handcuffs. Stars exploded in my head as someone kicked me in the side of the head, and someone else was pulling at my prisoner trying to set him free as I felt another sickening kick in the ribs.

I looked up to see the blurred image of Mossy standing over me, imitating a windmill lashing out with seemingly six-foot long arms at the seven or eight thugs who had decided to make the best of the opportunity. It looked bad for a while, as we were well and truly outnumbered, but in no time at least six familiar faces had emerged from the crowd and come to our aid. We were fortunate as these were all off-duty colleagues from Stoke and Longton, who were making use of the free tickets the management had given them.

My cowardly assassins turned out to be well known for assaulting police officers, and several of them would come to my attention many more times in years to come. A nice young lady returned my beautiful, but sodden, Stoke helmet, and my attacker, complete with bleeding head, and all the other thugs were taken away to be fined a few weeks later at Eccleshall Magistrates' Court.

* * * *

Often on Friday and Saturday nights until the pubs had turned out and the drunkenness and domestics had died away, town centre patrols would be 'paired up', meaning that two officers would patrol together because of the increased chances of a violent incident at these times.

It was an important and 'absolute' requirement that night duty officers should check the security of 'vulnerable property', both before and after 'meal break'. The problem was that the term 'vulnerable property' included pretty well anything that was locked up over night, so it meant that all the shops, business premises, clubs, offices and the like had to have their front and back doors and windows checked to make sure that they had been locked. By doing so, we would also occasionally discover if the property had been broken into and once in a while catch the odd burglar 'in the act'.

It really was surprising how often you would find the front door to a shop unlocked, and almost every night would reveal an insecure rear door or a window wide open. All such incidents had to be reported in by radio, whereupon the 'office man' would have to sift through the great list of keyholders in the enquiry office and then telephone the keyholder, or have a police car sent around to his house to ask him to visit the property to lock up. Even a light that had been left switched on in a 'lock up' property, which was not normally left switched on, would require similar attention to ensure that 'all was in order'.

Every incident that happened in the area covered by that police station had to be recorded in the 'Book Number 1', also known as 'The Occurrence Book' and, if the previous night's entries included a few 'insecure premises' or 'unusual lights', it meant that the property was being checked.

If there were no such entries then the day inspector would take a closer look to see if there was some reason why property had not been checked, such as a busy night with serious incidents that had kept patrols on the job elsewhere. The worst thing that could happen to you would be that it was discovered that a 'break' (break-in) had happened at a property on your patch and you hadn't found it.

Of course quite often you could be busy with a serious incident and not get the chance to try even one door handle, so it did happen. However, if you appeared to have no excuse, you could even expect a telephone call, or a visit from the inspector, waking you from your sleep, demanding an explanation. It was quite a harsh regime, but it did mean that you got to know the different areas that you worked literally like the back of your hand.

One Saturday evening on nights, I was paired up with fellow shift member, Mick, who was on a 5 p.m. to 1 a.m. shift, whilst I was on until 6 a.m.; it had been quieter than usual for a Saturday. We'd been sent to the Talbot and the Sea Lion to eject the same person from both pubs. He was drunk and mouthing off at the licensee, and was lucky to escape not being locked up, by the skin of his teeth.

We'd had the usual Saturday evening 'domestic' at 35 Lonsdale Street where the ninety-two-year-old father was yet again trying to throw out his sixty-year-old homosexual son onto the street. 'All was quiet on departure', but that was about it.

It was just after midnight and I was pleased when Mick offered to help me out with a bit of 'property checking' for his last hour.

"Yes, cheers, Mick, maybe I'll get chance to do a bit of paperwork later, if it stays quiet," I'd said.

As we walked down South Wolfe Street and passed the post office, I peered in through the 'policeman's window' at the safe and then we turned left through into the narrow alley that led to the rear of Woolworths. This was always in complete darkness and you simply had to use your torch. There were three levels to check as you turned the corner to the left at the end of the alley; one at ground level, which was very narrow and full of rubbish bins. The other two levels were up on rusty iron fire escapes giving access to various doors and windows.

As we started along the first few yards, which led to where the passage turned to the left, I clicked on my torch.

The hairs, not just on the back of my neck, but over the whole of my body, stood on end. I stopped dead in my tracks and automatically held out my left arm to prevent Mick going any further, as he didn't appear to have seen what I could see. There, clearly picked out in the beam, was the lifeless shape of a woman's leg laid on the ground in the mud. I could see the leg from the knee down sticking out from around the corner; a stiletto heel shoe was half on the foot, the heel broken almost completely off.

"My God, Mick, this looks bad," I whispered.

"Yes," he said, "we'd better take a closer look."

I was amazed at his coolness, for I was still trying to collect my thoughts as he strode forwards.

"Slow down, Mick," I gasped, "we've got to be careful, you know, the evidence, not disturbing anything."

We edged a little closer and then something about the skin texture made me start to think that things were not as they seemed. Yes, it was a shop dummy leg used for modelling stockings and shoes. Mick was suddenly laughing at the top of his voice. I was also elated that the situation was not as I'd thought, but couldn't believe the speed of Mick's recovery. I was still in shock, and then the penny dropped.

"You set me up," I shouted with relief.

Mick was still laughing as he wandered off at 1 a.m. to finish his tour of duty.

EIGHT

Friday, November 24th 1972 was to be a landmark day in my police service. I didn't know as I started my noons shift on that chilly winter afternoon that this day would result in PC Pye's exploits in the grimy Potteries' town of Stoke being on the front pages of newspapers across the world, and the subject of television and news reports on an international scale, and later the subject matter in various books and magazines.

It was about 6 p.m. when I got a radio call. It had been a pretty quiet shift and I was looking forward to finishing on time and managing a pint, so when Sgt Turner gave me instructions to go to 'number three, The Villas', where a middle-aged Polish immigrant lodger had not been seen for a few days, I suspected the worst - another form 12.

The house was directly opposite the home of Dr Wood, the police surgeon. The Villas was an avenue of huge Victorian mansions and was originally built for the millionaires of the day, mostly pottery barons. The road itself had never been adopted by the council and, consequently, was totally unmade and consisted of rocks, pebbles and potholes looking, no doubt, very similar to how it was one hundred years previously. Some of the houses had been kept in good condition, but most had deteriorated and been turned into flats.

Number 3, The Villas, Stoke

I had been to number three before and knew it to be owned by a Polish lady whose name was so long and consisted of so many Zs and Rs with hardly any vowels that she had become known to everyone as 'Mrs Rod'.

Mrs Rod rented several of her rooms out to fellow Poles, all males who had fled their country from the German occupation in the Second World War. Number three was a particularly large, dark and eerie-looking building with a gabled porch over the front door, the top of which was adorned by a large rusting iron spike rising a number of feet from the roofline as a form of architectural embellishment.

There were several large trees in the street, which was poorly illuminated by old-fashioned gas-style lamps. The trees cast shadows across the front of the house as I stood in the darkness of the porch awaiting an answer to my knocking. Eventually the figure of Mrs Rod appeared in the dimly-lit hallway and peered, squinting, through the opaque glass of the front door.

She hauled the massive door open and gestured me in, explaining in good English, but with her strong accent, that a Polish lodger who had lived in the house for several years had not been out of his room for several days and was not responding to her knocking at his door. As she showed me up the flight of narrow dark stairs to an equally dark and narrow passageway, Mrs Rod told me that the man had a name slightly easier to pronounce than hers - Demetrious Mykicura.

The passageway was illuminated by a light bulb of a wattage lower than I previously knew existed, and it barely lit the outline of a tongue-and-groove type door, as images of D Block and Dad's garage flooded back again.

This was Demetrious's door. I lightly tapped on the door in a friendly manner and called out a pretty hopeless attempt at his name.

"It's the police, Sir, are you okay?"

Silence…

I increased the volume and tried the door… Silence… Locked… After a few repetitions the inevitable had arrived.

"I'll have to break the door open," I said, turning to Mrs Rod, who was standing a few feet behind me, her hands clasped and with a worried, but knowing, expression illuminated slightly in the dimness.

"Yez, Offizer, it haz to be done," she said.

I firmly shouldered the door, which easily broke free from its lock at the first try. A musty, sickly smell crept out into the passage. There was no light at all inside the room, just total blackness. I fumbled around the inside wall with my outstretched left arm trying to locate the light switch. There was no way I was going over the threshold until I knew what to expect. Upon finding the switch I flicked it up and down - nothing.

Mrs Rod advanced a step closer.

"Zere iz no bulb," she said, "he iz frightened of elektrik, thinks it vil cauz expolzions."

My God, I thought, it gets worse. I pulled my torch out from where I kept it lodged between my greatcoat buttons, and clicked it on. The powerful beam revealed a sorrowful sight; the room barely measured eight by six feet and contained only a single bed and tiny wardrobe. The wallpaper hung in tattered leaves from the wall; Ryton had indeed been luxury.

On the bed I could see a small mound of bed clothing; a mound larger, however, than just pillows and blankets. I took another breath of the dank stale air and stepped over to the bedside, still calling out an attempt at the chap's name, and carefully and slowly pulled back the covers. Demetrious lay wide-eyed with congealed froth around his mouth, his arms up by his head, his fists clenched. He'd obviously been dead for several days.

I turned back to Mrs Rod, who was still silhouetted in the doorway.

"I'm afraid he's dead."

"Oh dear," she whimpered. "He had such a hard life."

She then spoke in Polish to herself for a few seconds as I carried out the officially required, but in these circumstances, totally unnecessary checking for a pulse.

As I drew back the bedcovers a little farther, I could see by my torchlight several small cloth bags in the bed with the corpse; each bag was tied with string at its neck and seemed to contain a powder. The contents trickled out from one torn bag - it looked like salt. Scattered in the bed, on top of the bed and on the floor were dozens of silvery, parchment-like fragments reflecting in the light of my torch. I picked one from the bed and felt how crisp it was as it crumbled between my fingers. It was garlic skin, and sure enough, there in the bed were several actual garlic cloves, too.

"Mrs Rod," I called out to the now composed silhouette, "what would this be for?" I asked, stretching out my arm into the passageway as I did so, and illuminating my handful of cloves, skins and salt bag with my torch.

"It woz for ze vampire," she said. "Demitri believed in ze vampire, zeese things would protect him."

My God, what next? I thought.

"Vampires, you say, Pork?" crackled back Sergeant Turner's reply to my radio summary of the situation. "You'll be needing Doc Wood then. I don't know whether it's for you or the corpse, perhaps you could send a bat over to him - he only lives over the road."

CID came; it was Dave and Jim again, and both smelling as though they'd already had the pint I was looking forward to. Jim was full of his usual sarcasm.

"Hope you've got this one staked out then, Porky."

Doc Wood ambled over from across the road, also smelling as though he'd had my pint. The police photographer was called out to take some photos of the scene. This was a detective sergeant with a terrible squint in one eye that often caused 'photographic misalignment', as he would term it.

Dave and Jim were satisfied that, although unusual, there was nothing suspicious about the death, and they left me to get on with the form 12. Doc Wood could find no sign of injury that could have caused the death.

"It will be up to a PM (post-mortem)," he said.

I had to go through the usual rigmarole of making a detailed plan with measurements and searching the room. Upon looking out through the tiny window I discovered that it led out onto a flat area where one part of the pitch of the roof joined another pitched roof. There, twelve inches or so beneath the window where the two roofs joined, was an upturned plastic washing bowl. I reached out, lifted the washing bowl and was puzzled to see what was definitely a human turd.

As my torch illuminated Demitri's turd I was even more puzzled to see that it had numerous garlic cloves sticking out of the surface. These were quite clearly additions and had not been digested. If this was to continue, perhaps I would become the 'expert on human excrement' that Mr Morley had been questioned about in court. I took statements from Mrs Rod and a couple of other Polish lodgers about Demetrious's background, his job, when he was last seen and so on, and was careful to include all the things known about his obsession with vampires. Eventually the ambulance service came and took the body away to the mortuary, and after writing up as much as I could, I finally managed to get off home at one thirty, completely pint free.

The case was unusual and had raised a ghoulish interest in me, so the next day I visited the library and managed to find a book entitled, *The Natural History of the Vampire*, by Anthony Masters.

I was in for some mickey-taking at work over the next few days; new nicknames were bandied about, such as 'Vampye' and 'PC Dracula' and even more so, when I was spotted reading my vampire book at meal break.

However, on the Tuesday following, I received a phone call from the coroner's officer, Mr Hibbert, telling me that the post-mortem had been carried out.

"He died from asphyxiation," exclaimed Mr Hibbert.

"What, you mean he was strangled?"

"No, no, he choked to death," said Mr Hibbert, "he choked. The pathologist found a pickled onion stuck in his throat."

"Wait a minute, Mr Hibbert," I said, "it's all here in the book, I'll bet it's a bulb of garlic, not an onion."

There was a puzzled silence from the phone as Mr Hibbert tried to piece together what on earth I was talking about. I told him of the book and updated him that I had learned that a method of protection from vampires was to sleep with a bulb of garlic in the mouth to stop the vampire's spirit entering the body.

I also expounded my newly found knowledge on 'vampire protection', regarding sleeping with salt bags and garlic cloves, and even the fact that vampires were believed to relish devouring human excrement (that word again). The theory was that a crafty vampire hater would mix a few garlic cloves in with a strategically placed turd, the intention being that the garlic, which was a poison to the vampire, would go unnoticed as the vampire tucked in to a tasty turd dinner, only to be killed by the unsavoury and poisonous garlic.

"I'll get back to Mr Brown, the pathologist, straight away and get him to look at it," said Mr Hibbert.

I'd met the pathologist previously and had noted that he had as many names as a good bank robber. Mr John Alexander Hunter Brown had been the humorous and clever man who had performed the first post-mortem I had witnessed. For some reason it was considered part of police training that we all had to go to see a post-mortem, and I recall how I just about managed to stay conscious.

It wasn't long before I got a call back from Mr Hibbert.

"You were right, young man, a bulb of garlic it is. Mr Brown sends his thanks and Mr Hales says he wants a very full report, as he will be holding an inquest."

Fred Hales loved a bit of publicity and this one was a sure-fire thing. I wrote up the report in great detail, picking the brains of my old tutor, Bill, who was still on tap to help me out when needed, and then Sergeant Turner could always be relied upon to fine-tune things.

Eventually the masterpiece was submitted, complete with numerous witness statements, detailed drawings, photographs and extracts from Anthony Masters' *Natural History of the Vampire*. That was the last I heard about it until I had to attend the coroner's court for the inquest on Monday, 8th January 1973.

The Stoke-on-Trent Coroner's Chambers had, until recently, occupied a building close to the town centre at the bottom of Stoke Road. My first inquest had been there, but now the entire office of the coroner had been moved up to Hartshill, which was about half a mile out of town, and occupied the former Hartshill Police Station. A new purpose-built coroner's court had been constructed at the side, together with a small car park.

As I arrived I saw that the newly-built courtroom was packed with journalists, and television and radio reporters. Doc Wood was there, together with Dave the detective, the squinting police photographer, Mrs Rod and all the other people I had taken statements from at The Villas. Fred Hales made great play of the incident and examined all the evidence and witnesses in full, including me. At the conclusion he said that it was 'this poor man's obsession with vampires that had led ultimately to his death, so perhaps they got him in the end'.

Fred Hales commended me for the thoroughness of my enquiry, which pleased me no end and delighted my mum and dad, who now had some more 'boasting material' for the pub. The press and TV were clicking and filming as I came out of court, and the next day each national newspaper had a column on the story. The newspaper seller must have thought it rather strange the following morning, when I purchased a copy of pretty well every different paper he had. The Mykicura Case was to follow me around for years to come, and featured in many books and magazines.

It was only a few months after the inquest when a chap from the BBC phoned me at work and told me that they were doing a programme on Bram Stoker, Mary Shelley and all things associated with vampires, Dracula and Frankenstein. He said that they intended doing a big piece about the case and wanted me to take part. Not being in charge of my own destiny, I duly reported the request and the very next week found myself summoned to the office of the chief constable himself at Stafford Headquarters.

Chief Constable Arthur Morgan Rees was a large man with a big round face and an even bigger smile to go with it; he was a likeable man, who enjoyed heaping praise upon those whom he thought deserved it. Mr Rees, as his name suggests, was a Welshman and a former rugby international, and played in the team during their 1935 victory over the 'All Blacks'. It was amazing how many Welshmen were employed as police officers in Staffordshire at this time; many were brilliant sportsmen and some, as a bonus, were also good policemen.

"We… ll, young man," said Mr Rees, with his strong Welsh accent, "I've heard from the Beee Beee Ceee and I knoww they want yooo to go on the tellee, but I don't reeeally like the idea of my officers being associated with vam… pires. So I caan't allow it, but never mind, you'll be on the tellee one day."

Mr Rees's broad grin signalled my departure from his office and, with an electromagnetic salute, complete with wobbling helmet and a floorboard splitting right turn as my left boot thundered into his carpet, I marched from his office, my first chance at the silver screen shattered.

"Well done, young man, well done," echoed the chief's voice, as I marched off down the corridors of power and headed back to the gloom of Stoke.

Arthur Morgan Rees, Chief Constable of Staffordshire, 1964 to 1977

I remember watching the programme on the black and white telly when it was broadcast several months later. Fred Hales was there in all his glory, complete with his monocle, and smoking a cigarette in a long holder. There was so much smoke billowing out of him that every so often the smoke would swirl away as if someone at the side and out of shot was wafting it away so that the cameraman could try to establish if Fred was still in the room. I don't think Fred as a coroner did much for the dangers of smoking and health that night, but he did give me a couple of mentions.

NINE

The next time I would get to hear from Chief Constable Arthur Morgan Rees would be in September 1973. I had been on a week's night duty and, whilst out on patrol on my own at 5 a.m., had come across a well-known and particularly vicious criminal hiding in a churchyard. He had with him a brand new lady's coat.

As I told the thug that I was arresting him on suspicion of theft, I fully expected him to attack me. However, this didn't happen. I took him in, and it later transpired that he had burgled a ladies' outfitters. The next night when I came on duty, there on the 'telephone message pad' (a form 27, if you're interested!) was a personal message for *me* from the chief constable himself, thanking me for 'a good arrest'. I cannot say just how much this little scrap of paper meant to me… To think that he had even got to know of such a minor matter way over there at Stafford HQ, never mind going to the trouble of ringing up in person to thank me, was the most encouraging action anyone could have taken.

John Pye

That 'Message' from the Chief

The police system for promotion to the rank of sergeant required that before you could even be considered, you would have to pass the 'sergeant's exam'; you would become eligible to take this exam as soon as you had completed two years' service.

I had put in for the exam at my first opportunity, but due to idleness and being more interested in 'other things', I had failed. The two visits I had made so far to the ballroom at the Trentham Gardens leisure complex where the exam was held had been pretty pointless and were taken more as an opportunity for a free lunch and a chance to meet some old colleagues whom I'd not seen for a while. As I came out from the exam cursing myself for not doing at least a bit of studying I felt like jumping into the same swimming pool that some idiot had tried to push me into on that 'special duty'. The failures were expected. I knew I had to knuckle down and get some studying done.

* * * *

There were many different characters in 'the job', and Stoke Police Station had more than its share. Sergeant Douglas Mathews was one on his own. Most of the sergeants and inspectors all seemed to me to be as old, or older, than my dad, and 'Dougie' fitted this category. He was a tall man, about six foot four and quite slim for his height. He seemed to have immensely long arms and legs, a long face and blond hair, which was always plastered into a solid quiff with handfuls of Brylcreem.

Dougie was no pushover and would stand nonsense from no one. Pretty well all the crooks and troublemakers on the patch had had a well-deserved thump from him at some time or another and most of them knew to keep their mouths shut. Dougie was a station sergeant on a different shift from me and he was noted as a brilliant snooker player (unlike me).

All the police stations then had a snooker table in them and Ray Reardon, who later became world snooker champion, served as a PC in the old Stoke-on-Trent force and could probably thank some of his time as a PC for the practise he got in on his meal breaks, which helped him towards his title. Dougie would often boast about how many times he'd beaten Ray.

Dougie's main claim to fame (albeit unknown to him) was his extremely noticeable speech impediment, coupled with his use of his own home-made vocabulary, which consisted of words quite similar to the words he really intended to use, but different enough to cause everyone around him to stifle their laughter until the opportunity arose for hysteria. Hardly a day would go by without somebody saying:

"Have you heard Dougie's latest?"

Dougie had an extremely high opinion of his own abilities and was never one to hold back on telling everyone around him about how good he was at football, driving, swimming, card-playing, or any subject that cropped up. Dougie could not sound his Rs and sounded all his Ls as Ws, so this, coupled with his home-made words (known as Dougie-isms) caused his fame to spread, not just throughout the county, but also farther afield. Quite often police officers visiting from other forces would break into a 'Dougie sentence' as a form of greeting to a Staffordshire officer, having heard the stories from someone they'd met on a course.

Dougie would affectionately refer to his wife as, 'the pwincess' and his two-up, two-down terrace house in Wharfe Street, Stoke, as, 'the wickle pawace' (little palace).

On one occasion, Dougie boasted about his forthcoming holiday as he, 'was taking the pwincess to Wugoswovakia' and the next year to 'Majowica', and on another occasion he was heard reading out a crime report on parade, where someone had entered the church and stolen a 'sowid (solid) silver candle-bwraa' (candelabra). He would often read out the MO of how a crime was committed when parading the men before patrol, and describe how, 'the offender cwimbed over the pwee-meter fence' (perimeter fence).

One day, the Stoke City and England goalkeeper, Peter Shilton, came into the station to enquire about something, and Dougie later told the story that he looked, 'just like a chimpaneez'. When everyone burst into laughter Dougie told them that they should not laugh, as it was not Shilton's fault.

On a summer police station outing to Blackpool one year Dougie told the lads that there was nothing he liked better than to, 'whi (lie) on the beach and watch the seagulls hoovering in the sky'.

Dougie's car was a 'Ford Angular' rather than a Ford Anglia. On another occasion a German lorry driver came in, apparently trying to get directions for the Michelin factory. As the office staff struggled to overcome the language barrier, Dougie muscled in and said he'd deal with the matter as he 'spoke a wickle German'. He then leaned over the counter and shouted, 'Vot iz your name?'. He then asked the man to, 'sit down on those tubercular chairs'. His Italian was no better, as when trying to impress an attractive lady at the counter, he greeted her with, 'Bournevitta, Senorita'.

PC Ray Reardon, complete with Stoke helmet
(photograph with kind permission of Ray Reardon)

I had now become a regular panda car driver. I could never work out why they were called panda cars because they were a kind of greeny blue and white, not black and white like a panda. There were three 'panda areas' on Stoke's patch; Panda Six, which covered an area called Hartshill and down into the town, Panda Seven, which covered the Trent Vale area and down into the town and Panda Eight, which covered Trentham. None of the areas was vast in size, but there were plenty of folk living in them, so we were kept pretty busy. There would be one panda car for each 'area' and two 'area men' per area.

The area men would, more often than not, be PCs who lived on that patch, and it was supposed to be their job to get to know the people on the patch. As a panda driver you got to know the area men well and you would often pick them up and drop them off at home for their meal, or when they'd finished duty (area men were the only ones allowed to go home for meals).

The pranks and mischief still continued when time allowed and I got caught out by area man, PC Roger Owen, who, in his efforts to teach me to lock my panda car whilst I was out checking property, once 'stole' it by releasing the handbrake and hiding the car around the corner. I nearly passed out when I saw it had gone and was just about to radio in to say what had happened, when Roger appeared from the shadows saying:

"I'll teach you, Porky."

It actually took another occasion to cure me. During my brief absence he'd got into the car through the unlocked door and hid in the darkness, lying down on the back seat, revealing himself only as I was about to start the engine, by grabbing me around the throat. I never left the car unlocked again.

Bertie was another area man and he had been having a lot of 'marital problems'. Bertie and his wife were always falling out. I'd often give him a lift home and he'd ask me in for a cuppa, but there'd always be an atmosphere. They'd both talk to me, but not to each other. It was about nine thirty one evening and I'd just dropped Bertie off at home for his meal, as he was on a 5 p.m. till 1 a.m. shift and I was looking forward to finishing at ten and then having a pint in the Copeland Arms. I had a drunken prisoner in the cells back at the nick, who had got to be charged before I went off duty. As I entered the enquiry office I could hear the sound of someone else's 'drunk' shouting obscenities at Sergeant Turner. I knew it wasn't my drunk, as mine had gone past the 'obscenities' stage, and was in the 'apologetic and feeling sorry for himself' stage.

"Flattery wunner get you bail," Sergeant Turner shouted down the cell passage, in reply to the drunken man's disgusting comments.

Just then the radio crackled into life and started to hiss.

"What's up with it, Sarge?" I said, slapping the blue metal casing.

"I don't know, Pork," replied Sergeant Turner, slapping it even harder.

"Right, I've bloody well had enough of you," shouted the radio.

"What's this, Pork? Who is it?" said Sergeant Turner as he twiddled the radio's knobs.

"Go back to your bloody mother then, and the sooner the better," shouted the radio.

"Is someone on a domestic, Pork? Who the hell is it?" Sergeant Turner said, with a puzzled expression.

"No, Sarge," I said, "I think it's Bertie and his missus. I think his transmitter button's got stuck in."

There then followed a detailed account of Bertie's fifteen years of married hell, interspersed with frequent colourful descriptions of all the things he hated about her, followed by his wife's broadcasts about what 'a useless sod' he was. We were subjected to a full five minutes of this before my frantic fumbling through the list of officers' phone numbers revealed Bertie's, and the argument was interrupted by the sound of a telephone ringing in the background, to which Bertie was heard to shout:

"If that's your bloody mother tell her from me to sod off."

Bertie was rather subdued for a few days after the incident.

* * * *

We were still using the original breathalysers back then. We'd keep a box in the panda cars. They were a sealed glass tube containing amber crystals; there was a halfway mark on the centre of the tube. Each of the small green plastic boxes would contain half a dozen tubes. There was a tiny hacksaw blade fitted into the side of the box, which you had to use to score the sealed ends of the glass tube and then push them into a tiny hole in the box to snap off the ends. Inside the box was also a folded plastic bag that you pushed on to one end of the tube, and a number of disposable mouthpieces that went on the other end.

After you had gone through a piece of legal jargon with the suspect, he then had to blow into the mouthpiece and completely inflate the little bag. If the crystals changed colour from amber to green past the halfway mark then you could arrest the person and, after a second attempt at the nick, he would be asked to give a blood or urine sample. It was a lengthy procedure and, coupled with getting the police surgeon out for the blood sample, could take hours. 'Blowing in the bag' and 'blowing a green one' were stock phrases then, but most police officers now would struggle to understand the connection with the electronic breath test of the modern era.

Another week of nights came around. It was May 1974. I had been married almost twelve months now and couldn't wait for the next few weeks to pass as the holiday in Cornwall, which wife Gladys and I had been saving for all year, drew nearer.

Staffordshire Police Austin 1100 Panda Car
(photograph courtesy The Potteries Museum)

It had been a warm evening and even as 3 a.m. approached was still quite mild as I slowly drove my

Austin 1100 panda car along Liverpool Road. By now the old areas numbered six, seven and eight had been changed to forty-one, forty-two and forty-three. I suppose there must have been some logical explanation, but no one knew why, so I was '42' instead of Panda Seven. I felt no different.

It had been the usual busy Friday night but had now quietened down, so I'd managed to get a few reports out of the way. I'd also been down to the main postal sorting office on Leek Road to post a blood sample by recorded delivery from a breathalyser that I'd had the night before.

The radio startled me back out of holiday daydreams.

"42, burglar alarm activated at Wengers, Cliff Vale," came Sergeant Turner's voice, "usually a good 'un, Pork."

"Okay, Sarge, on my way – over," I shouted back, as I gunned the frisky 1100 and sped away hearing the engine thump back into the bulkhead in between each gear change.

Sergeant Turner was right. This was usually a good burglar alarm, which had resulted in quite a few arrests; Wengers was a firm involved in the pottery trade, specialising in colour for glazes and decoration on crockery. The building itself was quite modern, but a bit isolated and the only thing worth pinching from these places, apart from a bit of petty cash, was the liquid gold that was used in colour.

I heard Sergeant Turner's voice directing other cars to also attend, and as I pulled into the large front forecourt, I realised I was first on the scene. At the rear of the building was a compound, completely enclosed by a six-foot-high, concrete sectional wall. Previously, burglars had always broken in through the back, after climbing over this wall. As I got out of the panda car, a patrol car and another panda pulled in onto the car park. I flashed my torch at the front doors of the building as I casually waved over at the other arrivals; suddenly there was a clatter of something metal in the compound.

With no thought other than 'burglar', I ran headlong towards the wall - I was a fit twenty-four year old and a six-foot-high wall was no obstacle at all. I took hold of the top of the wall with both hands and heaved upwards, jumping at the same time and hooking my left foot over the top. I was just easing myself up and readying myself for the drop down to the other side when everything went into slow motion. It was a bit like being back in Ian's car as a cadet when we had 'flown' over the roundabout and crashed through a garden wall.

Everything was slowly collapsing around me. There was a rumbling sound and a shaking as the wall on which I was perched folded backwards and down onto itself. I crashed to the ground as the concrete fence posts and the huge concrete panels tumbled down around me, pinning me to the ground trapping my feet and my left arm, and knocking the breath out of me. I was surrounded by a mountain of concrete slabs; my torch was still switched on and shone its beam skywards from within the posts and panels as a cloud of dust lingered in the air.

Three uniformed figures jogged over to me from their cars, half-laughing.

"You okay, Pork?" asked a voice.

"No," I mumbled back from within my concrete den.

It took several minutes to free me, and everyone looked up in amazement as a cat, which had probably been the cause of the noise I had heard, darted out of the compound through the hole I had made in the wall.

"Cat burglar!" someone joked.

There was no radiologist on duty when I arrived at the accident unit, so they bandaged both my badly swollen wrists and arms, and both my scraped shins, put a sticking plaster on the grazes to my forehead and soothed my dented ego, telling me to come back for X-rays after 9 a.m.

My wife, Gladys, usually a heavy sleeper, awoke with a start and a shout of, 'Oh, my God!', as the bandage-swathed 'mummy' hobbled into the bedroom to relate the tale. A visit to the hospital again later that morning revealed a fractured left wrist, and resulted in a plaster cast from the elbow with just my fingers and thumb poking out. It was going to take ten weeks before I was allowed back to work, as the broken scaphoid bone is a notoriously difficult one to heal.

I had so many jobs to do in the house that we had recently bought at Clayton near Newcastle-under-Lyme, but I effectively now only had one arm with which to try to do them. I was so bored that I decided I would try to dig an inspection pit for the garage that I'd got on order. Within a few hours I had mastered how to dig with one arm. By wrapping my right arm around the shaft of the spade and pushing the handle up into my armpit I could manage to make progress, if not a little slowly.

At the end of each day's digging my right arm ached, but the pit was taking shape and ever so slowly nearing the five-feet depth required. My right arm was taking on 'Charles Atlas' proportions as the left plaster-encased counterpart slowly withered away with the lack of use. I was eventually put on light duties, working at the coroner's office (more form 12s). I managed the trip down to Cornwall for the holiday I'd been daydreaming about, and at long last had the plaster cast removed for good.

I had to visit a consultant over my claim for the injuries that I had sustained. I removed my shirt as directed and saw the surgeon raise his eyebrows as he surveyed the injured wrist and arm, which through weeks of inactivity looked forlorn and stick-like. My right arm, however, looked as though it belonged to another person. The weeks of one-armed pit digging had sculpted it into a bulging muscular device more suited to a Greek statue. The consultant measured both arms at various places from the shoulder down to the wrist and then looked at me with a most concerned expression.

"There has been considerable wastage to your left arm and, consequently, this should increase the claim greatly," he said.

I didn't think he'd be very interested in my inspection pit, so I left it at that. After a few weeks out of the shade and a bit of exercise the left arm was almost back to normal.

* * * *

I had been at Stoke five years now. My third attempt at my sergeant's exam had been another waste of time (must study!). I had got myself pretty well known with my colleagues from around Staffordshire and with most of the crooks in and around Stoke, and I'd seen a lot of changes even in the short space of time I'd been there.

We'd got one personal radio now to take out on patrol, instead of the two 'Pye' ones. We now had a Burndept make radio that was both a transmitter and a receiver. It came with a great entanglement of straps to fit it to you. Finally gone was the old Stoke-on-Trent City Police Force that was supposed to have disappeared in 1968 upon amalgamation with Staffordshire. It had taken a long time and I suppose that there were still a few ghosts of the old force remaining for many years to come.

Once in a while an old Stoke form would turn up with the name of the old force on it, just to remind those who had forgotten, or those who never knew. Funnily enough those old Stoke forms always seemed to have been better thought out than the ones we had to use now.

Yes, gone were the beautiful old Stoke helmets, even within the long since non-existent boundaries of the old Stoke force. In fact, the badge on the helmets had changed a few times, as the official title of the force had changed. First it had been changed from Staffordshire County Police to Staffordshire County and Stoke-on-Trent Constabulary, and finally it had been changed to just Staffordshire Police. A lot of the old Stoke bobbies had said that the official changeover date of 1st April 1974 was 'well chosen'.

We all had 'buckets' for helmets now, and damned silly they looked, especially if you were a bit of a pinhead like me. The beautiful 'closed neck' old-fashioned, but 'dead smart', capes with the brass lion's head clasps that we used to wear were also gone, and gone too was the old police station itself. We were now in a brand new purpose-built, four-storey nick in Boothen Road just a ten second run from Stoke City FC's Victoria Ground.

Stoke Police Station 1974 (photograph courtesy The Potteries Museum)

Princess Margaret had officially opened the new police station on Tuesday, 2nd July 1974, and I'd gone and missed it by being off sick with my broken wrist. Princess Margaret had a close affiliation to the area, as she was Chancellor of the nearby Keele University. The old nick, sadly, was being demolished to make way for a big, new road scheme. The new nick had every modern convenience including its own garages and petrol pumps. It had a large cell block for both men and women, with a big prisoner exercise yard. There were dozens of offices upstairs, a proper canteen with 'real' canteen staff, a large and well-appointed bar-cum-function room and TV room, but no snooker room, which seemed to be a feature that was being dropped.

Another change that took place during this year was to the flat peaked caps that were part of our uniform and mostly for use when on car patrol. We were all given black and white chequered bands that had to be fitted around the caps; it was something that the Scottish forces had had for some time, and it wasn't until 1974 that the remaining UK forces went over to them.

We had an amazing computer system that had come online in February 1974. It was called the Police National Computer (PNC for short) and to start with we were just able to check on vehicles to see if they were stolen by telephoning headquarters where just two terminals were installed.

'The Box', the First Type of Computer Terminal used in Staffordshire
(photograph courtesy The Potteries Museum)

Over the next eighteen months or so the records from vehicle licensing authorities were also put on and eventually we could just ring headquarters and almost immediately find out the owner of a car. I expect the motor tax man, who we used to get out of bed all the time, had mixed feelings, as he'd get more sleep, but was missing out on all that overtime money.

After a few years each police station had its own terminal, which became known as 'The Box', and the names and records of criminals and wanted people went on as well. Ultimately all incidents were logged on, together with the details of staff on duty at any one time. The system was eventually called Command & Control.

* * * *

In July 1975 my dreams (and applications) were answered when I was temporarily posted to Stoke CID for an official four-month 'CID aide', which was par for the course before anyone could be considered for a permanent job in the department as a detective constable.

1975 was proving to be a busy year for me. I was interested in drugs work and had been on a drugs course shortly before my CID aide, and no sooner had I finished the 'aide' than I was put on an advanced driving course. I'd already been on two other types of driving courses, but this one was special; all the other guys on the course had applied for it, as they wanted to become traffic officers. I wanted it because I wished to become a 'crime car' driver.

The 'crime car' was a system that was used at that time as a quick response vehicle to all major crimes within the division, and to be a 'crime car' driver you had to be an 'advanced driver'. The other driving courses were good, but this was truly amazing. We had all the best, high-speed road cars of the day available to us, from the Ford Cortina 2000e, the Triumph Dolomite Sprint to the Jaguar XJ, which we would regularly perform in at speeds in excess of 130 mph.

There were nine of us on the advanced course, along with nine other officers who were on the intermediate course and another nine who were on the standard course. There were also some motorcyclists on a course. The set-up was in fact just as it had been on my intermediate course when I had lost my three friends in that terrible road accident three years previously.

Our bedrooms upstairs in the rambling, old, supposedly haunted, Baswich House were all dormitory style; some had four beds, some three and some two. Alan Smith and I shared a two-bedded room and were usually completely worn out after a day of intense concentration, some class work, oh, and a few beers in the headquarters bar, or at the Crossbows pub around the corner.

As I settled off to sleep one night after such a day, I could hear that Alan had already arrived in the land of nod, and I don't think I was all that long behind him. I think I must have been asleep an hour or so when I half-woke in a cold sweat, my heart pounding. Disorientated by the darkness of this seemingly unfamiliar room, I lashed out at whatever was gripping my feet. I could feel a heavy weight slowly enveloping me from the bottom of the bed. I pulled up violently, arching my back against the wall behind me, and let out a blood-curdling shriek, flailing my arms about in the direction of the black writhing mass at the foot of my bed.

"It's there, it's there!" I screamed out, pointing in the gloom at the *thing*.

"What… what… what the hell is it?" screamed Alan from his darkened corner.

"It's there, *it's there*!" I screamed back, leaping from my bed in semi-conscious confusion and fear.

"What is it? What the bloody hell is it, for God's sake?" shrieked back a petrified Alan.

"Look at it, look at it, it's *there*!" I shouted, leaping for safety onto Alan's bed and continuing to point and shout at the corner whilst Alan, who lay pinned to his bed beneath me, was now screaming loudly himself.

"What is it, for God's sake? What's happening?" shouted Alan's head, the rest of him being completely and tightly sealed in beneath his blankets and my weight.

Suddenly a calm came over me as I realised it was nothing more than a nightmare. Taking a deep sigh of relief I returned to my bed and immediately went back to sleep, leaving my poor colleague wide awake and shaking with fear.

The next day a very weary looking Alan proclaimed over breakfast that, 'any more nightmares' and he would be 'asking for a new room-mate'. It emerged later in the day that a fellow student in another room had claimed to 'have been frightened out of his wits in the night, as he saw a shadowy figure walk directly through a wall in his bedroom'. The position of the 'disappearing figure' led straight to the foot of my bed. Many beers were required before I could get off to sleep that night.

A View from the Staffordshire Police Skidpan at Hixon, near Stafford
(photograph courtesy The Potteries Museum)

The day following 'the ghost' was spent on the driving school skidpan. Staffordshire police had their own specially built skidpan, which consisted of a large smooth-surfaced track that had automatic water jets spraying the oil-laden surface. Different arrangements of track were made up with cones, and the cars that were used, usually old Ford Cortinas, had special 'slick' tyres. There was a control room from where instructions were given and assessments made, and it really was a laugh and undoubtedly helped us to achieve the high standards that were required.

Ghosts apart, it had been a great course and now as an advanced driver I returned to Stoke as a 'crime car' driver. I only spent a few weeks on this job when I was offered a post with the force drug squad. I was elated, although still a little sad to be leaving my friends at Stoke.

TEN

The force drug squad had two offices; one was at Stafford Headquarters, the other at Hanley Police Station. Hanley nick was a massive building, which had been built as the headquarters of the old City Force in 1964, consequently, its numerous rooms and offices, which were originally all designed for a specific purpose, were slowly being made use of for various different new departments and squads that were springing into life.

The drug squad office was by no means purpose-built. It was about eight feet wide by fifteen feet long, and was used as a base by up to six of us. I was to be teamed up with an old name from the past, none other than Jim, ex-cadet, bullshitter and never-to-be boxing champion. I hadn't seen Jim since the cadets. Jim was now a detective constable, which went some way towards proving the old police saying, 'You'll always slide further on bullshit than you will on gravel'. Jim hadn't changed his ways and still put more work into getting what he could out of the job rather than what he could put into it.

* * * *

During 1975 a series of major arson attacks took place in and around the Longton area of Stoke-on-Trent. The premises were nearly always pottery factories and there seemed to be a major fire almost every week during the summer. Many thousands of pounds worth of property was going up in flames on a regular basis, and lives were at risk and jobs affected. Longton CID was stretched to the limit with all their detectives involved on fire enquiries and despite their best efforts the attacks continued.

The bosses decided to arrange observation teams working nights to try to catch the firebug, but the attacks continued, so more and more officers were drafted in to lurk about in disguises in the shadows in every possible back alley and hidey-hole that existed.

Despite having only been a father for a matter of weeks, I was drafted in from my drug squad duties to also do my bit on the 'obs' teams working a full two weeks' stretch on nights, leaving my wife Gladys at home to look after baby, Adam.

I had been given my obs point for the duration of my stay, which was up in amongst the bushes and gravestones of St James and St Johns Churchyard on Normacot Road just outside Longton town centre. My position in the darkness gave me a perfect and concealed viewpoint of several small pottery factories and other industrial premises, including the front of the huge pottery factory of Hudson and Middleton. I could clearly see the large wrought iron gates of this factory, which were set into the blackened, but detailed, brickwork of the building.

Most of these factories had a night watchman or a kiln man working through the night, but this had not deterred the arsonist, who had often made use of the large quantities of cardboard boxes used for packaging to set his fires.

The first few nights of my duty had been as boring as hell. Nothing had happened and the only things of interest had been listening to my police radio to hear what else was going on in the world and watching the odd drunk stagger off up the road.

It was just after 1 a.m. as I tried to keep my eyes open and, as I flexed my shoulders to ease the stiffness, I thought I caught a glimpse of the very slightest of movements from the nearby junction with Chelson Street, where the black silhouettes of the old brick bottle kilns of Ashdale Pottery could be seen sticking up above the pitched roofs of the other buildings. I rubbed my eyes and tried to focus better in the gloom and then... Yes, there was definitely a figure peering around the corner.

As the figure slowly craned his neck around the edge of the wall, looking left and right, the tiny red glow of the pinprick of a cigarette could be seen in his right hand. The man stepped out halfway into the street, took a long drag on his cigarette, dropped it to the pavement, ground it in with his foot and, with a second furtive look up and down the empty street, stealthily made his way across the road towards the gates of Hudson and Middleton. As he neared the gates he pulled something from his pocket... It was a pair of gloves, he was putting on a pair of gloves! My heart rate started to increase... *This could be the man!*

My eyes were now wide and unblinking as the man went right up against the bars to the gate and peered through. He then took hold of the bars and started to climb up the eight-foot high gate using the cross bars as a form of ladder. I pulled my transmitter from my pocket and whispered the situation back to the control room at Longton Police Station.

"Okay, Pork," came back the radio reply, "stay concealed, keep us updated, I'm getting patrols to quietly close in around the place."

A hushed crackle of radio activity commenced on my low volume radio as different cars, foot patrols and obs officers were directed quietly, but quickly, to make their way to strategic positions around the factory. The figure had now climbed over the gate and dropped down into the darkened yard beyond. I vaguely caught a glimpse of him as he slipped back into the shadows, and then heard the distant whine of several different police cars being driven apace and obviously taking up their positions. Shadowy figures started to break the darkened stillness as up to eight officers waited for the command.

Suddenly my radio shouted out:

"Go, go, go!"

Figures appeared from every corner and alleyway to take up positions around every part of the building. Three of the figures ran directly towards the gate and I also broke cover from my bushes to join in.

Two powerful torch beams shone through the gate bars into the yard as one officer was almost over the gate already. Just as the officer dropped onto the cobblestones on the other side of the gate, a huge pile of cardboard boxes in a corner of the yard suddenly erupted into the air and a figure stood up from within it.

"Police!" a voice shouted…

"Police!" another voice shouted.

The cardboard box figure produced a torch himself and blazed it back at the three officers, who were now in the yard.

"*Police!*" he then shouted.

"*What?*" someone else shouted.

"Don't move!" one of the officers said.

"No, *you* don't move," replied the cardboard box man.

"What the hell is going on?" quizzed a different voice

"I'm DC Smith from Stafford," said cardboard box man, "this is my obs point. I was late coming in, got held up with a job in Stafford, so I just came on down and got settled in, next thing is all you lot appear, frightened the bloody daylights out of me."

I slunk back to my bush.

The arson attacks were never satisfactorily concluded, but the finger of suspicion had pointed towards a prominent member of the community, who was questioned and released, due to a lack of strong evidence. The suspect went missing shortly after his release and was found dead, having committed suicide by setting fire to himself - then the fires stopped!

After my two weeks on obs, it was back to the drug squad. It was at this time that the evil crimes of a man who had become known as the Black Panther were constantly in the papers and on the television. The Panther was responsible for the murders of three postmasters; offences that he had committed during post office robberies in Lancashire and Yorkshire, along with numerous other violent robbery offences.

On 14th January 1975, Lesley Whittle, the seventeen-year-old heiress of a coach travel company, was kidnapped in the dead of night from her home in Highley, Shropshire, and was then held to ransom. The kidnapper made a demand for £50,000, and a complex series of instructions led Lesley's brother, Ronald, under police surveillance, to Bathpool Park, Kidsgrove, within the Staffordshire Police area, to 'make the drop'.

A lot of things had gone wrong, both with the kidnapper's plans and the police operation to catch him. Suddenly there was no more contact, leaving Lesley's mother desperately wondering what had happened to her daughter and West Mercia Police, whose job it was to deal with the abduction, in 'stasis'. It was a week later when West Midlands Police contacted the West Mercia enquiry team to tell them that a shooting had occurred on the same night as the proposed ransom drop, during a robbery at a freightliner terminal in Dudley, and that security guard, Gerald Smith, had been shot five times, but was clinging to life. A car abandoned nearby and ballistic evidence, had now proved a connection between the post office murders, Lesley's kidnapping and, of course, Gerald Smith's shooting.

The officer running the kidnapping inquiry, West Mercia's Detective Supt Bob Booth, then ordered a full search of Bathpool Park, and poor Lesley's body was found hanging deep inside a drainage shaft. As the body had been found within the Staffordshire area, the murder inquiry officially fell upon the Staffordshire police to investigate. This massive inquiry severely sapped the strength of Staffordshire Police and was conducted from the small police station of Kidsgrove, which was a part of the Newcastle-under-Lyme police area.

So much paperwork had been generated by the inquiry and so many staff, both police and civilian, were engaged on it that structural engineers had to be called in to ensure that the upper floor of the building could withstand the weight. CID officers from all over the county had been drafted in to assist, and squads such as the drug squad had to supply manpower. Two officers from our squad were working full-time on the inquiry and, whilst greatly interested in it, I was still trying to get to grips with my new job, and found that because of the manpower shortage I had been thrown in at the deep end a little.

It was a December evening in 1975 when the Panther was caught. He was seen acting suspiciously on his way to rob another post office in Mansfield in Nottinghamshire and, whilst being checked out by two uniformed police officers, he had pulled a sawn-off shotgun from his holdall and turned it on them, taking them hostage and no doubt intending to murder them. However, during a struggle in which the gun was fired, the officers managed to overpower and arrest him with the help of some members of the public.

He was soon identified as the Panther and, with his real name of Donald Neilson now public knowledge, he was transported to Newcastle-under-Lyme Police Station for lengthy interviews, court appearances, remands and so on. As the inquiry was so vast and involved so many murders, attempted murders and robberies over such a wide area it would be many months before the matters were ready to go before the court.

One Monday morning, whilst I was at the Hanley drug squad office, I received a phone call telling me to report to the murder incident room at Kidsgrove. I arrived there within twenty minutes and was given a job. I was to drive to Dudley in the West Midlands and visit the home of Gerald Smith, the freightliner terminal security guard who had bravely tackled Neilson back in January 1975 and who had nearly lost his life in the process. His conscientious actions were turned against him, as he had disturbed Neilson in the middle of his criminal activities. Neilson had shot him and continued shooting him as he lay on the ground, pumping five bullets into him, clearly intending to kill him. Amazingly Gerald Smith had clung to life and somehow hung on until help arrived. He had undergone countless operations, but was now out of hospital and making a recovery.

It was with some excitement that I knocked on the door of the neat semi-detached house in Dudley in expectation of meeting this courageous man who had looked down the barrel of Neilson's gun, been shot and had survived. Mrs Smith, a slim fiftyish lady with tightly permed blonde hair and a pleasant smile, answered the door.

"Gerald's gorn back into hospeetal, my luv," she twanged in her Black Country accent. "Ayd got some bullights still in him, so they'n gooin ta tidy him up a bit more."

"I've got some exhibit labels that he's got to sign, nothing more than that," I explained.

"Oh!" she replied. "Yow'll be all roight, just go and see him at hospeetal."

Following Mrs Smith's directions I drove to Dudley General Hospital and arrived at Gerald's ward, clutching the handful of brown card exhibit labels, each one with its short piece of string for attaching it to the relevant exhibit.

"Police," I said to the ward sister, showing my warrant card. "I've come to see Mr Smith. Just got something for him to sign."

"Oh, that's fine," said the sister, "he's over there, giving out the teas."

She pointed to a tall well-built man wearing a brown dressing gown, who was standing near a tea trolley at the other end of the ward.

"Mr Smith, PC Pye, Staffs Police," I said. "I've just got some labels for you to sign, sorry to see you're back here."

"Oh, that's okay, nice to meet you," he said, extending his hand. "There were some bullets they couldn't get out, so they're just tidying me up," he explained as he warmly shook my hand. "How about a cup of tea whilst we sign?" he said, gesturing over at the tea trolley.

Of course I accepted.

Gerald Smith died two weeks later. It was blood poisoning; I must admit I was quite upset about it. I didn't know the man, but he'd been through so much and seemed perfectly okay and then...

An unusual piece of law, which very rarely came into play, had to be used because the shots fired by Neilson, into Gerald, which were clearly intended to kill him, didn't kill him until after a year and a day had elapsed, so Neilson could not be charged with his murder. He could only and was only, therefore, charged with his attempted murder. This law has now, however, been changed.

It was July 1976 before Neilson was eventually sentenced to five life terms for his horrendous string of murders and attempted murders, not to mention the nineteen armed robberies and many other burglary offences for which he was responsible. The attempted murder charge in relation to Gerald Smith was ordered 'to lie on file'. The judge added a 'whole life tariff' with no possibility of parole, although with another change in the law there does now exist a legal chance of his release, albeit a small one.

It was around this time when the force suffered another terrible blow with the deaths of another two of my friends and colleagues, PCs John Hunt, aged thirty, and Dennis Tunnicliffe, aged twenty-seven, both highly skilled police motorcyclists, who were killed in an awful road accident.

In April 1976, I was offered a permanent position on the drug squad and appointed 'Detective Constable'. However, that year's sergeant's exams came and went as in the other attempts – failure. I'd really got to sort myself out. It was then that I met Des Lewis, a PC who had been seconded to the drug squad with a view to a permanent position. Des would be my partner and comrade-in-arms on the drug squad for the next two and a half years, and my lifelong friend. Des had already passed his promotion exams and somehow seemed to inspire me into the 'study mode', so could this be my year?

The drugs squad was an interesting, laugh a minute, action-packed job, which was made all the better as I was now working with a man who shared the same sense of humour and passion for the job that I did. We were virtually our own bosses; we could do pretty well whatever shifts we wanted, according to what jobs we'd got on and we could go wherever we needed to and use our own initiative. We'd often work very long hours if a particular job demanded it, sometimes as much as twenty hours in one shift, and we'd cover an area over most of North Staffordshire, taking in Keele University,

Newcastle-under-Lyme, Stoke-on-Trent and right up to the boundaries of Derbyshire in the Staffordshire Moorlands.

We were, however, kept very busy just in and around the Newcastle and Stoke-on-Trent areas, but if the Stafford office had a big job on, we'd go over to help them, and they'd return the compliment if need be. You could, therefore, start your day early on observations on a cottage in the moorlands of Leek and finish off in some pub later that night in Burton-on-Trent or Tamworth. The other thing was that if there was a murder somewhere in the county that didn't look like it was going to be cleared up quickly, then the drug squad would be one of the first to be picked on to supply the extra detectives and, of course, all the drugs enquiries would have to be put on hold.

One person from the squad had to be on call on nights for the whole of the county, in case a major drugs problem occurred. We would share this cover between the Hanley and Stafford offices. This 'call out' rota was no perk, as you still had to do your ordinary duty and got no recompense for being on call. You just got paid overtime if you did get called out. In fact, you could just have got home at 1.30 a.m. after a long day and then get a phone call at 2.30 a.m., telling you to go all the way from Stoke to Lichfield where some bloke had been locked up with a big block of cannabis, or that some youngster had been found dead with a needle sticking out of his arm.

Search warrants were everyday occurrences for the drug squad and we had a great list of magistrates' addresses and phone numbers that we used to carry around in the van. We would choose whom to pick on to pester in the middle of the night to sign the search warrant to make it legal. Whenever possible we would use our favourites, usually the ones who weren't too full of their own importance or wanted to ask too many tricky questions before deciding to sign for us. Some of them were really nice down-to-earth people, who we would be on first name terms with and who would get the Scotch out while we told them the story, and would insist that we rung them back no matter what the time, so that we could let them know how we'd gone on.

The secret with a drug squad search warrant was the element of surprise, getting in quick. In no time at all the drugs would be thrown on the fire or flushed down the toilet and then you'd all end up with official complaints being made against you and claims of police harassment. It wasn't always a good idea simply to try to kick the door down because often drug dealers would have had their doors strengthened purposely. The only thing that you would achieve would be to make a lot of noise, giving the dealer plenty of time to dispose of the evidence. There could also be a big dog or children just behind the door. Sometimes cunning and stealth were the best way in.

Des had now been appointed 'Detective Constable' and we were working together on a 'suspected dealer'; a man who lived in Basford, Stoke-on-Trent. He had a large upstairs flat on the corner of a busy main road. The sturdy wooden door to the upstairs flat had apparently been strengthened with additional bolts. We knew that the door led directly on to a flight of stairs, which went straight up into the flat. This fellow was dealing big in cannabis resin and we needed to get him 'bang to rights' with the evidence. Trying to kick the door in was not the answer.

We'd got the search warrant ready, and managed to get a rough idea of the layout of the flat. We'd even got an idea where he kept his drugs, but, despite our efforts to blend in with the drug scene with long hair and tatty jeans, we had already become known to most druggies and dealers, so there was no bluffing our way in. We decided to adopt an alternative strategy and got the help of the local CID officer, Trevor Clowes, who was always immaculately turned out with neat hair, jacket, tie, well-creased trousers and highly polished shoes.

Trevor stood on the doorstep holding the search warrant on an official-looking clipboard, whilst Des and I stood either side of the doorway pinned to the wall out of sight. Trevor tapped a friendly tap on the door, and a short while later the muffled sounds of footsteps descending the stairs could be heard.

"Who is it, what do you want?" a voice shouted from inside.

"Council. It's about your rent, Sir," replied Trevor in his nicest of tones.

"It's not a council flat," came back the voice.

Trevor looked at me with an anguished wide-eyed expression as the script went out of the window. The letterbox had now opened from the inside and Trevor, thinking on his feet, smiled down at the letterbox and cheerfully explained.

"Yes, I know. We're doing a survey on private landlords, just a few questions, it might be beneficial to you."

From my 180-degree angle I could see Trevor smiling down at the letterbox as he was being 'scanned'.

"Hold on," replied the letterbox, as I heard the sound of bolts being slid and locks clicking open.

I looked over at Des, who was pressed into the brickwork and quivering like a sprinter in the blocks waiting for the gun.

As the lock clicked, the door opened two inches to reveal the pasty white features and long lank hair of drug dealer, James Ottey. I could see that there was still a security chain on the door and suddenly Ottey's features tightened from that drooping dope-smoker's gaze to one of electrified horror - he had seen me. In a blur Des shouldered the door open, ripping the chain off at once and knocking poor Trevor to the ground.

"Drugs squad!" I shouted rather unnecessarily, as the six-foot three-inch, gangling Ottey was off up the stairs in seemingly one stride with Des a few steps behind, closely followed by me after I'd disentangled my feet from the prostrate Trevor's writhing mass of legs, jacket and flapping papers on clipboard.

Trevor was left lying on the ground in a heap, still clutching the search warrant and looking for his spectacles.

Ottey had turned left at the top of the stairs into a bathroom, and this was immediately followed by the bang of the door and the instantaneous *clunk* of a bolt. I reached the top of the stairs just in time to see Des run straight through the closed bolted door, which splintered completely off its hinges, leaving him standing inside the bathroom on top of the flattened door.

Ottey stood frozen like a rabbit caught in headlights, mouth agape, eyes wide open and clutching a huge bag of cannabis resin in his left hand, which he was holding above the toilet.

"Need a bigger toilet than that, youth," said Des, as Ottey accepted defeat and handed the bag over.

The haul was later found to contain two full imperial pounds of cannabis resin or 'two weights' to use the druggie vernacular of the day, a pound being a 'weight'. By the standards of the day this was a large seizure and sent a minor shock wave around the drugs community locally.

There were many small-time dealers in the area, mostly users who made a bit of extra cash on the side to subsidise their own habit, but there were a few 'Mr Bigs', most of whom were known to us, who were very wary and difficult to pin down. One of the main dealers in Stoke-on-Trent at that time was known as 'Flake' and oddly enough also lived in Basford, the same area as Ottey. Could Basford, Stoke-on-Trent, be the drugs capital of the world? No!

Flake had been convicted for only minor drugs offences and that was quite a while back, but the information kept coming in and he'd slipped through the net several times, even despite carefully planned operations. When new information came in that he had a huge stash of cannabis resin and 'bush' (cannabis vegetation), and was being brazen enough to deal to selected buyers from his house, we decided to obtain a search warrant and try to get in rather than wait and watch as we had done so many times in the past.

Flake lived in a moderate semi-detached house, together with his wife and two small children. He was very 'police conscious' and his doors were strengthened and had additional bolts. He was always looking over his shoulder and would drive around roundabouts two or three times or suddenly pull up to see if anyone was following him. We'd decided that the worst we could do would be to lose out again, so Des and I, along with our Detective Sergeant 'Ernie', two other lads from our office and a couple of lads from the Stafford office, all arrived close to Flake's house on a dark, very wet winter's evening.

I was armed with nothing more than a soggy search warrant on a clipboard, a pair of spectacles with no lenses in them and an umbrella. I knocked on the door as the other team members took up various positions around the house. The hall light came on as the familiar outline of the curly-haired bearded Flake came to the door, pressing his face up against the glass, squinting through at me.

By this time the rain was thundering down and I couldn't believe my luck as he unthinkingly started to unlock and open the door to the miserable, rainswept umbrella-toting figure.

"Hello, what can I do for you?" Flake asked, in a friendly welcoming manner, clearly not seeing through my intricate disguise.

"Good evening," came the voice from beneath the umbrella. "I've got this for you," I said, showing the clipboard and rain-sodden warrant.

"What is it?" asked a puzzled Flake.

"Search warrant, Flake, *drugs squad*," I shouted, pushing my way in before the door could be slammed in my face.

"You bastard, Pye! *You bastard!*"

He didn't have time for a third 'bastard' before the entire house was swarming with us. We had to put up with the usual 'police harassment' shouts, together with screams that he, 'had no drugs and never did have any' that accompanied the tired old, 'I will sue you for every penny'.

In addition, Flake tried a new one, saying he was just in the process of bathing the kids and that we surely wouldn't interrupt this family activity. We could get the search done, he suggested, whilst he kept this disruption of his family life away from the children. A look around the bathroom door revealed two small boys splashing about in the bath and Ernie, our sergeant, agreed that it might look bad on us, especially if we didn't find any drugs. After a cursory search of the bathroom it was agreed that he could continue in private whilst we searched the house, but Des was to be positioned outside the bathroom door, which was to be left ajar.

We started to carry out the search. I was in the kitchen with Ernie when suddenly there was a tremendous commotion as the kitchen ceiling started to shake and buckle.

"Outside," I heard Des's voice shout from upstairs.

At the same moment a figure fell past the kitchen window from above. I darted out through the back door thinking the SAS had arrived, as a second figure fell from the sky, this time it was Des. The door to the nearby garage hung open and all three of us attempted to enter through the doorway at the same time. There stood Flake inside holding a massive heavy bag and intent on shouldering all three of us out of his way - he tried.

The bag contained a huge haul of bush cannabis and cannabis resin. He had been keeping it in the garage and had tried to get to it by climbing out of the bathroom window onto the flat kitchen roof, intent on disposing of the evidence. A wrap of cocaine, no doubt dumped from Flake's pocket, was also found floating in the bathwater - so much for Flake's impersonation of a caring father. Flake got twenty-one months in prison. I got a cold.

It didn't always go right, though. Des and I took out a search warrant on a terraced house in Leek Road from where a chap was dealing LSD. We'd decided that we'd do the warrant at 8 a.m. and thought the back door looked pretty flimsy, so we'd go in that way. LSD was easy to 'flush' or to burn on an open fire, and the suspect was an old hand, so we'd got to get in quickly. We climbed the wall into the rear yard and on the count of a whispered 'one, two, three', kicked the door off its hinges with one kick. The door lay flat on the kitchen floor and there at the kitchen table sat an old gentleman wearing a cloth cap with a spoonful of cornflakes just up to his lips. We'd got the wrong house, we'd counted one too many, we should have been next door. After a quick, but very sincere, apology, we did the same again next door where we recovered one measly LSD tablet and a tiny deal of cannabis. We spent the whole afternoon repairing the chap's door then took him to the pub for a couple of pints and heard no more about it.

I really had studied for the sergeant's exam this year. Nearly all my spare time would be spent down at my mum and dad's in the quiet with my books out. The exams were now held at Bingley Hall, within the Stafford County Showground, and when the results came through on teleprinter message a few months later with the list of names of those who had passed, I was elated to see mine was included. Bingley Hall featured in my life at this time not only as the place where I had sat my promotion exam, but also as a regular pop concert venue, and the drug squad was required to attend most of these concerts. It was a great perk because we'd all get in free and were allowed to go backstage and pretty well anywhere we wanted. I saw Queen, Bob Marley, Cat Stevens, David Bowie, Genesis and Pink Floyd, to name but a few, and only occasionally did we get *interrupted* by having to arrest someone for possession or dealing.

I was now not only eligible for promotion to sergeant, but also eligible to sit the only other exam there was in the police promotion procedure, which was the inspector's exam, and I enrolled for this immediately. The 'job' still went on, however, so I tried to keep up the studying in the few short months leading up to the next exam whilst working all the usual long hours.

We had a call one summer's evening from the Stafford office; they'd got a job to do in Burton-on- Trent. The 'info' was supposedly very good on a big dealer, who was operating from a house on the outskirts of the town. It was a massive house to search with loads of students living there and the potential for many prisoners, lots of documents to go through, together with vehicles and a huge garden. The entire squad met up at Burton nick, a lovely old character-filled building that adjoined the even more impressive magistrates' court building.

The parade room was full at the briefing, and so big was the job expected to be that half a dozen uniformed officers were also to be involved. We got in on the warrant quite easily just by knocking on the door, but then we had to go through the usual abuse and swearing (mostly from the occupants). However, as time went on, we all got to know each other and cups of tea were produced by the students and pleasantries exchanged with us as we diligently went through all their personal belongings.

Some of the uniformed officers were 'rookies', just out of Ryton, and they were keenly interested in what was taking place, as they had not been part of a drugs search before. One of them produced two, dead-looking potted plants from the kitchen windowsill, which he thought might be cannabis, but which were pretty obviously tomato plants. Not wanting to dampen his enthusiasm we agreed to send them off for analysis.

As I went out into the enormous back garden, complete with a shed, a pergola, a greenhouse and a fishpond full of frogs, it was now dark and various uniformed PCs were probing bushes, bins, flowerpots and anywhere that the powerful light from their Maglight torches could get, in the hope of being the first to discover a huge stash of drugs. The beams of light cut across the garden like a return to the Blitz; childish laughter could occasionally be heard as someone acted the fool by doing ghost faces behind the torch, and other such daftness.

As I scanned my own torch across the flower borders, something white that was just poking out from the soil reflected back towards me. I knelt down and tugged at the object. As I did so, I was unaware that I was already being closely watched by two of the uniformed officers, who were now standing by my side.

"What's this?" I muttered to myself, recalling that several times previously we had recovered drug stashes buried in plastic bags. "Looks interesting!" I exclaimed, as I tugged a little harder at the weighty object.

By this time I was surrounded by a crowd of torch toting uniformed PCs, plain clothes officers and occupants from the house.

"Yes, we have found a substance - over," I heard one of the young officers enthusiastically report over his radio, before I could stop him.

"Thank you for that," came back an official sounding voice over the police radio. "Superintendent wants a quick report from you as soon as you know what it is - over."

I pulled harder at the thing, which I could now clearly see was a white plastic bag containing a heavy object several inches beneath the surface.

"It'll be Moroccan cannabis," I heard one voice say.

"Must be worth a fortune," said another.

With a little more probing and tugging, I eased the complete bag free from the soil, only to hear the same voice I had heard a few seconds before reporting into his radio.

"Yes, this looks like a large haul we've got here – over."

As I struggled to open the bag the same voice was heard with another premature radio report.

"I think we should consider the police photographer to photograph the item in situ - over," said the now very annoying 'creep'.

The bag contained a solid heavy object about eighteen inches long and tubular in shape. The light of so many different torches from so many different angles made it difficult to get a proper perspective as I unrolled the bag and opened the top. The item was jammed sideways into the bottom of the bag, and complete silence now enveloped the whole scene as I carefully put my hand inside the bag to free the object. My hand grasped a slimy solid object and the word 'errrr', or something similar, involuntarily came from my mouth as I pulled out the maggot-infested family cat that had departed this world some three months earlier.

The word 'errrr' was closely followed by several different voices, some emulating my 'errrr' and some others showing their own distaste with much worse expletives and howls of laughter. We never did find any drugs, the tomato plants were just tomato plants and 'The Voice' was given the job of telling the superintendent what had really happened.

We debriefed in the Coopers Arms until the early hours. Funny how no one wanted to share my crisps, but I did buy drinks all around, as I'd received the news just before we set off to the pub that I had passed my inspector's exam.

* * * *

Des and I had now both undergone intensive firearms training and were authorised firearms officers, although the need to carry weapons was a very rare occurrence in those days. The best thing that used to come out of it was that about once a month we would go to the Swynnerton Army Camp just outside the town of Stone, or to the Whittington Army Barracks at Lichfield, for a day of weapons training. Here we would be allowed to use the firing ranges for practice, but in later years the force acquired its very own shooting range near Uttoxeter. The weapons training was great fun, and we'd spend the whole day practising on the outdoor ranges with various different firearms, including revolvers and shotguns.

There was a special indoor range at the Swynnerton Army Camp, which was housed inside a large building and was constructed just like a street with shops and houses. There was even a Reliant Robin car parked in the street and a pub at the end of the road with the corny name of The Skillat Arms. The range had been built to train troops going out on duty in Northern Ireland. There was a big control room at the other end of the street, with bulletproof glass. They could control the lighting to make it day or night, and would make the different mechanical targets pop up from different locations. We used .22 calibre revolvers on the range and if you hit the target it would automatically go back down; you had to be very careful, as often a false target would suddenly pop up in one of the windows. It might be a man holding a Black and Decker or a woman holding a baby, and if you shot one of these you'd never hear the last of it.

The control room staff could introduce 'crowd noise' and even make the car suddenly flash its lights, and make small 'controlled explosions' go off to try to unnerve you. The range had been used for the filming of one of the episodes of the hit TV series *The Avengers*.

There was also an indoor firing range at Whittington Army Barracks near Lichfield. This used a different system whereby a cine film of a supposed armed robbery would be projected onto a large screen in front of you and when one of the robbers in the film posed a threat to you (by appearing to point his gun at you), you'd fire your revolver at the figure. The noise from the shot would automatically make the film freeze and then shine a light through the back of the screen to show where, or if, you'd hit the gunman. These days out were always a welcome change, but often we'd have to continue with our normal work after we'd finished.

LSD (lysergic acid diethylamide, to give it its full name) kept cropping up fairly regularly and always went hand in hand with cannabis; wherever you found LSD you would always find cannabis. In 1977 a huge operation took place in North Wales where, after months of surveillance and undercover work, the drugs squad had uncovered the largest LSD factory known. The drugs raid on the property, a remote farmhouse, recovered enough LSD for thirty million doses. This illegal drugs factory was responsible for the majority of the LSD that was turning up throughout the globe. The tablets produced there were known to the druggies as 'pyramid' due to their shape, and came in different colours. So much LSD had been produced by the gang that 'pyramid' still kept turning up for a long while after the operation.

I had attended a drugs course at the Hertfordshire Police HQ at Welwyn Garden City back in 1975. It was whilst I was on this course that I met Detective Inspector Dick Lee, who was one of the leading lights in the operation entitled 'Operation Julie'. The success of Operation Julie was so profound that LSD virtually vanished from the drugs scene for a very long time.

Des and I had had a good year with plenty of good 'busts', a few 'cock ups' and plenty of fun, but that was all to change when another big inquiry hit Staffordshire Police on the 20th September 1978 with the terrible, ruthless and unnecessary murder of young paper boy, Carl Bridgewater, at Yew Tree Farm near Stourbridge.

Thirteen-year-old Carl had been delivering his newspapers as usual, his round taking in the isolated Yew Tree Farm, near Stourbridge, just within the boundary of Staffordshire Police not far from the town of Wombourne. It appears that he disturbed a team of burglars stealing antiques from the farm during the temporary absence of the owners. One of the burglars shot the poor boy in the head at close range with a twelve-bore shotgun, killing him instantly. This turned into a massive and lengthy inquiry involving many, many Staffordshire officers drawn from all over the county.

The fact that we lived almost at the other end of the county was no bar, and within a few days of the crime, Des and I had been drafted in to work full-time on the inquiry. Starting out at 7 a.m., we'd drive to Wombourne Police Station every day, seven days a week for several months, usually getting home around midnight.

I was now a dad with two very young children and a third one very imminent. Eldest, Adam, aged three, and Julie, aged two, seemed increasingly puzzled at the strange face that would occasionally appear - the one called 'Dad'.

I had in fact only been involved on the Carl Bridgewater Inquiry for a few weeks when our third child, David, was born. I was allowed just four days off from the inquiry and then it was 'back to Wombourne'.

Des lived in the single men's accommodation that was provided; this was situated above the old magistrates' court premises in Water Street, Newcastle. Part of the building had originally been built as the old County Police Station in the days when there was a separate Newcastle Borough Police Force. There were quite a few single bobbies living there, and their rooms in the upstairs part of the building had probably been built as offices originally. There was a bar downstairs, which was the Newcastle Police Club, and of course a snooker table. The police canteen was there as well, until it was later moved to the upstairs of the police station in Merrial Street, the rest of the building was still used as the magistrates' court.

If it was my turn to have the drugs squad van overnight, I'd have to pick Des up in the morning, before our journey over to Wombourne. He'd usually be a bit late, due to too many beers the night before, and I'd end up hammering on his bedroom door.

Wombourne nick was built to the same plan as Kidsgrove's and, consequently, had to undergo the same sort of additional stresses that were imposed on Kidsgrove during the Black Panther Inquiry. The place was simply groaning under the weight of all these overweight detectives, filing cabinets and all the other paraphernalia that went along with the inquiry.

Our job was to track down and interview suspects given to us, on 'action forms'. The action required on the action form was arrived at through all manner of varied permutations of possibilities: descriptions of people seen near the scene of the crime; people using or owning vehicles that matched in some way a blue estate car seen near the farm; people owning shotguns; crooks who were suspected of having shotguns; criminals with 'form' for farmhouse burglaries or antique theft burglaries, and so on.

A detective inspector would be the appointed 'action man' and it was his job to compile the actions with whatever information he had and then allocate them to the various teams, depending on what type of particular enquiry that team was earmarked to do.

Each team of two detectives had reams and reams of 'actions' to deal with and, as our job mostly involved tracking down particular suspects, we could find ourselves travelling all over the country with the aim of finding a particular person. More often than not, these were quite vicious and nasty hardened criminals from whom we had to take statements as to their whereabouts on the day in question, together with a full description and their fingerprints, whether they were on file or not.

The list of suspects being churned out was endless. There were numerous teams like ours, all with dozens of actions to complete. To make things worse we were working mostly in and around the Black Country in the West Midlands and only very occasionally in Staffordshire itself. It was all new territory to us and the language took some understanding; that accent took some time to get used to.

After a while we had begun to get to know our way around places like Cradley Heath, Bromsgrove, Walsall, Dudley, Wolverhampton, Brierley Hill, Gornal, oh, and Lower Gornal. We had also perfected our own version of the Black Country accent, which seemed to require the mouth to be set turned down, with the top lip straight (you're doing it, now aren't you?) and the bottom lip slightly protruding with a half-inch bit of open mouth showing. This we called 'Brierley Mouth', and it was all that was required to set you off on a near perfect Black Country accent.

In among the scores of 'no hope' suspects we did have the occasional one who had a bit of a chance, but of course each one had to be treated with the same suspicion. One such suspect who came on an action to us was Leslie Gaiter, a man with a lot of convictions for house burglaries involving antiques. It also came to light that he had a blue estate car similar to one seen near the murder and he was of a similar description to a man seen nearby. It was also the case that Gaiter had most definitely been responsible for a nasty and expensive burglary at a farmhouse in Shropshire two years previously, but the police had never been able to prove it. Gaiter lived in the suburbs of Liverpool in a nice semi-detached house with his wife and teenage children.

We showed what we'd got to our detective inspector and it was decided that we would take a team over to Gaiter's house in Liverpool with a search warrant, arrest him on suspicion of murder then take him back to Wombourne for interview if need be - nothing could be more simple. Famous last words!

With meticulous planning we all arrived at Gaiter's house one Wednesday lunchtime, having discreetly found that he was not in work on this day. Detective inspector, detective sergeant, Des, myself, three local DCs, the Liverpool Police firearms team, police dog, a Black Maria - the works.

Gaiter Junior greeted us at the door with:

"Oh, me dad's gone to the match at White Hart Lane in London, Tottenham versus Liverpool, they went this morning."

This was a blow, and it meant we'd have to get on with the house search, looking for evidence connected to the murder, but it was also vital that Gaiter was arrested before he was tipped off. Whilst the search team got on with a detailed house search, a flurry of phone calls took place between Staffordshire, Liverpool and the Metropolitan Police. Later that evening a call came back from the Met.

"We have your man; he is detained at Shepherds Bush Police Station."

Apparently he had been in the crowd waiting for the match to begin when he was surprised to hear the PA system announcing, 'Will Mr Leslie Gaiter from Liverpool please report to the security office'.

Amazed and worried as to what catastrophe had happened at home, and well before the days of mobile telephones, he had gone straight to the security office where he was greeted by a Met superintendent who knocked the wind out of his sails with:

"Mr Leslie Gaiter, I arrest you for murder."

It was 10 p.m. that evening before the DI, Des and I arrived at Shepherds Bush Police Station and were shown into the cell where Les was detained.

Les stood up from his bench with a worried expression as we walked into the cell.

"What the f***'s going on?" he said, with a quivering Scouse accent. "I come down here to see the match - been in the ground twenty minutes, hear me name called out in front of me mates and thirty thousand other bastards and then there's this giant 'bizzy' (Scouse for policeman), who tells me he's arresting me for *muuurder*, I mean *f***ing muuurder*, then I get chucked in here and that's f***ing that for the next six hours. I've been straight for two years and then *muuurder*, what's going on?"

After an hour and a half interview it was decided to keep Les in custody and then take him back to Wombourne for further interviews the following day. As Les was bedded down for a sleepless night in his cell, the three of us were directed to the Shepherds Bush police accommodation block about a mile from the nick. This was an old

Victorian building used as lodgings for single police officers and as stopovers for situations such as ours.

We were each given a small room, complete with a washbasin and, yes, I could hardly believe my eyes - khaki-coloured lino - they even had it here. We dumped our belongings, which consisted of nothing more than a briefcase each. I washed my hands and face, and tried my best to clean my teeth by rubbing them with my fingers; we then all bolted for the nearest pub.

It was well after closing time already, but the licensee, Mick, a dumpy little Irishman, had been warned of our arrival by the Shepherds Bush CID, who were his best customers, and he welcomed us in. The pub was full and the doors were locked. When we enquired if any food was possible, as we hadn't eaten since breakfast, he produced a huge bowl of tomatoes. Tomatoes were all that he had, so we ate tomatoes and, of course, downed a few beers.

The beer and tomato feast went on into the small hours, interspersed with various fun and games created by Mick. Most of the fun and games seemed to be at the expense of our DI, as Mick told him to put his thumbs on the bar and then carefully placed a beer mat on the thumbs followed by a full pint of lager as the mystified DI looked on wondering what would happen next. Mick walked off leaving him puzzling how he was supposed to get out of this; the whole room, which now seemed to have even more people in than when we first arrived, erupted into laughter as, inevitably, the DI tried to get out of the fix and the bar was flooded with lager.

We simply could not believe it when Mick got him again with another full pint of lager, which he carefully pressed up against the ceiling with a pool cue, beckoning the DI over and inviting him to take over the pool cue with both hands pressing firmly so as to keep it against the ceiling, and casually walked back behind the bar to pull more drinks. There was, of course, no escape, and everyone dived for cover as, after a full five minutes, the DI had decided there was again no way out - more spilled lager and some broken glass.

At 2 a.m., replenished with our tomato and beer diet, we all retired to bed for a few hours. Not much was said in the Staffordshire Police Ford Cortina on the way back to Wombourne between the three stubble-chinned, bleary-eyed, BO-laden detectives and the worried, but relatively fresh-looking murder suspect. After a couple of hours of interviews, all the other forms, fingerprints and so on, it was decided that Les was not our man, but that wasn't the end of it for Les as, whilst under the pressure of a murder arrest, he had tried to impress us with his honesty by admitting in full to the antique farm burglary in Shropshire. Detectives from the town of Wem were delighted at the news and duly came over to Wombourne to elongate Les's day a little more.

It was many months later, many long days, many late nights, many miles up and down the country, many suspects, prisoners, interviews, statements, a few pints, many bacon sandwiches and bags of chips later, before the inquiry would close with the arrest and charging of a group of men whose conviction for Carl's murder would, many years later, be the source of conjecture by the media, leading to their eventual release. Staffordshire Police did not reopen the case.

After the charging of the men, a lot of the teams were sent back to their divisions to resume their normal jobs, but a few of us were retained for a while to clear up some of the outstanding 'actions' that still needed to be done. It was at this time, when a well-known BBC TV newscaster, Reginald Bosanquet, was going through a difficult patch in his life and often appeared reading the news whilst tipsy and sometimes even downright drunk. Des and I would always do our level best to get back into the nick in time for the news, and sometimes would end up howling with laughter at Reg's latest gaffe. As a result of this, following an evening of too many beers, the nickname of 'Reg' was born into the Staffordshire Police and, in fact, the nickname would spread to some other forces as well.

Both Des and I were now known as 'Reg', in addition to any other nicknames we possessed, and it was found that the name could quite acceptably be used as a nickname for just about anyone. It effectively took on the usefulness of the term 'mate', especially in police circles.

So it was back to Hanley, a return to drug squad duties and a little more normality, but now, with my inspector's exam passed and out of the way, I could try to devote just a little more time to my family.

Tablet abuse was rife at this time. The Northern Soul music scene was still very active and was used by a lot of dealers, both big and small, to feed the habits of unfortunates, who were gullible and naive enough to gamble with their lives, just so they could keep awake and dancing throughout the all-night discos that they would travel many miles to visit. Northern Soul was great music, but its association with drugs gave it a bad name.

Chemist shop burglaries were taking place throughout the county on most nights of the week and the DDA (Dangerous Drugs Act) cabinets were forced open, or ripped from the wall and taken away. Everything was used from the cabinets, from diamorphine (heroin) right down to barbiturates (downers) and, of course, the amphetamines (speed), which was the drug most sought after by the Northern Soul scene.

A detective sergeant at our Stafford office had the job of going around the county examining the DDA cabinets in all the chemists' shops. Often when visiting some antiquated old shop that had served the community for many years, he would come across all manner of strange drugs and potions that had lain there for many a long while; arsenic and even cyanide were not unheard of, and even the odd bottle of something called 'tincture of cannabis' dating back to before the Second World War would sometimes come to light. It was used as a form of 'cure-all' with all kinds of claims written on the label, but the druggies would dip their cigarettes into it and smoke it if they got their hands on it.

The Wigan based Casino Club was the main Northern Soul club in the country at this time, and most of the 'speed' stolen in chemist shop burglaries locally would ultimately end up there. The remaining stolen drugs would, more often than not, end up being cut, watered down or generally very unhygienically messed about with, before being sold on for ridiculous sums of money in some pub or club in the Stoke area. Our very own local Northern Soul club, The Golden Torch in Tunstall, had by this time already closed down.

The flood of strong dangerous drugs that became available led to many deaths and overdoses, which usually came in clusters whenever a very strong uncut drug came into the hands of dealers who were unaware of its strength or what it really was.

I was awakened from my sleep by the telephone early one Sunday morning and asked to attend the scene of a suspected 'drugs death' at Norton, Stoke-on-Trent, where a young man, whom I had previously dealt with for drugs offences, had been found dead. This was followed by further reports of another two deaths and six serious overdoses, all involving people I had dealt with or knew because of their involvement in drugs. It was later established that all the victims, thinking that the drug was of the strength to which they were accustomed, had taken what turned out to be pure uncut methadone crystal in quite large quantities.

One of these deaths resulted in the arrest of one of the overdose survivors. Some weeks later I charged him with the manslaughter of his late friend, whom he admitted to having injected with the lethal mixture. I spent several weeks on the inquiry, which was headed by Detective Chief Inspector Keith Houlston, a humorous and likeable man.

As it was so serious, the case had to be heard by a high court judge and, consequently, Shrewsbury Crown Court was the eventual venue. It was quite a long drawn-out court hearing lasting almost two weeks and afterwards I often used to laugh to myself, despite the drama and sadness of these events, when I recalled the journeys between Stoke and Shrewsbury. Keith and I used to play a game he'd invented to play with his kids whilst going on holiday. This entailed every time you passed by a pub on your side of the road that had the name of a creature - such as the Red Lion - you got points for how many legs it had. So if you passed the King's Head, you'd get just two points for his legs; I often wished we could go past the

Shropshire Fly for some bonus points, but there were only so many ways you could get to Shrewsbury.

Keith came over in the courtroom as very serious and rational, which of course was in keeping with the elements of this tragic case, but all I could remember was, 'Right, Porky, White Horse, that's another four for me'. I often wondered what the judge would have made of it. The accused was found guilty and received a lengthy term in prison.

The druggies would try anything for a 'buzz', but without exception each one, even the 'pill heads' of the Northern Soul scene, all started out on cannabis. Without cannabis there would hardly be a drug problem.

The use of 'magic mushrooms' would come on to the scene towards the end of summer or early autumn. These tiny, beige fungi with pointed caps would grow wild in patches, usually sprouting up following a wet spell. Their real name was *Psilocibe Semilanceata* and when eaten would produce LSD-style hallucinations. Most weekends at the right time of year would result in a handful of wide-eyed, arm-waving youngsters being examined at the North Staffs Royal Infirmary by some puzzled doctor who was trying to make a diagnosis.

One of the more unusual substances the druggies found they could get a buzz from was a perfectly legal asthma cigarette that could easily be purchased over the counter. It was found that if they broke the cigarette open and poured the leafy contents into a hot drink, the resulting beverage would produce hallucinations and weird behaviour. The concoction became known as 'goon dust' and my first encounter with it was when I was called down from the drug squad office at Hanley one afternoon to give my opinion on a young man who had been brought into the police station for his own safety. Apparently he had been found riding a bicycle along Marsh Street in Hanley whilst wearing nothing other than a woman's flowery dress. As he had no underpants on, and the bicycle was a racer with drop handlebars, it must have been quite a sight. For some reason he was also equipped with an aerosol tin of fly spray that was fitted into the drinks holder between the handlebars and which he had been using to give any onlookers the occasional squirt. He had consumed two large mugs of goon dust tea; the manufacturers soon took the asthma cigarettes off the market.

Towards the end of my time with the drug squad, Des and I, together with another good friend and colleague, DC Bernie Pearce, had been investigating a drug-dealing ring working out of the Dresden area near Longton. We had good information that cannabis was being sold from the house, and that the dealer was also receiving stolen property and sometimes taking this as payment for drugs. We had been watching the house using the force's observation (obs) van on and off for the best part of a week. The obs van was a tatty-looking, green Commer van. It was made to look like a tradesman's van and had a partition between the driving compartment and the rear, with a little door in it so we didn't have to get out of the van to take up our places in the rear.

There was a spyhole through the partition, to look through the windscreen from the back, and it had one-way glass in the back windows to prevent people seeing us. It also had tiny spyholes in the sides. There was a flap in the partition on the driver's side, so you could reach through and flick the ignition key on to wipe the windscreen occasionally, if need be, but this meant leaving the ignition keys in.

We had been watching the house from the obs van for three days on and off. The neighbours must have been a bit annoyed as this tatty van kept appearing and being dumped outside their houses for hours on end. Often when we parked someone would come out with an annoyed expression and look around the van, puzzled as to how they never caught anyone leaving the seemingly empty van. On one occasion an inquisitive neighbour got his face right up to the one-way glass, (which incidentally wasn't completely one-way) trying to peer in as we all lay on the floor hoping he couldn't see us.

It was in the middle of a red-hot summer. We were all sweltering and would often strip to our underpants when the heat got too much. There was no toilet in the van. We would usually take a bottle of beer each, and had to use our initiative (and the empties) when the call of nature arrived.

We had to park the van opposite the gates of a haulage firm to get a good view of the house we were watching. Early one evening, as the hot spell continued despite a bit of drizzle, a large lorry appeared and parked some way up the road from us.

"What's he doing?" whispered Bernie.

"That's a lorry from the haulage firm," Des said. "Oh, no! He's not going to be able to get into the yard because of how we've parked."

The driver jumped down from his cab and stood looking over at our van with a puzzled and annoyed expression.

Shaking his head, he walked over to the haulage yard and started to undo the gates.

"Quick, Reg," said Des, using the universal nickname and directing his speech towards me, "give the windscreen a wipe."

I reached through the flap and flicked the ignition key on and off causing the wipers to sweep across the windscreen just once and giving us a clear look at the situation as the driver disappeared into the yard for a moment.

After a minute or so the driver emerged from the yard and walked over to our van. We all held our breath as he walked around the vehicle, peering in through the front window and putting his face right up against the so-called one-way glass in the back doors. We pinned ourselves to the floor hoping he would not see us, and held our breath as he then squinted in through the driver's side window. Upon seeing the keys dangling from the ignition, the driver tried the door, which swung open for him. I deftly pushed the small viewing flap in the partition closed and we then felt the van settle down on its suspension as the burly driver climbed into the driving seat.

In our gloomy hidey-hole in the back of the van just feet away from him, the three of us sat on the floor, glistening with sweat, wearing nothing but our underpants and trainers. We heard the engine start, and all shared the same anguished expression as we quietly took hold of our individual urine-filled beer bottles to prevent any further catastrophes.

The driver crunched the van into first gear and then, not being familiar with the clutch, kangarooed it off up the road as we held onto our bottles and tried hard not to make any noise. After about thirty yards the driver, also not being familiar with the brakes, threw us all up against the partition in a jumble of arms and legs as he came to a very sudden halt.

The thought suddenly struck me that here I was wearing nothing other than my underpants and trainers, covered from head to foot in sweat, entwined with my two sweating male colleagues, who were similarly scantily clad and each holding a bottle of urine. Should the driver find the viewing flap and peer through there would be *no* acceptable explanation.

The driver pulled on the handbrake and jumped out of the van, leaving the keys dangling, and banged the door as hard as possible as he stormed off back to his lorry, annoyed that he had been inconvenienced so much. The three of us looked at each other in disbelief and started to snigger.

"We've just been taken and driven away!" I quietly exclaimed.

The next day we returned to our 'plot', being more than careful not to park inconveniently. We now had additional information that the drug dealer had received a quantity of valuable stolen paintings and, as we were now also 'armed' with our search warrant, were ready to go in when the time looked right.

As we watched, we discussed the best way to go about the raid and were troubled that, even though we had spent many hours, we had not seen any sign of paintings being taken in. We looked on with interest as we saw the dealer and his girlfriend leave the house by the front door and drive off in their car.

Des and I decided to go and have a look to see if we could see anything through the back window of the house, so, with the two-way radios that operated between us and Bernie in the van, we quietly slipped out of the van - now fully dressed!

We casually wandered down the street towards the house and, when we were sure that no one was watching, dodged into the alleyway running along the backs of the row of two-up, two-down terraced houses. Peering over the locked gate into the backyard, I whispered into my radio to Bernie.

"Okay, Reg, we're just going over the wall."

"Righto!" came back Bernie's voice. "I'll keep you informed."

We both clambered up and dropped down into the small backyard, confident that as the dealer had only just left we were in no danger. I peered in through the kitchen window as Des looked into the living room.

"See anything?"

"Not sure," replied Des. "There's a big picture hanging on the wall, but with these net curtains I can't make anything out."

In the kitchen window a piece of cardboard was stuck into one of the small mullioned panes, which had obviously been broken previously.

"What about this, Reg?" I said to Des, with a smile.

Des looked over at the cardboard windowpane.

"Why not?" he said, "We've got a warrant anyway, and there's no reason for them to know we'd already been for a look around."

I poked the cardboard and it fell away into the sink. Des reached in and undid the window, climbing into the old Belfast-style sink and down onto the kitchen floor. I radioed through to Bernie what was happening then followed Des through the window and into the kitchen. Bernie's voice returned from the radio, which was now turned down to its lowest volume.

"Okay, all quiet for the mo."

The kitchen door was closed and the family cat, being rather perturbed by this sudden uninvited intrusion, whirled around the kitchen in panic with its fur standing on end and tail bolt upright. There seemed nothing of interest in the kitchen, so we opened the door and went through to the small living room as the cat flew in after us and continued its imitation of what a cat on hot bricks probably looks like.

We looked around the room. *Bingo*! There were paintings everywhere; at least a dozen all standing against the walls around the room and the one Des had seen hanging - yes, these were definitely the stolen ones. Two luxuriant cannabis plants flourished in pots in the corner and a set of brass scales sat on the table, together with several small chunky objects wrapped in silver paper.

"They're back! They're outside now!" Bernie shouted over the radio.

"What?" I instinctively shouted back into my radio as I started to head for the kitchen with Des almost pushing me out of the way.

"He's getting something out of the boot," came Bernie's voice again, "and she's standing by the door getting her keys out."

"The bloody cat," hissed Des, as we both struggled to get into the kitchen. "If it's not in the kitchen they might suspect something."

Des turned and stepped back into the living room to see that the cat, which had become a little more at ease with the intruders, was now lying peacefully on the arm of the sofa.

Bernie's voice, although on low volume was shrill and anxious.

"She's got the key in the door."

Des made a grab for the cat, got it by the scruff of the neck and winced with pain as it somehow managed to dig its claws deep into his thumb.

"*Bloody hell!*" he whispered, as he dropped the cat onto the kitchen floor, closing the door behind him.

I was now outside and, having retrieved the cardboard windowpane, helped Des out through the window just as Bernie's voice piped up again.

"She's in and he's right behind her."

I pulled the cardboard back into place as I heard the front door close, and followed Des over the gate and into the alleyway as Bernie's voice kept on repeating:

"Speak to me for God's sake."

As we wandered casually back up the street towards the obs van (if it is possible to be casual when your heart rate is five times the norm), Bernie's relieved voice came over the radio.

"Thank God, I nearly had a breakdown."

He did?

We quickly followed up the 'recce' with an official search, and duly recovered a lot of cannabis, some LSD, the plants, scales and a lot of stolen property including, of course, the paintings - *phew*!

It was around this time that great news was received. The high-level inquiry and report into police pay and conditions, which had been undertaken by Lord Edmund Davies, had been published and we would be getting a substantial pay increase and other benefits, including overtime payment.

I was also on the move again. After three years of drug-related deaths, drug busts, stop searches, long hours, not much time off and involvement in some interesting major inquiries, my drug squad time was at an end.

ELEVEN

The force had a policy of not keeping anybody on one department for too long and when I was offered a place on a CID course at the West Midlands Detective Training School in Birmingham, I knew it would mean that I was soon destined for a transfer from the drug squad to the CID.

It was April 1979 as I dragged my suitcase out from the back of my tatty brown Hillman Avenger estate after parking on the large car park of the detective training centre on Pershore Road. The building was named 'Tally Ho' and resembled one of those 1950's high-rise blocks of flats; it was also the location for all manner of other types of police training.

Situated on the outskirts of Birmingham city centre, Tally Ho was literally just around the corner from Edgbaston Cricket Ground and, with my suit over my arm, I walked past the giant statue of Sir Robert Peel and into the foyer through the double front doors. A uniformed PC slid the glass widow hatch to one side as I pinged the bell. He gave me the key to room 405.

"You've to be in classroom number seven at 11 a.m."

He then shut the window with the usual air of dislike that often seemed to exist between uniform and CID in those days.

My room on the third floor looked out over the busy Pershore Road and would be my home now for the next ten weeks with just weekends at home. The room seemed vaguely familiar as I looked around; wardrobe, bed, sink, mirror, mat and oh, *green* vinyl lino tiles - different.

Down in classroom seven, the twenty-one desks were filling up with mustachioed look-alike detectives. In those days it was the done thing in the CID to have a 'tash', and one of the few people in the class without one was the lone woman detective on the course, although there could just have been a hint of six o'clock shadow.

Most of the 'tecks' (detectives) in the class had short 'police' haircuts - apart from one or two of us who had been working on crime squad or drug squad. Smart suits or leather jackets were the CID dress of the day and always a collar and tie.

Sitting behind me on that first day in the classroom was the giant figure of one who was to become my friend for life. Graham Timson from Kettering in Northamptonshire had an infectious laugh and the same bizarre, childish and stupid sense of humour as my own.

Our class instructor introduced himself.

"Detective Sergeant Jim Evans, lady... and gentlemen, nice to meet you all, lots of work to do over the next ten weeks and I'm sure we'll have a few laughs along the way. We'll be starting some proper work shortly, but on an important note, do we have any wholesalers amongst us, anything to sell?"

By this, Jim was referring to the fact that as we had come from all over the country, and being detectives, we would often have contacts for all manner of cheap goods, especially ones that were produced in the area from where we came. Courses such as this were the ideal market place where it was accepted that we would sell the goods at a little more than we got them for, and everybody was happy.

Jim continued.

"Graham Timson, you're our Northampton representative, any shoes?" (Northamptonshire is the country's foremost area for shoe manufacture).

"Yes, Sarge, got a bedroom full, all good prices," was Graham's reply.

"Okay then," Jim said. "John Pye, our Stoke-on-Trent rep, any pots to sell?"

"Yes, Sarge," was my reply, "got a car load, dinner services, tea sets, mugs, you name it, all good prices."

I had been tipped off about this nice little earner by previous course-goers, so had visited Beresford's pottery in Longton. Beresford's would let detectives going on courses have whatever they wanted on sale or return. Various other wares were also on offer, including suits, and someone was able to get all manner of saucepans and other kitchen equipment.

"Okay," said Jim, "we'll have a sale after tea tomorrow night in this classroom. I'll make sure all the other classes know, and the cleaners and kitchen staff."

One desk remained empty.

"You'll note," Jim said, "that we have someone missing. David Dunwoody from the Royal Ulster Constabulary, Northern Ireland, is stuck on a court case, but hopes to be with us for Wednesday."

We were all given a large lever arch file of 'law notes' and massive piles of other legal papers and notes. We then all had to give a cameo picture of ourselves, and our careers so far, what departments we'd worked in and any interesting jobs we'd worked on. It was a good way of getting to know everyone and we soon realised that many of us had met before, or spoken over the telephone. There was another CID class running at the same time as ours, with another twenty-one detectives, many of whom also had wares to sell and stories to swap.

Most of the people on the course had already been working in CID for some time before being allocated their 'coveted' position on a course, and they already had a lot of experience to share. We didn't get stuck into much 'law' for the first day or so; the pressure just seemed to build up gradually.

The first evening was spent in the large police club bar, which was also within the grounds of Tally Ho, and we all got to know each other over a few drinks. By the end of the night everyone had had quite a few beers and shared quite a few stories.

The Tuesday sale went well; the classroom was full of crockery, shoes, suits and saucepans. Dozens of staff and students attended, and could not believe the cheap prices. Both Graham and I boosted our beer money and took orders throughout the entire course.

By Wednesday the RUC officer, David, had arrived. He had frequently been working on crimes involving the IRA and had been involved with this type of work for some time, so this course was overdue for him. He had been involved in the most awful, sickening and horrible IRA crimes imaginable. He was a very likeable and humorous man, who clearly had had a really difficult and stressful time, as he had worked throughout some of the worst of the atrocities.

Many of the RUC officers who had been involved in this type of work were completely worn out mentally. These courses were often looked upon as a holiday for them. David was used to wearing a gun virtually twenty-four hours a day, and admitted to feeling undressed and uneasy without it. His laugh was infectious, and after every joke or funny story he would automatically throw in the comedian Frank Carson's line, 'Hey, hey, it's the way I tell 'em'.

As the course got into its stride we developed a routine. We were bombarded with huge amounts of criminal law, legal practice, police procedure and practical exercises. We delved into each aspect of crime from simple theft to robbery, blackmail, burglary, deception, murder, manslaughter, rape, various types of assault and perjury - the list went on and on and on.

We learned in detail exactly how an ID parade really *should* be performed. It was nothing like my attempt with the Salvation Army several years previously.

We had huge amounts of homework every evening and every weekend, when most of us would return home. Our daily routine would start at 7.30 a.m. and finish usually around 9 p.m. In this time we would fit in meal breaks and perhaps a game of volleyball between lecture upon lecture. After 9 p.m., unless there was something difficult that required more work, it was time for a pint, so we would escape for a few hours, often to one of the local pubs down into Birmingham or, if the worst came to worst, just to the bar.

We took David out for a curry in the first week; it was the first time he'd been able to relax properly for a long time. He was utterly drunk as we sat around the table with various steaming curries in front of us, and after his first mouthful of vindaloo, he exploded into a spluttering cry of, 'Tooo hot' and then poured a jug of water over it. We had to compensate the waiter for the mess by having a whip-round; we came up with a fiver in total, so the waiter was remarkably pleased.

Quite often we'd collect a takeaway curry or a Chinese from one of the nearby restaurants on Pershore Road. This was okay, but usually led to everyone borrowing some of the large meat plates from my crockery stock, and I'd wake up next morning to a sink full of dishes splattered with rice and curry.

There was a large lecture theatre at Tally Ho for special talks and films, which both classes would attend together; the seats were tiered down just like a proper theatre and there were no windows so as to produce the necessary darkness.

In keeping with the responsible and sober attitude that is synonymous with being police officers, some of us had visited a joke shop in Birmingham and had brought back all manner of things that might come in handy for a laugh.

One afternoon both classes were in the theatre watching a film on murder investigation. It was the old-fashioned cine-type film, which was clicking away with the bright beam of light being cast from the projector onto the screen.

We had been watching for about half an hour when strange puffy shapes started to drift across the screen. At first people thought there was something wrong with the film, but as time went on it became more puzzling, as in the gloom you could make out odd cloud formations, which seemed to be actually floating around the room. A murmur of laughter had developed into full-blown hysteria as the instructor switched on the lights to reveal that the room was indeed full of large fluffy white clouds, which were the product of a purchase from the joke shop; the seemingly innocent-looking white tablets when placed onto the tip of a burning cigarette would, as if by magic, turn the cigarette into a 'cloud machine'.

We had a very interesting visit from the army bomb disposal unit one day, which was conducted by an army captain and his corporal. Both men were great company and made the full afternoon's lectures extremely interesting. The chain-smoking corporal insisted on being called by his nickname, 'Ziggy'. The lectures started outside on the rugby field with a tiny amount of Semtex explosive, which Ziggy detonated with us all standing a very considerable distance away. Having seen and handled the tiny amount of the explosive beforehand, we were all astonished that it could produce such a tremendous bang.

As we trooped back to the lecture theatre some of us were suspicious of pieces of paper lying about, together with a strategically placed torch and briefcase. One small detective, who seemed to have enormous feet for his size, just bowled into the class without a care in the world and plonked his giant foot squarely on one of the pieces of paper. A tremendous 'bang' echoed around the room and everyone dived for cover, but David Dunwoody was first to the floor. This was, of course, Ziggy's little trick, a way of showing us how simple it could be to plant and conceal explosives and how easily they could be disguised. It wasn't long before we had endured several more bangs from the innocent-looking items, leaving us nervously twitching as we lurched, hands over heads, down to the canteen for half-time tea break.

It was now time to hatch our own plot and get our own back on Ziggy. The visit to the joke shop had indeed been fortuitous because, of course, we had also purchased several packets of 'exploding cigarette pellets'. Many people's cigarettes had already been detonated on previous days, but there were still three pellets left. God was smiling on us, as Ziggy had left his Benson and Hedges on the lecture dais, so it was a simple matter for Graham and I to nip back into the room and 'seed' his packet, hoping that he would pick a 'live one' before they had finished for the day.

The lecture continued after the break, with Ziggy and the captain imparting their interesting and useful knowledge in a professional and entertaining way. Every time Ziggy lit up another one we all waited with squinting eyes for it to happen; Graham was quietly laying bets as to which numbered cigarette would explode, when on the fourth one we got him.

Ziggy casually 'pinged' his Zippo lighter and drew in, eyes closed as he filled his lungs.

Bang!

Ziggy dived beneath the dais, his papers tumbling to the floor. The captain fell backwards, stumbling against the table and the whole room let out an ear-splitting cheer then broke out into sustained laughter. Ziggy, choking on the half-consumed lung full of smoke, looked up from the floor and coughed.

"I've never been caught out with my own tricks before," he said, and when breathing normally joined in the laughter.

The captain was laughing more than anyone and could not stop saying:

"Just wait till we get back, they'll never believe this."

Another childish prank that was especially suited to the lecture theatre was that of making small paper hats that would then be ever so carefully placed onto the head of the person sitting in front of you. As the room was tiered down, the head in front was just at the optimum height for covert hat placing. On one occasion we had a line of eight detectives sitting attentively listening to a lecture all unknowingly wearing a neat little hat. Often the giveaway would come when a hat wearer asked a question of the lecturer, who would not be able to control his own laughter at having a grown man asking a pertinent question about a crime or legal matter whilst wearing a small paper hat. The other offshoot of this was that everyone then became paper hat paranoid, and any new lecturers would be extremely puzzled as to why everyone in the room kept patting the tops of their heads.

There were shower blocks on each floor of the residential block, which consisted of a group of four open showers, each with a transparent plastic shower curtain. On the wall of each corridor was fixed a large, sturdy, red steel fire hose reel complete with many yards of thick, red rubber heavy-duty fire hose. The reel was mounted on a massive metal hinge, so that it could swing out away from the wall whilst in use; there was a large chromium tap fitted to the end of the hose and the water pressure was massive.

When the reel was swung outwards it automatically engaged the water pressure. It then remained only to turn on the tap to achieve a tremendously powerful blast of water. This most useful 'tool of torture' was often used on fellow students, just as they were in the middle of a soothing, hangover- relieving, steaming hot shower. Suddenly the plastic shower curtain would be blasted to the ceiling by the full force of the ice-cold jet of water, which threatened to remove your skin. People were often seen, towel under arm, sneaking off to another floor for a 'safe shower'.

It was on one of these water raids when, in an attempt to retrieve the flailing water hose that had been dropped in mid-spurt, I received the heavy metal nozzle sharply on my foot, sending me hopping away in excruciating pain. As David turned off the nozzle tap there was a hissing and tearing sound, followed by an explosion of water as the hosepipe ripped open, sending gallons of water spraying out. Everyone ran for cover, including David, who fell to the floor cracking his head open on the window ledge, leaving Graham, who had a badly sprained ankle from playing volleyball the previous night, grappling with the writhing hose whilst hopping on his good leg.

It was several minutes of high-pressure water, before it was discovered that all that was required was to swing the reel back to the wall to cut off the supply, but the damage was done. The fourth floor was literally inches deep,

David's head was badly cut with blood dripping into the water, which was successfully making its way towards the lift shaft, my big toe was like a balloon and Graham was wincing with pain as he splashed about trying to retrieve his walking stick, which was in danger of being swept away. All three of us went to hospital. David had six stitches, I had an X-ray on my badly bruised toe and Graham was found to have an even more sprained ankle than before.

When we returned later that evening, we couldn't believe it. Fearing the worst, we were expecting to see the fire brigade, plumbers' vans and probably a superintendent ready to send us back home, but no, nothing, no one, and on floor number four everything was just as it was before, apart from a little mopping here and there.

"Did we dream it?" I said to the other two.

"Nightmare, more like," said Graham, leaning on to his walking stick.

We were just settling down to a small tot of David's poteen (moonshine Irish spirit) to celebrate the fact that we didn't appear to be in trouble, when all the lights in the entire building went out.

"*Shit*" said the three voices in the darkness in unison.

Apparently an inspector in a room below had come in after a night over at the bar, switched on his light and 'bang', water was found to be running through the ceiling rose in his bedroom, cascading down his light shade and onto his bed. Two feet of water was found to be at the bottom of the lift shaft, and someone had mentioned our names 'in dispatches'.

At 9 a.m. the next morning the three of us were lined up in front of the desk of the course commandant, Detective Chief Inspector Ray Dyde. Beside the seated chief inspector stood a poker-faced Detective Sergeant Jim Evans.

David had a huge black lump on his forehead with the six stitches that were holding together a nasty gash clearly visible. I stood to attention in my best suit, which didn't go at all well with the size twelve white pump I'd borrowed from Graham on my left foot and my own brown shoe on my right. Graham stood next to me, his massive frame bent over as he leaned more than usual on to his buckling walking stick.

DCI Dyde kept looking down at his desk as he spoke to us.

"What the hell have you three been playing at? All the lights are out on the second and third floors, the lift's out of action, we might have to get the police bloody frogman out to fix it. We've got an assistant chief constable staying over tonight and I've got to try and find some way of keeping this from him, and look at the state of the three of you."

He looked up at us over his half-moon glasses, his tight mouth creasing and eyes crinkling at the sides as he looked back down at his desk. Jim Evans's grim expression was slowly cracking as he fixed his stare on a mark on the ceiling to avoid looking at us.

"It was all my fault, Sir" David explained. "I threw a wobbly and the lads were just trying to becalm me."

"So they hosed you down then, did they?" retorted the DCI with a slightly cracking voice.

"Well, err-" David started back.

"Sorry, boss," I said, "we were larking about a bit and it all went wrong."

"Yes, boss, we were just-" said Graham.

"*Enough!*" shouted the DCI, almost laughing. "Just get out, and consider yourselves lucky."

We all right turned in true drill fashion, Graham and I without banging our left foot down, and hobbled out. No sooner had we closed the door behind us than we could hear the two of them rocking with laughter. Nothing more was said of the hosepipe incident, and the bonus that came from it was that anyone could take a shower in uninterrupted peace whenever they wished.

Yes! There had been a lot of fooling about and a lot of laughs, but there had also been a lot of very hard work done, and the accumulation of the huge amount of detailed practical and theoretical knowledge would help us all in the years to come. The end of the course culminated in a week of exams, practical tests and presentations. Everyone had done well and I was surprised to have come second on the course.

We all had a comprehensive record of achievements throughout the course to take back to our respective forces and fortunately there was no mention of hosepipes and other such misdemeanours. The friendship and camaraderie that had developed between everyone on the course during those ten weeks would stand us in good stead many times in the years ahead as we bumped into each other on various different enquiries.

The end of course party was held at a pub in nearby Selly Oak and was, of course, a very rowdy beer swilling 'do'.

We had various 'acts', which comprised of selected members of the course doing what they all did best - taking the mickey out of each other and making us all laugh. I had to dress up as Pam Ayres and recite a poem in that Pam Ayres' style, southern rural accent. The poem had been composed jointly by several of us, and contained details about the instructors and the pranks that had been played during the course.

On the Friday lunchtime, the last day of the course, we said our goodbyes, lumped our suitcases, boxes, bags, books and unsold stock of pottery, shoes and whatever else, into our respective tatty cars and left Tally Ho to return to the real world.

CID Course 'Tally Ho' Birmingham. I'm three rows up, second from left, Graham Timson front row on left (look at that tie). Much beer was consumed by this 'mob'

John Pye

TWELVE

I did a few months more back on the drug squad before my CID posting came through - Hanley. I was being posted to Hanley CID, so my actual physical 'move' was only a matter of yards down the corridor from the drug squad office that I had worked from for the past three years. Hanley CID was housed in a huge office; it was a very large and very busy department. I knew most of the guys who worked there already and I knew things wouldn't be too different, with strange shifts, long hours and not much time off.

I arrived on my first day, complete with the first smart haircut I'd had in three years and wearing a suit - no more jeans and trainers.

I was given a desk, complete with the usual in-tray already piled high. There was a phone on each desk, and most of them seemed to be ringing constantly. The sheer quantity of jobs that just kept coming in was ridiculous. Of course, much of it was the same minor stuff that I'd had a taste of whilst doing my CID stint at Stoke - things like gas

243

and electric meter breaks - but each day there was a constant stream of burglaries, both at houses and other properties. There were dozens of thefts, cars being pinched, assaults, criminal damage, con tricks, major frauds and sexual offences, to name but a few, all of which had to be investigated at any one time.

One of the everyday priorities was that of any prisoners who had been arrested during the night for offences that it was thought required CID's expertise. Such prisoners could often take up your entire day, leaving all your other paperwork to mount up.

The detective whose turn it was to do nights for a week was literally run ragged from the moment he started at 10 p.m., as he'd have to dodge about between Hanley, Burslem and Tunstall all night long on different crimes, and then try to compile a report for the day staff in time for the early CID man. He was supposed to finish at 6 a.m., but was more often than not was still typing away at 9 a.m. or 10 a.m.

At Hanley CID in addition to the existing staff, we had the luxury of an office detective sergeant named Ken Lawton, but known as 'Lawt', a wise and cunning man who would often take the mickey out of you before guiding you into the 'best path to take'. Accompanying Ken was office DC Charlie Edwards whose job was to classify the various crimes and see that the daily paperwork found its way to the correct destination.

It soon became a routine for me, along with the other detectives, to go out on morning visits to the various burglaries that had been committed overnight. All burglaries had to be attended by CID. The same old villains' names would crop up time and again. Quite often these were people I knew only too well from the drug squad, as they would be burgling to fund their drugs habits. There were frequent court appearances, both at the magistrates' court, which was at Fenton, and at Crown court, which was part of Hanley Town Hall.

I hadn't been all that long at Hanley when a young PC from the uniform branch came into the office clad in his new Burtons suit ready to start his four-month CID aide. Young Geoff White - 'Whitey' and 'Chalky' were his two predictable nicknames – oh, and of course, 'Reg', was an extremely witty and intelligent man with a common sense attitude beyond his young years. Whitey spoke with a slow nasal drawl and could make a joke or a funny story out of nothing. He had a liking for beer and a dislike for criminals, shirkers, skivers and thugs. We got on very well.

Whitey had worked in Hanley town centre for almost all his two and a half years and had firmly planted in his memory the full names, nicknames, addresses, vehicle numbers and everything there was to know about almost every crook that dared to step over the boundary line onto his patch. Whitey's only real problem was that he was, and still is to this day, the most frightening, terrifying and hopeless driver ever to have been behind a steering wheel, and it still amazes me that he did, even at his fifth attempt, obtain his police driving permit that would allow him to drive the CID vans. On the scale of alarming drivers, Whitey would even be several points ahead of my old inspector from Stoke, 'Wild Bill Holdcroft'.

I met Whitey one Saturday morning as I came in through the front doorway of the nick. He was 8 a.m. 'early man', and was heading down towards the cells with a great bundle of papers in his hand.

"Loads of bloody prisoners in, Reg," he drawled, "could do with a hand."

"Okay," I said, "I'll just go and sign in, and dump my coat."

It was well after midday by the time we'd got all the problems sorted out in the cells, and the rest of the day staff had been kept busy with burglaries, thefts and all the other usual stuff, so it was pretty annoying when, after catching a bite of lunch, we found that there was still an outstanding burglary that hadn't been visited. It was Newbolds, the optician's in the town centre. Realising that the incident had to be visited, I quickly grabbed the van keys before Whitey could get near them, thereby possibly increasing my life expectancy by at least one day.

I parked the CID van around the corner from the optician's shop and we both made our way in through the front door.

"CID," I said to the manager, Mr Thomas, "sorry for the delay, we've been up to our necks."

"No problem," said Mr Thomas, "your fingerprint man came around earlier, but the whole thing has really messed us up."

"What's been taken, Mr Thomas?" Whitey asked.

Mr Thomas frowned as he looked at us.

"Two hundred pairs of spectacle frames and a clock."

"What," I said, puzzled, "just the frames, no glass in them?"

"Yes," said the bemused manager. "They're quite valuable in total, but absolutely no use to anyone other than an optician, and the clock was only worth about fifteen quid."

Whitey looked over at me with a furrowed brow and a concealed grin. We were both thinking, What the hell would anyone want with two hundred pairs of spectacle frames? We checked the shop and found how the offender had broken in through a back window, rifled through drawers, stealing petty cash as well, and gone out by opening the back door; all pretty usual. Whitey took a statement from Mr Thomas and we made our way back to the office to try to get on with all the other stuff we hadn't even touched.

It was only a couple of days later when following a few phone calls, questions in the right direction and a few pints bought for the right local crooks, that the names of two Scottish men were being mentioned. We had never heard of Duncan Adams and Tommy McPhee before. Apparently they were newcomers to the large council estate of Abbey Hulton, which was about one mile out of town. Abbey Hulton was a rough area and we'd often find ourselves down there, kicking in someone's door armed with a search warrant, or dealing with a serious domestic assault.

The word was out that these two had amassed a huge quantity of spectacle frames, which they were having great difficulty in offloading at pubs in the area in return for pints of beer or whiskies. Suspicions seemed justified as the hilariously laughing Tommy McPhee unknowingly answered his front door to the two strange men. Tommy had tears of laughter rolling down his cheeks as he stood on the step wearing a large and flamboyant pair of blue spectacles - with no lenses.

"Good evening, gentlemen," he said, his smile beginning to recede as the penny was dropping that Stoke-on-Trent coppers look a lot like those in Scotland. "What can I do for-?"

"CID - Mr McPhee, is it?" I asked.

"We've got a search warrant," said Whitey, "nice glasses, Mr McPhee."

Despite the implications, Tommy insisted that he had bought the spectacles from a man in a pub, along with the other pair that was found Sellotaped onto the pet dog's head. However, a further search of Duncan's nearby house turned up an additional three pairs of the glasses and, after a night of 'reflection' in the cells, the two of them were in agreement that they would get all the frames back for us the following night. True to their word the 'Scottish connection' arranged a 'meet' in the Corner Cupboard pub the very next evening where they handed over to us two Tesco bags brimming over with the missing specs.

Hanley CID office was an enormous office and it was quite usual for there to be as many as thirty people in there at the same time, sitting at desks, answering telephones, standing in groups discussing operations and so on. It was, therefore, amusing the following morning to see two detectives from another force enter the office, and to capture the bewilderment on their faces as to why every single person in Hanley CID from civilian staff, cadets, typists and detectives were all wearing some form of spectacles, be it John Lennon style, horn-rimmed or blue butterfly-winged.

It was later quite amazing to get the news through that both Tommy and Duncan were going to plead 'not guilty' at Crown court, despite all the evidence and even their previous admissions.

Crown court is always a bit of a nail-biting affair, even if you're totally sure of your ground. There will always be some smart-arsed barrister trying to score arrogant, toffee-nosed points in an effort to discredit you.

In a 'not guilty' case, witnesses are not allowed to go into court until they are called and are not allowed to speak to people who have already given evidence, so they have no idea what's going on or what has been said.

Whitey was called to give evidence first, and even though I knew we'd done everything by the book, I still sat fidgeting pensively outside, wishing I could hear what was going on and what nit-picking thing that had nothing to do with the case the defence was probing into in an effort to throw up a smokescreen.

"*Detective Constable Pye!*" shouted out the court usher.

Straighten tie, deep intake of breath, notebook in hand and enter courtroom.

I was very familiar with Hanley Crown Court by this time, but it never made any difference. The dark Victorian wood panelling and lofty carved plasterwork ceilings, the seemingly dozens of piercing sets of eyes peering from bewigged heads and a sort of haunting echo to the acoustics, always made my pulse race.

The prosecuting barrister led me through my evidence and I was allowed to use my pocket notebook, but not before the usual stock questions.

"And these are your original notes, are they, Officer?" he asked.

"Yes, Sir," I replied.

"Made as soon as possible after each event?"

"Yes, Sir."

All went well - not a hitch - and then it came to the defence's turn.

"Original notes, then, Officer - made, you say, as soon as possible then, Officer?"

"Yes... Yes, Sir"

"So, Mr. Pye..." droned the defence barrister, "you and DC White had been in this public house with Mr Adams and Mr McPhee, and this so-called handover of the spectacle frames had taken place, and you and Mr White then religiously went and made up your pocketbooks together, did you, as soon as possible?"

"Y-yes. Y-yes, Sir," I stammered, wondering why he was dwelling on this point, and also just what Whitey had said.

I could feel a trickle of sweat run down my temple.

"How long, Officer?" demanded the barrister.

"What, w-what? Pardon, p-pardon, Sir."

"How long after the pub meeting, Officer, did you and Mr White make up your pocketbooks?"

"Well, Sir, erm..."

My mind was now racing, trying to recall whether we'd been called to another job, or did we go back to the nick.

"I'm waiting, Officer", demanded the barrister.

"Erm, er…" My mind was now racing even faster. "About forty-five minutes, I should think, Sir. Yes, about forty-five minutes," I finally managed to say.

"Thank you, Officer," said the barrister, "no further questions, you may sit down."

With a slight tremble I walked from the witness box and headed towards where Whitey was sitting on one of the chairs reserved for police. Whitey fixed me with an emotionless tight-lipped stare.

"How was that?" I whispered out of the corner of my mouth, as I sat down next to him.

"Crap!" was Whitey's corner-of-the-mouth reply. "You've really dropped us in the shit."

"Why?" I pleaded in an almost normal volume voice. "What did you say?"

"Three quarters of an hour," came back Whitey's reply in a stifled spluttering laugh.

"*Bastard!*"

The Scottish connection were convicted and sentenced to a short term in prison, despite a suggestion from other colleagues that they'd been framed!

One afternoon, together with Whitey, I visited the home of a well-known crook on the Abbey Hulton estate, following an enquiry into a burglary at an off-licence around the corner.

The off-licence management were so fed up about the number of times the place had been screwed that they were considering closing the branch down, and now someone had broken in during the night, and had taken away the safe and stolen a few hundred cigarettes.

By knocking on doors we had found a neighbour, who, on hearing a noise in the early hours, had looked out of his bedroom window to see two men walking along the street, one of whom was pushing a wheelbarrow that contained a safe. The question had originally sprung to mind, 'well, why didn't you ring the police?', but apparently wheelbarrow safe-removing had become quite a regular occurrence on the Abbey Hulton estate during the hours of darkness.

The witness had identified the man we were visiting as the man accompanying the wheelbarrow-pusher - hence our visit.

"Oh! It's you bloody pair again, is it?" was our greeting as the man opened the door, recalling us from another recent visit. "Come in, do what you like, I'm watching the racing," he said as he slumped down in his chair in front of the TV.

I reiterated some of what we knew.

"Oh! That youth with the safe, the other night, the one in the wheelbarrow?" he said, without removing his stare from the screen.

"Well," I sarcastically said, "just how many different safes were being shifted about that night?"

"Well, I only saw the one," came the humourless reply, "and I don't know who he was. I just got talking to him; I was on my way back from the club."

Whitey looked over at me and I knew we both had the same vivid picture in our minds of dozens of people all walking around the estate of a balmy evening, each pushing a wheelbarrow loaded with a safe.

The house was a tip. There was stuff everywhere, from dirty dishes and old takeaway cartons to dog turds in the hall. There was a nauseating smell permeating the whole place. We unenthusiastically started the search in the living room, wandering back and forth, passing the man as he sat glued to the television. As I approached the settee, the nauseating smell wafted towards me in waves.

"What the hell is that stink?" I said.

The man looked up briefly from his chair.

"Yes, I noticed that the other day, it's bloody horrible, nearly put me off me takeaway last night."

I pulled back the settee and saw a large brown dog lying outstretched on the carpet.

"Bloody hell!" I said, startled, expecting to be savaged, as I had disturbed its sleep, but the dog made no movement.

Whitey came over and with a bigger frown than normal, drawled:

"It's bloody dead, Reg."

The man continued to watch the TV, gripping the arm of his chair as his horse came up on the rails with a chance of being in the frame.

"There's a bloody dead dog behind your settee," I shouted, to overcome the noise of the commentary.

"*Yes!*" shouted the man, jubilant at the fact that his each-way bet had got in the first three. "What's that you say, youth?" he finally said.

"I said there's a bloody dead dog behind your settee."

The man lifted himself from his armchair and peered over,

"So that's where he's got to. I'd been thinking only the other day, I wonder where he is."

"The dog's dead, mate," shouted Whitey. "Didn't you think to look for him? When did you last see him?"

"Oh! It's got to be a week or more. It's a shame, but he was getting on," replied the man with a shake of his head.

"So, you've been living in this house for a week with a dead dog behind the settee then?" I said.

"Yes, it's a shame, but he's had a good life," was the man's reply.

The wheelbarrow safe-pincher was eventually traced and charged with burglary after making a full admission about how he had spent a full two days chiselling open the back of the safe, only to discover that it contained a small bottle of Baby Bio plant food.

* * * *

Alan (Owly) Howell, also known as 'Growler', had now been the detective sergeant on our shift for some time. He was another character. Dedicated to the job, passionate about the job, loyal to the job, Alan was incredibly smart, always wearing a beautiful suit, or blue blazer with brass buttons. He was gifted with a supreme sense of humour and a rather high-pitched laugh that caused everyone within earshot to laugh without even knowing why. Alan, however, had frequent tantrums whenever he saw or heard of something not to his liking, and would concoct the most amazing tortures, which he would like to carry out on certain criminals, or even police officers, who in his mind had not 'carried out their duty correctly'. He would continue to a captive audience with the description of such punishments, whilst all of us around him cried with laughter and begged him to stop, for fear that some injury be brought upon us through laughing too much.

With the spread of the universal nickname of 'Reg', confusion was occasionally inevitable. One morning the office was its usual manic self, with upwards of twenty people, including detectives, uniformed officers, civilian staff and some members of the public. Telephones were ringing and there was the usual bustle.

Owly sat at his desk by the window engrossed in his paperwork and as the telephone on his desk made the slightest of pings, he had grabbed it and answered by bellowing into the phone in his normal over-emphasised manner.

"Ceee Eye Deee, Sergeant Howwwool speeeking."

No one ever found out why he did this!

A short conversation then ensued, following which Owly looked over at the rest of the office in general and spoke in a loud voice.

"Phone call for *Reg*."

Twenty people stopped what they were doing and started towards Owly's desk... Owly returned to the caller.

"Everyone's called bloody Reg around here," he said, and promptly replaced the receiver.

Early one summer's evening, when Geoff White and I were on noons, a report came in of a robbery at a Chinese takeaway in Birches Head Road in Hanley. It was a nasty job. The Chinese lady owner and her husband had been bundled into the back room and tied up, then taken upstairs where a mattress had been placed over them, pinning them down and nearly suffocating the lady.

Her young son, shouting out from the bedroom window for help, had raised the alarm. A lot of violence had been used, and the owners, who did not speak good English, were clearly petrified. Cash had been taken, and other members of the public had seen the offenders fleeing, and taken a car number. The strange thing was that the offenders were Chinese themselves.

We contacted our local Chinese interpreter whom we had used several times before. He was a very friendly man who had lived in Britain for many years and had adopted the name 'Frank' in preference to his Chinese name. Frank joined us in the interview room on the ground floor at Hanley nick, where we were sitting with the Chinese lady and her husband. Frank had his usual big broad grin.

"Hiya, Mr Plye, you okay?" he said.

"Yes thanks, Frank, see if you can ask them what's gone on tonight, sounds nasty."

Frank chatted away in his native tongue to the couple. A heated exchange took place and the couple became more frantic the more they blurted out, at lightning speed, whatever it was they were saying. Frank's mouth was by now wide open and he had stopped talking. He seemed speechless. Gone was his usual broad grin as he turned to us.

"This was the work of Triads," he said, with real fear on his face. "These people are so frightened I don't even know if they'll give you statements."

"Triads, Frank?" said Whitey. "How can they be sure, I mean, here in Hanley?"

"Oh, yes, Mr Whitey," said Frank, "there's a big Triad organisation in this country. These people know they were Triads all right, and they'll stop at nothing; they're vicious evil men."

It became apparent that, had it not been for the presence of the couple's children shouting out of the window and causing the incident to be reported by neighbours, the couple would have been too frightened to report the matter themselves. With a lot of reassurance the couple made the necessary statements, and shortly afterwards the car used by the Chinese gang was traced to a chef at a Chinese restaurant in Chester, who was quickly arrested and the car seized.

Although clearly petrified at the involvement of Chinese Triads, Frank was interested and keen to be of assistance and would turn out at a moment's notice to help out. Initial enquiries revealed that the Triad organisation in this country was indeed very active and clearly was responsible for numerous similar robberies at Chinese businesses nationwide. The usual theme was that the Chinese owners would be so terrified that they would fail to report the matters to the police, so the little bit that we knew of these incidents was probably the tip of the iceberg. There had been murders involving the Triads and reports of victims of crime having fingers chopped off to instil further fear into them.

A search of the car involved in our robbery revealed few clues, but one was a page of foolscap paper upon which was some Chinese handwriting.

Frank was clearly shaken when he examined the paper.

"The man you have is a very important and dangerous man," Frank said. "He is a member of the 14k, the very worst of Triads. He is a 'Red Stick', a high-ranking member. This also shows lists of Chinese businesses that may be potential victims, or previous victims."

Any dealings with our prisoner, Cho Sang Lee, were difficult. He would feign an ignorance of English or would just stare blankly at the wall throughout an entire interview. Although trying to be helpful, Frank was frightened for his life, and any interviews we held with Lee had be done with a large cine-projection screen on the table between Lee and Frank, with Whitey and myself either side, so that Lee could not see Frank's face.

It did inevitably become hilarious, as Frank did not wish to be known by his name of Frank, and we, therefore, decided to call him 'Reg', a name that Frank could only pronounce as 'Ledge'. Unfortunately on a couple of occasions we slipped up and referred to him as Frank. Frank immediately corrected us by saying:

"No, no, I am… *Ledge*."

Our enquiries took us to many different parts of the country, including Liverpool and Blackpool. It was in Blackpool that we met a young police constable who, having being brought up in Hong Kong, could speak Chinese fluently. The bearded, completely 'English'-looking officer's expertise was in great demand throughout the country and it was occasionally very useful to have him listen in on conversations for us.

Owly, being our supervisor, took great interest in this serious and unusual case, and would occasionally come with us on enquiries concerning it. As Whitey and I planned a trip to Chester Police Headquarters the following day we were pleased to hear that Owly would accompany us, despite the fact that he had been suffering terribly with gout for several days and had been seen limping badly.

As I came into the office at 8 a.m. the next day I could see Owly standing at the far end of the office resplendent in his usual immaculate blue blazer with brass buttons, crisply ironed white shirt, red tie and razor-edged grey slacks. I was puzzled, however, as I caught sight of Whitey sitting at his desk convulsed in laughter, hiding his head in his hands and pointing his finger towards Owly.

As I walked a little closer to Owly, who was busily talking into the telephone and writing with his free hand, I was able to see his feet. He was wearing a pair of blue velvet carpet slippers! I looked back over at Whitey and, shaking my head in disbelief, pointed at Owly and mouthed the word, 'Chester?'.

Whitey nodded.

The entire day over at Chester seemed to be taken up with different reactions from different people, including members of the public, uniformed officers, detectives and some very high-ranking Chester officers, who were all interested and puzzled by the sight of this extremely smart detective sergeant from Stoke who was traipsing about around their headquarters wearing carpet slippers.

One of the turning points of the inquiry would be through the inevitable use of one of my pet hates, an ID parade. My mind would always go back to my first hopeless attempt, but the thought of trying to arrange an ID parade for a Chinese man was daunting. Where on earth were we going to find another dozen or so Chinese men, let alone, ones who resembled our suspect? However, after many futile attempts to find even one who was willing to help, because of the Triad connection, someone came up with an idea.

Located some ten miles away, near to the town of Stone, was an establishment that was looking after and housing a large number of Vietnamese boat people; refugees who had fled their country to escape persecution. Although the skin colour was slightly darker, they did have similar oriental features to our Chinese man, their language was, however, totally different.

An approach was made to them and the response was overwhelming; literally all of them wanted to be involved. Two police personnel carriers were dispatched to make a good selection and bring the 'chosen ones', back to the assembly hall of Hanley Police Station where the parade would take place. The assembly hall was a huge room, originally designed as a ballroom and still used as such at that time for dinner dances and other entertainment.

The chosen boat people duly arrived and were settled for the time being in the adjoining bar-room, whilst the other arrangements were organised. The room was busy with uniformed and plain clothes officers, police photographers and solicitors. Of course Frank was there, too. The clamour of unintelligible voices coming from the bar-room where the boat people were waiting was growing by the minute, as they all excitedly chatted away about what was taking place. After a while we were ready to start the parade, and Whitey and I went over to Frank to tell him that it was time to bring the suspect up from the cells.

"Okay, but he must not be able to see me," was Frank's worried reply.

"How the hell are we going to get around this?" I said to Whitey.

"God knows," came back his reply.

Eventually the solution was arrived at, thanks to a pair of scissors and a brown Manila folder. Frank was handed his 'protective' folder, which now had two eyeholes cut in it and was to be held in front of his face at all times.

Frank followed us down to the cell block, together with the suspect's solicitor, and rigidly kept his folder up to his face, interpreting what was going on from behind, after carefully reminding us to ensure that we called him 'Ledge' at all times.

Frank stumbled a couple of times whilst climbing the cell block steps and really did look ridiculous as he wandered about the assembly hall, interpreting from behind his folder with just a flash of his eyes occasionally to be seen through the eyeholes.

Owly limped about the room, shining with a lustre in his expensive charcoal grey suit and colour-co-ordinated bright red slippers as Whitey and I found it difficult to contain our laughter. The afternoon's proceedings and the day's hard work proved fruitless, as neither of the Chinese witnesses picked out the man.

On the other hand, all the boat people seemed to have had a great day out and after being paid their £3 fee, which had increased since the days of the Salvation Army, they were delighted to be allowed to spend it in our bar, and they turned it into quite a party. The case culminated at Stafford Crown Court with Lee being found not guilty. You can't win 'em all!

* * * *

One bitterly cold winter's morning I arrived at Hanley. It was just after 8.30 a.m. as I entered the CID office. Whitey was early man and was sitting at his desk with a phone pressed to his ear, continuing to talk into the handset as he gestured over to me in his left-handed manner to look at what he had written on his notepad.

He tapped his pen onto several lines of his distinctive scrawl, with which I had become so familiar, as he carried on urgently with his phone call.

I read from the page:

Naked man's body, wasteland, side of Carmount Inn.

Within ten minutes we had made it to the scene (I drove!).

The Carmount Inn was a big old public house in the middle of the Abbey Hulton estate where we seemed to spend most of our time. At the side of the pub was a large area of wasteland that was littered with rubbish, old sofas, bottles, bits of old cars and anything else that nobody wanted.

Everywhere was covered in a thick white crusty frost. A couple of panda cars had already arrived and closed the scene off from the public. The licensee, Clive, was out on the front of the pub. Clive had spotted the body and rung in to report the matter, and now he was engaged in 'tea-making' for the boys.

Whitey and I picked our way through the rubbish, frost-covered beer bottles and cardboard boxes, bricks and bits of wood, and eventually arrived alongside the scene of the crime officer, who was standing making notes and taking details.

This was the strangest of scenes. The body lay on the ground curled up on his side in the foetal position with his head resting on his clasped hands, he was stark naked. Had he not been in the middle of a field of rubbish and covered in frost you would have thought he was in bed at home and fast asleep. His jacket, trousers and underwear were all folded and piled up neatly near his feet, along with his neatly placed shoes, each one of which contained a sock.

It didn't take long to establish the man's identity; his dole card was in his trouser pocket. He turned out to be a fifty-nine-year-old alcoholic who lived alone only about three hundred yards away.

A lengthy day of enquiries established nothing suspicious or of concern about the man, and the eventual cause of death and consequent answer to the strange circumstances was that the man had died from hypothermia. It appears he had wandered off from the pub the previous evening very drunk and must have collapsed unseen by anyone. Being only lightly clothed in what was bitterly cold weather it hadn't been long before hypothermia had set in. In the delirious state bought on by the condition, the body loses heat at such a rapid rate that the person starts to feel unbearably hot as the core of the body rapidly loses heat through the skin.

We later learned that removing the clothes and folding them neatly is a classic example found in hypothermia cases, as the disorientated mind tries to make some order of the situation to relieve the unbearable heat.

* * * *

Whitey had badly injured his right ankle some years previously and this, coupled with his compulsion to play sport whenever possible and a natural flair for clumsiness, meant that his right ankle was always lurking… waiting… ready to be sprained at the slightest opportunity. He was a very fit young man, but seemed to lack any co-ordination and when running his legs seemed to shoot out sideways from the knees.

It was just after 6.30 p.m. one evening when Whitey put down his pen an hour and a half later than he should have done, and drawled in that nasal voice:

"Right, you lot, I'm off home."

It wasn't many minutes later before we were all called over to the window.

"Looks like someone's been hurt," said Ken (Lawt) Lawton, the office sergeant.

We peered through the window to see a small gathering of people, including a couple of uniformed PCs, clustered around a prone figure on the pavement in St John Street opposite the nick.

"It's Whitey!" exclaimed Charlie Edwards.

"Is he pissed again?" asked a frowning Lawt.

"No, Sarge," I chipped in. "He's been in court all day, looks like he's done his ankle in again."

I darted downstairs and soon established that this was indeed the case, and helped an ashen-faced Whitey to limp painfully back upstairs to the CID office.

"Done it this time, Reg, good and proper," droned Whitey with a pained expression.

Whitey slumped down into a chair, his right foot at a strange angle and his ankle swelling by the second.

"Right, Charlie," commanded Lawt, "first aid book."

Charlie promptly produced a 'force issue' first aid book, and the comedy continued as Charlie flipped through the index looking for 'ankle'.

Lawt then took the book and read from it in a loud voice.

"Make a triangular bandage."

Whitey gasped in pain as someone removed his shoe, whilst Charlie scrabbled about in a drawer for a first aid kit. Upon finding the kit, Charlie pulled a dirty-looking small paper package from it marked 'bandage'. Ripping it open he pulled from it an off-white square of gauze cloth that he placed on the desk and folded over to one corner making a tatty-looking triangle.

"Done," said Charlie.

"Place the top point beneath the ankle so that it points up towards the back of the knee," said Lawt, reading from the book, which he was turning around in a clockwise motion as he spoke, with his head slightly tilted, lining the diagram in the book with Whitey's leg.

Whitey gasped in pain as, following Lawt's instructions, Charlie lifted his melon-sized ankle upwards and slipped the dirty crumpled rag beneath it, the patient's ashen pallor now taking on a dark greenish grey.

"Reg," said Whitey, "take me to the hospital. This triangular bandage thing's not going to work."

I arrived at the North Staffs Royal Infirmary Accident Unit some fifteen minutes later with Whitey in the CID van, and wheeled him through to the waiting area in one of the cumbersome, red leather wheelchairs provided.

After booking in my forlorn-looking colleague at the reception desk, I positioned his wheelchair alongside my grey plastic chair, looked around at the multitude of variously injured folk around me and resigned myself to a long wait. We talked for a while about various subjects and different cases we'd got on the go to try to keep off the subject of the painful ankle and then, quite suddenly, Whitey went strangely quiet.

After several minutes of seemingly deep thought, Whitey spoke pensively.

"Reg…"

"What?" I replied.

"Reg… do you think I'll have to take my trousers off?" he drawled, with a worried expression.

"Yes, bound to," I said, "they'll have to X-ray it and all that. You might have to have it in plaster, why?"

There was a long pause before he looked at me, swallowed, and said:

"Reg… I've got no pants on."

There was quite a long pause from me as I tried to visualise Whitey sitting waiting after his X-ray naked from the waist down, with other people sitting either side of him reading magazines and so on, but after these visual images all I could muster was:

"Oh dear!"

"Reg," said Whitey, quite firmly now, "Reg, can I borrow your pants?"

Well, the things you do for mates!

Knowing that there was not much time left, as we were getting near the front of the queue, I dashed off to the gents and as quickly as possible removed my underpants, restoring my appearance back to normal in record time. I boldly strode back out, hoping that no one would know that I now had my underpants crushed into a ball in my right hand ready to pass them on to Whitey so that he could struggle into them in the gents.

I dashed down the corridor with my hand outstretched like a relay runner ready to pass on the baton. As I turned the corner, all I could see were the grey plastic chairs and a gap where the red wheelchair had been. He'd gone; he'd been taken, possibly by a beautiful young nurse. I caught up with him at the X-ray department, just as a giggling nurse was in the process of slicing through his grey flannels with a pair of scissors. A grinning, but still a bit ashen faced, Whitey proclaimed:

"Too late, Reg, I've had to cough it."

* * * *

On Wednesday, 3rd June 1981 I was on a 'special duty' along with a great many more detectives and uniformed officers, when Prince Charles came to Hanley to open the newly built City Museum and Art Gallery. The building was just one hundred yards from the police station, and upon seeing the prince I was amazed at how small he was. We all had a full day just standing about and then had to start a real day's work when he'd gone.

With my exams out of the way it was now time for a stab at promotion, so after attending a promotion board at headquarters, I suddenly found myself back in uniform and on shifts as 'acting sergeant' at Hanley (this is promotion?).

THIRTEEN

After two months of 'acting sergeant' I was summoned to see our chief constable, Mr Charles Kelly. Our previous chief, the Welshman, Arthur Morgan Rees, had retired in 1977. Mr Kelly told me he was promoting me to uniform sergeant and sending me to - Biddulph.

Biddulph was a market town in the Leek division. It was quite a distance to travel every day and the work was going to be completely different from anything I had known before.

I arrived at Biddulph Police Station on Monday, 17th May 1982. The Falklands War was in full swing and it was just in the news that a twenty-eight-year-old naval petty officer from Biddulph had become the first local casualty of the war. Fortunately he was only injured, but it put my own minor discomfort into perspective.

I had a shift of six PCs at a small, but newly built police station on the outskirts of the town. Our territory covered quite a large area of mostly farming communities and it had more than its fair share of nutcases, sex offenders and extremely violent men (oh, and women!). It was, however, pretty quiet compared with Hanley.

Biddulph Police Station (since demolished)
(photograph courtesy The Potteries Museum)

On my first day I scanned the six PCs who made up my shift; one older chap, who was near retirement, two fairly new to the job and three of a similar age to me. I had intended using the 'smartness and punctuality' speech that I had had drummed into me over the years, but stopped in my tracks at the sight of one scruffy young constable with baggy flapping trousers, filthy boots and unkempt hair. I sent him home with the warning not to come back until he looked like he used to do at Ryton.

I disliked having to discipline someone, especially on my first day, as I had always felt that I could get the best out of people with good humour and self-respect, but realised there would always be exceptions.

The lads on the shift were, however, a decent bunch, apart from sadly the same constable I had to send home, who turned out to be a sex fiend and was arrested off duty, up to no good on the fire escape of the local squash club, peering into the ladies' changing rooms through the extractor fan. He, of course, got the sack.

There was a distinct lack of entertainment in the town, so when anything was 'on', people tended to go over the top. I remember one night there was a function at the town hall. We had been a bit short-staffed due to time off and illness, so when John Caddy, one of the shift PCs, turned up for duty, despite his bandaged hand due to an injury at home, I was more than pleased to see him.

John was out on town centre patrol near the town hall. It was about 1 a.m., just as some of the revellers were turning out from the fancy dress party that had been held there, when he spotted a German SS Officer in full uniform, urinating against the monument in full view of a party of maids, schoolgirls, a lady in a crinoline dress and Dr Who. Aware of being outnumbered, and thinking of his disability, he decided to just tick off the SS Officer and send him on his way.

"Sorry, Mein Fuhrer," came the reply, as the officer clicked together his heels with his willy still hanging out and thrust up a Hitler salute.

John was still intent on just sending the miscreant on his way.

"Just go... now!" he ordered, and was surprised to feel someone tightly grip his arm from behind.

He swirled around to see the local troublemaker, busybody, drunkard and loud mouth, who was known by his strange nickname of 'Bunty', swaying back and forth.

"Leave him alone you, leave him alone, bloody copper, he's not hurt you," shouted the tottering Bunty.

"Keep out of it, Bunty," replied John, "it's got nothing to do with you."

At that Bunty launched himself at John and tried to pull him to the ground. As John struggled with his attacker, trying to send a radio message through for help, Bunty suddenly spotted John's bandaged hand and immediately stopped his attack and loosened his grip.

"What you done to your hand?" Bunty spluttered.

"Burned it on the iron," was John's reply.

"Is it okay?" enquired Bunty.

"Yes, not too bad," gasped John.

With that, Bunty continued with his attack, tightening his grip and trying to take John off his feet. After a few seconds more, he stopped again.

"Hand okay?"

"Yes, it's okay."

More struggling... stop... struggling...

"You're sure now?"

"Yes, I'm still okay."

This ridiculous scene continued until I arrived, whereupon Bunty was arrested and driven back to the police station, passing by the SS Officer, who was happily, but unsteadily, marching back home minding his own business with his willy now safely tucked away. En route to the nick Bunty continually asked as to the state of John's hand.

The whole situation culminated in the custody office of the police station with Bunty removing his false teeth and throwing them at the cell block wall smashing them on a radiator pipe... I'll never know why.

There were some strange duties that were the responsibility of the police in those days, such as visiting shops to examine their licences that allowed them to sell fireworks before November 5th. All manner of duties concerning, 'diseases of animals', were the responsibility of the police. Of course, now I was out at Biddulph and surrounded by farms, such matters were of much more importance than they had been at Hanley. One such duty was the requirement for a police officer to be present during sheep dipping at the various farms, to ensure that the farmer was carrying out the procedure fully and correctly. This was a real change from murders and drug swoops.

I longed to get back to CID work, but tried to make the best of my lot. Things were never consistently busy, but did often come in waves and catch you unaware. How true this was one summer Sunday afternoon as I strolled down to the town centre with the inspector who had come over from Leek. As we chatted, I mentioned that I was a bit cheesed off and hoped to get back to CID, as nothing much ever happened at Biddulph. The words had hardly left my mouth when we heard the unmistakable sound of the nearby blast of a shotgun. The inspector narrowed his eyes as he looked at me and was about to make a comment when right in front of us a car, with tyres screeching, smashed into the rear of a van that had pulled up rather abruptly at a pedestrian crossing. A wheel trim flew off the car, skimming between the two of us as a motorcycle then ploughed into the back of the car sending the rider flying up onto the roof of it.

The radio crackled into life.

"Report of a shotgun being fired in Diamond Close. Any patrol to attend."

I raised my radio to my mouth, intent on reporting the accident and mentioning that we had heard the shotgun, when a man dressed in running shorts appeared in front of me.

"There's a bloke down here in the garden," he gasped. "I think he's dead, looks like he's been electrocuted by his lawnmower."

The inspector looked at me.

"Not much happening?"

This proved to be a long day.

* * * *

One morning one of the PCs on my shift, Kenny Harper, came into my office.

"Seen this, Sarge?" he asked as he placed a glossy covered hardback book down on my blotter in front of me; the book was entitled *The Hamlyn Book of Horror* and depicted a demonic-looking Dracula figure with a wooden stake embedded in his chest.

"What the hell's this, Ken?" I asked, laughing.

"It belongs to my lad, he's pointed out to me that *you* are in it."

Kenny flicked through the pages and opened the book at an article entitled 'The Man in Stoke-on-Trent', which was a complete short story of my vampire encounter that had occurred some ten years previously. The article even included a black and white drawing of a policeman entering a bedroom with torch in hand to the sight of a body lying on the bed.

We both laughed at the article.

"And this is me, then?" I said, pointing at the picture.

"Guess so, Sarge. Will you autograph the inside cover for the lad?"

Fame at last!

I was on duty in the police station one summer's evening when a man came into the enquiry office with a large brown cardboard box, which he placed on the counter.

"Good evening, Sir, and how can I help you?" I said with my most welcoming of Biddulph smiles.

"I'd like you to have a look at this please, Sergeant," he said, gesturing towards the box, which I was almost sure I had seen move slightly under its own power.

He opened the lid of the box, and as I peered inside a gigantic snake rose up from within, right in front of my face. I staggered backwards, knocking the nuclear attack early warning box from the shelf and ending up sitting on the floor against the table.

"Why the hell have you bought it in here?" I shouted, my welcoming Biddulph smile now replaced with a look of total disbelief.

"Well, we found it in the fields at Knypersley and thought you'd know what to do."

The man was ordered to return the creature, a three-foot long grass snake, to where he had found it.

I was once again on duty in the station one evening, taking the opportunity to get through some boring paperwork and daydreaming about drug squad and CID days, when one of the shift members came into my office.

"Sarge, there's a strange woman at the counter, says she wants to speak to the person in charge, she's got a box with her and she won't speak to anyone else."

"I hope it's not another bloody snake," I said, as I made my way through to the enquiry desk.

Through the sliding glass window I could see a petite woman in her mid-thirties with her back to me, clutching a shoebox to her chest as she looked out through the glass front doors.

"Hello," I said, being ready to take up my 'grass snake' defensive position.

The woman swirled around.

"You in charge?" she demanded.

"Yes, at the moment, what's the problem?" I answered.

"And you're a sergeant, are you?" she quizzed.

"Well, yes," I said, puzzled as I checked to see that no one had torn the bright silver stripes from my sleeves.

"How do I know that you're a real police sergeant?"

"Well, I'm here in a police station wearing a blue uniform with stripes on my arms, is that not good enough?" I replied, with a degree of sarcastic annoyance.

"No, it's not... this is serious, I shall have to see your identification," the woman demanded with a wide-eyed expression as she clutched the box ever more tightly to her chest.

What the hell is in the box? I thought to myself, *somebody's head or something?*

"Very well, madam," I patronised, "I'll get my warrant card to show you."

The two PCs who were also in the office at the time looked at each other, thinking, We've got a right one here!

I returned within a few seconds and produced my warrant card, which the woman examined in detail then opened the box and pulled from it... a gun... a silver heavy-looking revolver, which she pointed directly at me through the open sliding window. I dropped to the floor beneath the counter thinking that this deranged woman must have heard voices commanding her to go and kill a police sergeant.

"This gun," she said, slamming it down onto the counter, "is my husband's and he's a stinking bastard."

Realising that the gun no longer presented a problem, I picked it up and made it safe by pushing the bullet chamber outwards, noticing that it contained no bullets.

"What's this all about?" I said with relief, now realising that I was not the intended victim of some Biddulph-based, police sergeant slaying cult.

It transpired that her husband, who was an accomplished engineer, had actually made the gun as a training project many years before. It was beautifully crafted, but highly illegal, as it worked perfectly with .22 ammunition. After years of mental problems and domestics, the woman had taken this path as a way of getting her husband 'into trouble'. He had to make a court appearance over the unlicenced gun, received a fine and the gun had to be destroyed.

I had now become highly suspicious of people entering the police station carrying cardboard boxes, so when an elderly lady slowly and carefully tiptoed in through the front doors holding yet another cardboard box, which she held out at arm's length, I didn't know if I should just drop to the floor as a matter of course or run off. The lady placed the box down onto the counter with great care.

"I think you should take a look at this, my dear," she said.

After my two previous 'box' experiences, I cautiously moved closer as the lady produced a copy of the *Daily Express* from her pocket.

"Read this first, young man," the lady said, pushing the newspaper over to me, which was folded over at an article entitled, 'Exploding Treacle Tins'. A photograph accompanied the article, showing a tin of Lyle's Black Treacle, which had somehow become distorted into an almost perfect spherical shape. The article explained how, in recent weeks, several similar very old tins had blown up with considerable force in people's pantries. Apparently the fermentation created by the hot summer and the considerable age, had generated such massive pressure that some of the tins had eventually swelled up and burst. I carefully lifted the lid of the box to reveal an almost completely round tin of black treacle. The wording and colouring of the tin gave it an obvious pre-war appearance. It seemed astonishing that the lid had not just eventually popped open on its own.

With even the slightest movement of the box, the tin rolled from one corner to another as there was now no flat side for it to rest upon. The pressure inside must have been immense. I carefully carried the box out into the backyard of the police station and set it down by the wall in the full knowledge that, should it explode, the flimsy cardboard box would offer no protection at all.

The detective sergeant suddenly appeared from his upstairs office after hearing about 'the incident', and offered his previous military and bomb disposal experience to us by throwing the tin as hard as he could at the garage wall. The tin exploded with a dull thump leaving a two-feet wide, black treacle splatter on the garage wall and several dollops on one of the panda cars. Beware of people carrying boxes!

One Sunday afternoon whilst out on patrol with Kenny Harper, I received a call over the radio saying that someone had been seen in the compound at the back of a motorcycle spares' garage in the town centre. As we were close by it took only seconds to get there. As we jumped out of the panda car, I could clearly hear the sound of a powerful motorbike revving up. I ran around the corner into an alleyway leading to the rear of the garage with Kenny in hot pursuit and saw a figure astride a large red motorbike facing towards me and about twenty yards away. Upon seeing me the rider opened the throttle with a roar, the front of the bike lifted and he drove straight at me.

The alleyway in which I stood was narrow, and littered with machinery and other rubbish. As the machine raced towards me I instinctively pressed myself into the brick wall on my left, the front mudguard of the bike caught me a sickening blow to the right leg as the handlebars hit me in the ribs. I grabbed the rider around his helmeted head and clung on as the machine charged forwards, dragging me along with it. The engine note changed as the rider started to lose control with the added weight of Kenny, who by now was somehow perched on the handlebars. The machine and the three of us were all flung violently in different directions as it smashed into a pile of wooden pallets. The engine roared at full revs and the rear wheel spun dangerously as the machine lay on its side, whilst Kenny and I struggled violently with this madman who'd just nearly killed us.

We overpowered him and turned off the machine. He had been stealing motorcycle parts, and a later search of his home and garage revealed an Aladdin's cave of stolen motorbikes and parts. I ended up with bruised ribs, a badly gashed shin and a commendation from the judge at the later Crown court hearing. I also lived in hope that the incident might spark a memory in some distant senior detective in the faraway headquarters that the name 'Pye' was a name that used to feature in the Criminal Investigation Department.

Maybe it did, I really can't be sure, but after enduring twenty-two months at Biddulph, I received a call one day from 'God', well, God's deputy, Detective Chief Superintendent Malcolm Bevington, the man in charge of the CID, asking me if I'd like a job as detective sergeant at Stone CID - silly question.

FOURTEEN

I started at Stone in early 1984. It was a very old building full of character, and yes... khaki-coloured lino, how nice to see some again. The nick was just outside the town centre. There were stairs and corridors leading everywhere. Apparently part of the building had originally been the magistrates' court and the actual CID office was in fact the old courtroom itself. It was a very large echoing room with a high ceiling.

The area covered by the sub-division of Stone was immense, as it actually covered a third of the county of Stafford, but, of course, the policing boundaries were worked out on population rather than square miles. We had other 'satellite' police stations at Great Haywood, Gnosall and Madeley. Madeley even had its own little CID office with two of our DCs working from there. We had a detective inspector, a detective sergeant (me) and eight DCs.

Stone suffered more than its fair share of crime, burglaries in particular, the reason mainly being that it was such a big area with a lot of isolated expensive houses and it attracted the attention of 'travelling crooks'. We had a bad time, particularly with Scouse burglars, who would just come down the M6 from Liverpool and drop off on our patch to see what looked worthwhile. We seemed to be forever travelling back and forth to 'Scouseland' to arrest some of their villains.

I hadn't been long at Stone when I was offered a place on an advanced CID course, which would be at Wakefield in the West Yorkshire force and would last six weeks. It was just one hundred miles from home and, as my tatty old mini was not up to the job, my dad loaned me his brand new Ford Capri. I had to put the back seats down flat to get all the pottery in. The course was very intense and was on at the same time as the 1984 Miners' Strike.

The training school was another historic old building on the outskirts of Wakefield, known as 'Bishops Garth', but the accommodation block was within another nearby building. The theme of the course was much the same as my previous course years before at Birmingham, but we were all a little older and, supposedly, a little more responsible - perhaps boring would be a better word. Nevertheless, we had a great time, but all had to work very hard. There were twenty-six of us on the course from all over the country, including two RUC officers. We would get woken up most mornings at 5 a.m. as the dozens of police personnel carriers, which assembled on the giant car park, all trundled off every morning, laden down with hundreds of uniformed officers going on picket duty for the Miners' Strike. We did manage to have more than a few beers on the course, and gained some new and useful contacts, who we'd be in touch with over the years to come.

In January 1985 I was to lose another two friends, PCs Bob Owen, aged twenty-eight, and Graham Whitehurst, who was thirty-three. I had served with them both at Stoke.

They were both killed when their vehicle was involved in a high-speed accident, whilst answering an emergency call on the A500 near the city centre.

I was back at Stone and the real world again after the course. Stone CID had its fair share of characters. Peter Rowley was a detective who should really have been on the stage, as he was a born comedian who always had a joke or funny story at the ready and would often break into a brilliant rendition of Dame Edna Everage at the most inappropriate of moments - not that there were many occasions when such a rendition would be appropriate anyway.

Peter was a brilliant detective. He did, however, suffer from 'builders bottom' and, consequently, would often be seen showing the crack of his bum when the necessity to bend over even very slightly occurred. Many times I have, with some embarrassment, had to shield Peter's rear from the astonished gaze of some member of the public whilst attending one crime scene or another as Peter found it necessary to bend down and pick up some clue or other.

Patrick (Nult) McNulty, another DC on the shift and another character, was always extremely smartly turned out; never a jacket, not even a leather jacket, always a suit and quite often two-tone shoes. If some annoying or amusing incident happened (which was most days), in no time at all, Pat would have composed a suitable poem encapsulating the incident and bringing everyone to hysterical laughter.

One grey, miserable, wet autumn afternoon, Nult and I were on our way back to the office in our CID Ford Escort after dealing with an assault in the nearby village of Yarnfield, when we spotted a young man who was wanted for several burglaries around the town centre. Pat was his usual dapper self with a light grey suit, white shirt, dark blue tie and expensive-looking light and dark, grey leather shoes.

The villain, Darren Hulse, spotted the CID car and was immediately off like a rabbit around the side of a car repair garage. I flung the car onto the garage forecourt and Nult was out of the passenger door and away after him as the puzzled garage employees dashed outside to see what was going on. As I escaped the seat belt and got around to the other side of the car, I was in time to see young Hulse leap over a farm gate at the side of the garage and make off across the muddiest, wettest, most unpleasant-looking ploughed field I had ever seen. Undeterred, Nult, in all his finest regalia, but not being up to leaping, quickly climbed the gate, splashed down into the field and made off after the rapidly diminishing figure of Hulse.

Nult had gone only a few yards before his beautiful shoes had become so heavily laden with mud that he could hardly pick them up... With another struggling step his right foot came up minus the shoe, he stumbled, arms waving wildly, as his forward velocity was suddenly held back by his left foot, which had disappeared completely from view and was held tightly in the grip of the mud. His body quivered momentarily and then he shot forwards as his left foot was freed from the shoe, leaving him stumbling on for several yards shoeless, arms flailing about for balance as he inevitably churned into the mire face down like a 'human plough'.

I had only made it to the gate; my cunning sergeant's instinct had made me realise that this was a futile pursuit, coupled with the fact that this had been such a wonderful spectacle. I could not contain my laughter as I radioed in with the direction in which Hulse had been seen heading. I was immediately aware that I had been joined by all the staff of the garage, who were also hysterically laughing. The laughter increased as Nult turned around, his front completely plastered from head to foot with thick black mud and corn stalks. He tentatively tiptoed forwards a few steps, losing a sock and then finding his shoe. He pulled with all his might to release it from the suction, falling on his backside as he did so. On finding another shoe, he managed to release it only to discover it was one of Hulse's trainers, which he also had lost.

Nult, tarred and feathered now, both back and front, looked skywards with clenched fist and threw Hulse's trainer an amazing distance into a nearby stream as he shouted:

"Bastard!"

After recovering his other shoe and covering the car seat with a blanket, I drove Nult back to his home at Stafford for a shower and change of attire. I really wanted to take him back to the nick first, so everyone else could have a look, but he wasn't having any. Strangely he never did compose a poem about this one.

John Cowan was another member of the department, another character; a muscular, strong and very fit man who facially slightly resembled the rugged features of film star, Charles Bronson, the name by which he was often referred. John was a gentle, well-mannered, inoffensive man, but was capable of 'sorting out' even the most violent of criminals when pushed to the limit. He would laugh uncontrollably at the slightest opportunity, until tears literally ran down his face.

One Saturday afternoon, whilst I was on noons, a report came in that burglars had been disturbed at the isolated home of a wealthy jeweller in the village of Butterton, some six miles out of Stone. John and I attended, and it was found that the two offenders had broken into the beautiful detached house during a brief absence of the elderly owner.

In fact the eighty year old arrived' back as the burglars were in the middle of deciding what to take. They had fled the scene, fortunately without harming him, and had made off in a car, which they had cheekily parked within the driveway of the house. The sprightly old gent had been able to take down the registration number of the car, but didn't manage to get much of a look at the offenders, one of whom he thought may even have been a young woman. A lot of jewellery and ornaments had been taken, along with a yellow candlewick bedspread that had no doubt been used to pack everything up in. The thieves had also hauled a very heavy safe out of the house onto the veranda, where it remained perched on top of a creaking wicker chair; had it not been for the owner's arrival, this would probably have been lumped into the boot of the car.

The MO fitted very closely with other burglaries we'd been having over the past few months and might well have been the answer to a lot of crime. The possibility of a starting point with the car registration number turned out to be a let-down, as we only got as far as discovering that it had been bought from a Manchester car auction by a man named Mr Smith with a false address. All was not lost though, when a computer check on the car number revealed that the car had been towed away after being parked illegally in Manchester City Centre three weeks previously, and had been collected from the police pound by a Mrs Michelle Waylan from Middleton.

A call to the Middleton CID came up trumps. Mrs Waylan was the wife of a very well known burglar, Shaun Waylan, who was known to specialise in jewellery. Middleton CID agreed to have a look at the house and see if there was any sign of our burglar's car. They came back to us the very next day. There had been no sign of our car, but a white van was found parked outside the house, which again had been purchased by 'Mr Smith' and was wanted by Derbyshire Police after it was seen leaving the scene of a burglary at a house up in the moors where a lot of jewellery, along with two expensive fur coats, had been taken.

Middleton CID needed no prompting and had raided Waylan's house, arresting him and recovering, from beneath the floorboards, huge quantities of valuable jewellery and other property. John and I joined up with Middleton CID the next day and had soon identified some of Waylan's floorboard cache as being from our Butterton burglary, along with a few other items that were from other burglaries on our patch. We also found a rent card for a lock-up garage that Waylan owned, again in the name of Mr Smith. A search of the garage, which was just around the corner from Waylan's house, revealed the yellow candlewick bedspread from our burglary. This was all beginning to look very interesting.

Waylan was doing his best to keep his wife Michelle out of it, whilst admitting to nothing himself. Michelle actually worked as a cashier in Barclays Bank in Manchester and appeared, to the untrained eye, to be perfectly innocent. A jewellery valuation certificate was also found under the floorboards. This had been stolen, along with the jewels it described, from a house in Blackpool and, whilst none of the actual jewels were still to be found, it was also discovered that chequebooks had also been taken during this burglary. Enquiries with the owners in Blackpool revealed that all the stolen cheques had been used to purchase items from stores in Leeds on one particular day a week after the burglary. We now had a great list of household goods to look for as well as untold amounts of jewellery, and the 'fur coat' list was also on the increase.

A further search of Waylan's house resulted in the recovery of a great deal of this property, including curtains, ornaments, rugs, lights and very expensive clothing. It appeared that they had beautifully fitted out their entire house with the proceeds of various burglaries and items purchased with stolen cheques. Even a stolen camera was found to contain photographs of a gloating Waylan standing next to a pile of obviously recently stolen booty. For some reason he was pictured with his willy hanging out.

The net was closing in on Michelle too, as she was clearly in up to her neck, and it was just a matter of time before the evidence came to the surface.

Shaun had now been connected to dozens of high-value burglaries, and the property recovered from beneath the floorboards was nothing compared with what was still missing. We then found that Michelle had a safe-deposit box kept at the branch of Barclays Bank where she worked - we wanted a look in there.

Together with John I visited a magistrate and applied for a search warrant on Barclays Bank in Manchester. You can imagine the disbelief on the magistrate's face. However, he signed, and away we went. The bank manager's jaw dropped as we stood in his office and related the story to him, with a pensive-looking Michelle standing in the corridor outside the office and clearly visible through the office window as she occasionally looked up at the now well known and hated 'two Johns'.

The box was duly brought into the manager's office and, with several other senior members of staff present, the security ties were removed and the lid opened. An air of disappointment went around the room as the contents were shaken out onto the manager's table. Not a single item of jewellery, just a small handful of scraps of paper with writing on. After a closer inspection, however, it was seen that these were lists of cash adding up to many thousands of pounds.

"These look like account numbers," said one learned member of staff, pointing to the number written above some of the lists. "Probably a building society, the Leeds at a guess," he went on.

Michelle spent her first night suspended from her job in the cells back at Stone Police Station.

Enquiries the next day revealed that three building society accounts had been set up, again by Mr Smith. We were even provided with CCTV photos of Mr Smith at the counters of the building society, opening the accounts. Mr Smith was, of course, none other than Shaun Waylan. It began to look increasingly likely that Michelle had actually been on some of the jobs with her husband, including the Butterton job, but proof in this direction was lacking.

Yet another bloody identification parade! We hoped that this one would prove that Shaun and Michelle were the man and woman described by a Scottish lady who owned an expensive ladies' outfitters in Leeds. The Scottish lady had been duped by the couple, who had purchased several hundred pounds worth of top-notch ladies' clothing from her store using cheques from the stolen chequebook.

We had already recovered the clothing from Michelle's drawers and wardrobe, and as the irate Scottish lady had said during statement taking, 'I'd bloody well know those two thieving gits anytime, even in a hundred years I'd spot them,' we thought we'd got a chance.

This time the ID parade was well organised. Everything was done perfectly, and we now just had to hope that our Scottish friend was as good as her temper. As she walked into the room at Newcastle-under-Lyme Police Station and took just one glance at the line-up of similarly dressed, petite and attractive young women, her eyes widened with anger as she spied Michelle.

"That's the little bastard," she shouted as she strode straight over to Michelle. "*Number bloody seven,*" she shouted in her broadest Scottish accent, pointing to the number at Michelle's feet. "Thought you'd got away with that one then, you little cow," she shouted over her shoulder as she was directed out.

The Scottish lady managed a repeat performance on the next parade for Shaun, with even more expletives, and afterwards, as I took a statement from her about the two parades, she confessed to having enjoyed every minute.

The case was strengthened even more with the discovery of yet another car bought by 'Mr Smith' and connected to Waylan, which had been issued with a parking ticket in Leeds on the day of all the cheque cashing. I had never had a case where so many clues had been left and where everything fitted so well into place, so it was a blow when I was telephoned at home on a rare day off to be told that Waylan had escaped from Newcastle Police Station whilst on one of his weekly court appearance-remand sessions. He had been slippery throughout; someone had dropped his guard and he'd gone.

Things carried on; there were still a lot of other enquiries that had to be completed, not to mention all the other everyday stuff that was always coming in.

The words of my old chief constable, Arthur Rees, were proved correct when I appeared on the telly. *Granada Reports* did a feature for us on the huge amount of recovered jewellery, and I was interviewed, showing and describing the jewels in the hope that we might prove where they had come from and so detect a few more cases. My kids were loaning out the video of 'Dad on telly' to their schoolfriends, and my mum and dad even after all those years were waiting for their turn to show their friends in the pub. I cringed as I waited to see the recording for the first time, wondering if I had subconsciously slipped in a few robotic police style phrases such as 'associating' or 'frequenting', but it wasn't too bad.

One morning, months later, as I trawled through the great pile of teleprinter messages that had come in over the weekend looking at the various crimes that had happened in other parts of the country, I saw it - *'fur coats'*.

I was looking at a teleprinter message about a burglary at the isolated home of a racehorse trainer in Exeter. It had Waylan's MO all over it and, as well as jewellery, two valuable fur coats had been taken. Waylan was the only burglar I had ever known who had an eye for fur coats and he clearly knew how to get the right money for them, as we had never recovered any of them.

I was on the phone to Exeter CID within minutes, telling the interested DC the story and giving him the issue number of the *Police Gazette* that featured the photo of Waylan. Two days later the same DC rang me back with the news that, following a high-speed car chase after a burglar had been interrupted at the home of a wealthy landowner, a man had been arrested. He had driven through fences and across parkland in his efforts to escape and was refusing to say who he was, but despite a few lumps and bumps he fitted the photo of Waylan. After a few more miles for John and me, with a trip down to Exeter and a few more celebratory pints, Waylan arrived back in Staffordshire. He received a lengthy sentence, as did Michelle for her part in these crimes.

It was interesting how the silly mistake by Waylan's wife of collecting the car from the police pound had given the breakthrough to all this. It was, therefore, equally interesting how the strangest of things could end up solving another case, even such an innocuous item as a camping tent.

On hearing of the report that a branch office of a building society, out in the village of Ashley on the road to Market Drayton, had been burgled over the weekend, I journeyed out to the crime with DC Phil Simpson. En route we discussed how ridiculous it was that such a place was covered by the CID in Stone, as it was so many miles away. We arrived at the small, isolated branch office to discover that intruders had broken in and completely removed a very heavy safe containing a few hundred pounds. The thieves had left behind several two-feet long, hollow metal tubes and from the marks on the floor these had been used to roll the safe along.

Within an hour we had received a second report that a car had been abandoned in a field some half a mile away and, upon arriving at the scene, found that the car, a small tatty saloon, had been driven off the road and right down a steep embankment. It had been raining almost constantly for over a week and the bank side was a slippery, muddy churned mess.

The doors to the car hung open, papers were strewn everywhere and there, near the back of the car, partially embedded in the mud, was the safe. The door had been chiselled off from its hinges and could be seen lying nearby in the mud; bankbooks and documents lay all around fluttering, but fixed to the ground in their sodden state.

Inside the car were more of the same metal tubes that we had found at the building society office. There were deep ruts in the mud where the thieves had been trying to drive the car back up the embankment, but they clearly never stood any chance, and must have driven down there in the first place so that no one could hear the noise they made as they chiselled away for possibly hours.

Enquiries into the car came back with the usual blank, as it had been purchased in a false name, but then it was discovered that a 'police interest marker' had been put against the car's computer record showing that it had been seen in the possession of two young, very active, burgling brothers from Preston. Yet again armed with a search warrant and aided by the enthusiasm of some members of Preston CID, who were more than keen to see these two, well known, arrogant thieving louts put behind bars, several members of the Stone CID and I made an early morning visit to their flat.

The reception was the usual unpleasant, rowdy shouting-match with swearing and threats, most of which turned to silence at the sight of a strangely jubilant Detective Sergeant Pye rejoicing at finding nothing more interesting than a tent with no poles. Other evidence supported the case, including a perfect imprint of one of the brother's footwear patterns being found in mud inside the building society office and also on a map inside the car.

At the Crown court case, months later, the judge watched with interest and some enjoyment as the executive from the tent manufacturers, together with the help of Phil Simpson, swiftly erected the tent at the front of the court. This added to the mounting evidence that the poles were of their manufacture and designed only for this model of tent.

The judge, of course, was not aware that only days prior to the case I nearly had my evidence jeopardised by none other than a fellow colleague. The uniformed inspector at the station had undertaken a spring clean of the property store and without much thought had deposited 'exhibit A' (one metal safe door) at the local scrapyard. Finding out just in time, I managed to retrieve the door. The brothers went to prison, and as it was too far to join up for a celebration with Preston CID, both offices separately enjoyed a few beers.

In November 1986, yet another friend and colleague would be killed on duty; twenty-six-year-old PC John Taylor died when he fell through a window of a block of high-rise flats in Honeywall, Stoke, whilst struggling to arrest a burglar. The burglar survived. A commemorative stone for John now stands in Kingsway near Stoke Town Hall.

* * * *

It was in June 1987 that, as a firearms officer, I was told that I would have to perform 'armed protection' duty for two days for members of the Royal Family, who were to be taking part in a televised charity show, along with dozens of other celebrities. The show was to follow the format of the television show *It's a Knockout*, hosted by British television presenter Stuart Hall, and was conceived and organised by Prince Edward.

The show featured Prince Edward, Princess Anne and the Duke and Duchess of York as team captains, and a great list of TV and film stars as team members. Along with Stuart Hall, the *Royal It's a Knockout*, as it became known, was hosted also by comedian, Les Dawson, and comedy actress, Sue Pollard.

I was ferried up to Alton Towers on the first day of my 'armed duties', along with the other armed officers and a large contingent of other CID. It was 6.30 a.m., the weather was simply appalling. It was just a constant cloudburst as we ran for cover from the police bus into a small flapping marquee, which had been pitched on the side of a slight incline (why were all the tents I have ever been in always on a slope?). Our seemingly second-hand or possibly 'borrowed' tent looked pretty shabby against the fire service's beautiful inflatable and heated accommodation, which was positioned some distance away on a level piece of ground. Even the short run into the tent had soaked us. There were dozens of plain clothes officers, but only about eight of us were to be armed. There would also be a large number of uniformed officers.

The firearms officers were all handed shoulder holsters that we had to fit to our own comfort beneath our jackets. We then had to sign for our Smith and Wesson .38 revolvers. The smaller version we were using for this duty carried five bullets, and we also had to sign for the bullets and some spare ammunition.

Considering this was June, it was not only very wet, it was also cold. We were told that we all had to be inside the big top-style circus tent for our 8 a.m. briefing. The big top was a good quarter of a mile from where we were and, as a few of us started to ask the pertinent question of how we were to get there in view of the now unrelenting torrential downpour, it dawned on us that the bosses had made no provision for this. The police bus had gone and we were expected to walk. We stuck it out as long as we could, but eventually some senior officer ordered us all to make our way.

I was already slightly damp from my first run from the bus. I was wearing my best suit with my camel Crombie overcoat. None of us had an umbrella and I guess it would have been rather in the way if we had to draw our guns and take aim with an umbrella in the other hand. With every step each and every one of us took on another half gallon of rainwater. The gun strapped to my left breast was now becoming very heavy and I was feeling ever more uncomfortable.

Eventually we all slopped into the big top and took up our seats for the briefing as small rivulets of water streamed away from our feet. I was so wet now that I feared that should I have to shoot anyone, my rusting gun would not have gone off.

During the briefing all the armed officers had to stand up, so that everyone knew who they were just in case anyone should require someone to be shot.

After the briefing had finished I went and found a new-looking gents toilet and proceeded to try to dry myself out at least a little. Taking off my socks and shoes, I used my initiative by fitting the socks over the nozzle of the hand drier causing the sock to billow out as it dried. The shoes took longer and were so wet that they started to curl up at the toes like a clown's shoes – perhaps I should go back to the big top.

When I had done my best at drying out, I took up my place in one of the tents as various celebrities, including John Travolta, Christopher Reeve, Michael Palin, John Cleese and Rowan Atkinson, wandered in and out taking little notice of the dripping detective. I was completely unconcerned as a figure strolled past me with a casual, but precise, 'Morning', which was clearly directed at me.

Being more concerned with the wetness of my trousers and underpants, I instinctively replied, 'Ha do, mate', looking up to discover I had just 'Ha do mated' Prince Edward himself. The prince looked back at me with a puzzled expression, possibly thinking that I was a foreigner or the local lunatic, and then carried on about his business.

The first day was really a rehearsal, although some filming was going on; I was never so pleased to get home and into a hot bath at the end of a very long, wet and uncomfortable day. We were allowed to take our empty holsters home with us so that we could save time and fit them as we got dressed the following day. The kids were full of it that evening, with the two boys each taking turns at trying on the holster, whilst my daughter Julie wanted to know which film stars I'd seen.

Early the next morning I was dried out and spruced up again complete with shoulder holster, suit number two (good job it was only two days!) and Crombie coat dried out from all night on the radiator.

As I joined the other firearms officers in the still flapping, but not so wet, police tent, I was handed my revolver with its chamber open and empty. I signed for both the gun and the ammo as I had done the day before.

For safety, we had been taught to 'go down on one knee' whilst loading, making sure the safety catch was on, and then holstering the gun. I went through this procedure meticulously then carefully pushed the barrel of the gun down into the holster for a nice snug fit. The gun didn't want to go down into the holster, something was stopping it; I carefully removed the gun and, feeling down inside my holster, grabbed hold of the unknown object and carefully withdrew it. It was a pink plastic toy gun, one that I had seen only the night before at home. Carefully and swiftly before anyone had chance to see, I thrust the toy into my Crombie pocket with a snigger to myself, imagining what could have happened had I been called upon to draw my weapon 'in anger'. The thought crossed my mind of a manic assassin screaming towards one of the Royal Family and me with my chance of becoming a national hero, shouting, 'Freeze arsehole!', standing legs apart, both hands firmly clasping a pink plastic water pistol.

It was another wet day. Nothing much happened apart from one or two princes and princesses, together with dozens of film stars and TV personalities rolling around in the mud, dressed up as giant vegetables - no one got shot.

* * * *

During my time at Stone we'd had plenty to keep us all busy; some interesting and unusual jobs, some terrible and sickening cases. There were many bizarre deaths and each one had to be investigated to find out what the cause had been and if there had been any criminal involvement.

There were many suicides; it was that kind of 'patch', for some reason! Our area was vast and covered a great deal of farming land. There were, of course, a lot of shotguns and, therefore, many of the suicides were particularly unpleasant, many involving heads being blown off.

As Stone also covered a huge part of Cannock Chase, which was many square miles of thickly wooded and dense forest, bodies could lie undiscovered for months or even years. All manner of strange stories and reports would filter back about people involved in 'satanic rituals' on the Chase, and other incidents where some weirdo had pulled a gun on a courting couple in a car.

Once I had to deal with the discovery of a man's body in a car on one of the Chase car parks. There was the usual Hoover-type pipe in through the window connected to the exhaust pipe, and the man lay dead in the driving seat. Simple... another suicide... No, the engine had been switched off and the ignition keys were in the driver's door compartment. Both the driver's seat and the passenger seat were halfway in the reclined position and I noticed that the rear passenger side window was down just enough for the pipe to feed in, but the glass window had been forcibly pulled out of its guide in the door, leaving it loose enough to put an arm through from the outside.

It turned out that the man had died from poisoning by the exhaust fumes, but he had a secret of which none of his close family or workmates knew. Despite being a family man living with his wife and children in a neat semi just outside Lichfield, he had been involved in a gay relationship with a young man from Birmingham for some time. This man was traced and found to be a rent boy, and despite this fairly long-running relationship with the man, he didn't seem to care in the slightest that his lover was now dead. There was never a suspicion that the rent boy had killed the man. The strong possibility of a suicide pact, which is a criminal offence, did enter the inquiry. Why was the passenger seat down, who had turned off the engine and who had put the keys in the door compartment?

It was ascertained that the pipe would fit comfortably over the passenger seat only when it was reclined, and the rent boy had a sound alibi - he was with another man.

The car was covered in a film of dust, as the weather had been hot and dry for weeks. The only disturbance to this layer of dust was on the driver's door, the front of the bonnet, where someone, in a panic, may have tried to lift the bonnet to stop the engine, and around the damaged window, where someone had undoubtedly used considerable force to pull the glass out then opened the door allowing them to get in and turn off the engine.

The dead man clearly intended to kill himself, as he had also consumed a large quantity of paracetamol and a bottle of sherry. The theory was that a courting couple, probably having an illicit affair, had stumbled across the scene and did what they could, but it was too late. Despite press appeals stating that identity would be kept secret, no one came forward, but to this day someone knows what really happened.

On another occasion I was called to a report of a burnt out car on a car park frequented by courting couples in the large wooded area of Hanchurch Woods, which was much closer to Newcastle, but again covered by Stone. The report said that there was a body in the car. I arrived at the scene at about 6 p.m. on a balmy summer's evening. The fire brigade were just leaving and two uniform cars were still there, together with the police photographer and the scenes of crime man.

In the corner of the car park I could see the still-smoking remains of what looked like a family saloon. The nearby trees were badly scorched, and the stone and earth around the car formed a lighter colour due to the intense heat. The heat had lifted every scrap of paint from the contorted shell of the car, all the glass had melted and the tyres and number plates were completely burnt away. The entire inside of the car was gutted, leaving only the metal framework of the seats and the cores of the wiring.

On the wire frame remains of the rear seat was a large, black smouldering mass; perched precariously on top of the mass was the unmistakable shape of a human skull, blackened and wafer-thin due to the heat. Two wisps of smoke trailed upwards from the eye sockets, and blackened stumps of bone protruded from the black mass where arms and legs had previously been.

On the ground a few yards away, far enough to still be relatively intact, lay two empty cans of Tennent's extra strong lager. Inside the car in the back with the body lay the fragmentary remains of another two beer cans and what was left of two metal oil-type cans. The distinctive smell of petrol was still apparent, even despite the intensity of the fire.

With the help of the police computer it didn't take too long to establish from the barely legible chassis number that the car had been a Ford Sierra, owned by a Longton-based firm. The case had initially looked very suspicious with the body being discovered in the back seat. However, it soon emerged that the corpse was that of a rep of the firm, who had been disillusioned with his job and was being treated for depression.

The problem of positive identification could only be overcome by using dental records, and it wasn't until the following day that I managed to track down a dentist who had treated the man several years before. The dentist turned out to be a rather irritating arrogant man who initially declined to assist until being warned that his actions 'may be considered to be obstructing Her Majesty's Coroner'. His attitude changed somewhat as I led him through into the mortuary examination room where the blackened remains lay in pieces on a white porcelain slab. After regaining his composure he was in no doubt from the dental chart he had with him that the remains were those of whom we thought them to be.

There were many more similar tragic episodes, one where a jealous boyfriend lay in wait for his vivacious young girlfriend in the village of Madeley and then viciously attacked her with an axe. She survived after months of surgery and intensive care, but was destined thereafter to a life of disability and disfigurement; he served a few years in prison - so unfair.

Another was the discovery of the putrefied body of a newborn child in the bedroom of a schoolgirl in the village of Eccleshall. The thirteen-year-old girl had become pregnant by her fifteen-year-old boyfriend, but had not realised until the baby was born one evening whilst she did her homework. She insisted that the child had been born dead, and the condition of the body prevented any other opinion being proved. She had tried to carry on with her life for six months before the body was discovered in a plastic bag in her bedroom by her horrified mother.

With the main West Coast railway line running through our patch, we had several horrific death scenes to attend. I recall the tragic sight of the body of a thirteen-year-old boy lying at the side of the track. The train had arrived at the station with its door hanging open, and the father had alerted the authorities when his son did not appear at the station as he waited for him. The boy had been seen fooling about previously by opening the door and hanging out of the window. The father's grief was so disturbing.

On another occasion I had to visit a terrible scene where a middle-aged man, who had been diagnosed with terminal cancer, had committed suicide by throwing himself in front of a train as it passed through the hamlet of Stableford, a few miles out of Stone. The man had parked his car on the nearby roadside and climbed down onto a concrete parapet at the side of the track. He had left his jacket, trilby hat and cigarettes, together with a suicide note, on the parapet and then launched himself from it just as the express train came past. He was smashed into a thousand pieces, the largest piece I found being half of his head.

What was so disturbing about this was that as I walked along the track dictating the scene into my portable Dictaphone, I heard a familiar voice shout to me from the nearby bridge.

"Hey up, Reg!"

It was Glyn Machin, a detective I had served with at Hanley and who lived close to this vile scene.

"Hiya, Reg," I replied.

"Looks like you've got a bit of a job on," shouted Glynn from the bridge, all too aware of such atrocities from his own experience.

There then continued a short exchange of pleasantries between old friends who hadn't seen each other in a while, including, 'You going away this year?' and such like.

I continued my dictation.

"Left hand lying on railway sleeper, portion of intestines hanging from bushes."

Had fifteen years of police work changed me so much from that silly nervous boy who had sat waiting for his cadet's entrance exam?

Despite this near constant association with tragedy, there was always some fooling around, mickey-taking or practical jokes being played, and it may in fact be this that helped to keep one's sanity intact.

I had visited the scene of a nasty burglary out in the village of Woodseaves near Stafford. It was the second time in a month that the frail eighty-five-year-old lady had fallen victim to thieves. The raiders had beaten down her back door and pushed her out of the way as they stole one hundred pounds – her pension money for two weeks. During the raid one of the men had worn a very tatty pair of hand knitted socks on his hands to prevent fingerprints being left and had then left the socks behind in the garden.

The local *Evening Sentinel* newspaper had been concerned about the incident, and published an article on it in which they included a photo of me wearing the socks on my hands.

It wasn't long before photocopies of the sock-clad DS were published on every police noticeboard between Newcastle and Stafford with suggested titles, including 'Reg examines the wife's handiwork' and 'No, Reg, on your feet'.

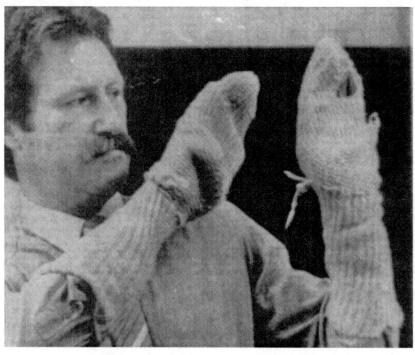

'Sock Man' (photograph courtesy Sentinel News & Media)

We had several different detective inspectors in charge of Stone CID during my time there. They were all nice guys who you could get on with and have a beer and a laugh with at the end of the day. One, however, would often let his enthusiasm get the better of him before he got his brain into gear.

We had received a report of a woman being raped whilst taking her dog for a walk in Hanchurch Woods. Everyone in the office was working on it and we weren't getting very far with enquiries when Harry, the DI, suggested we should have the case put on *Police 5*.

Police 5 was a five-minute television programme presented by Shaw Taylor, giving the details of serious and interesting cases, and requesting witnesses to come forward. The programme was in a way a forerunner to the later *Crimewatch* programme. Shaw would finish off each programme with his catchphrase of 'Keep 'em peeled' as he pointed a finger towards his eyes.

The programme had been successful in helping to detect many crimes and Shaw had been to Stone a few times previously on other cases, and would usually buy us a beer after the filming.

Shaw and his team arrived in our big, old courthouse CID office in the morning and we explained the case to him as he made notes and decided the best way to get the message over. They did some filming and interviews, and we were just about out of ideas when Harry rose from his chair with a beaming 'eureka-look' on his face.

"I'll tell you what we could do," he exclaimed as everyone looked on with straight faces, knowing from previous experience that this type of reaction usually led to the rest of us being involved in some totally unnecessary wild goose chase. "We could," he said, "have the police helicopter; they could take one of the film crew up and it would give the public a proper look at the area we're talking about."

Whilst it might have held the public interest a little bit and it would have been interesting for us, we all knew only too well that there weren't that many people on our patch who had the luxury of a helicopter, so the panoramic viewpoint wouldn't have made a lot of difference to them.

Harry's enthusiasm, however, seemed to win Shaw over and, still beaming at his good idea, Harry grabbed the nearest phone and rang the Air Support Group. The helicopter was shared between other nearby forces and in no time Harry was through to a sergeant in their control room. We all sat without saying a word as he explained the situation and what we required.

"Oh, so our force would have to pay then because it's not a normal job... Yes, I see... So how much would it be? "Right... Is that all? Two seventy-five an hour... Oh, plus VAT. Well, that's nothing, I'll pay that myself," said the beaming Harry.

We all looked at each other, each with worried and astonished looks on our faces. He really and honestly did believe that he was going to get the services of a three-quarters of a million pound helicopter for two pounds and seventy-five pence per hour plus VAT.

Harry made a few more arrangements before replacing the telephone handset and looking up with a huge round beaming face.

"*Sorted,*" he said to the bemused and disbelieving group that surrounded him.

"You do realise, do you, Boss," said Nult, with his usual deadpan expression "that he was telling you it's going to cost the force *two hundred and seventy-five pounds* an hour plus VAT?"

The colour drained from Harry's face as the reality dawned.

* * * *

I'd done yet more courses whilst I was at Stone. There had been a big change in the law over how the police had to deal with prisoners, legal rights and all that sort of thing, so the new Police and Criminal Evidence Act, which demanded all these big changes, needed a course all of its own, albeit only a 'one-weeker'.

I'd also been on a month's course at headquarters to learn all about the new police computer system that had been introduced following some of the severe problems that had happened on big murder inquiries such as the Yorkshire Ripper and the Black Panther. The system was a national one and was called HOLMES, which stood for Home Office Large Major Enquiry System. It was all very new to me, as the nearest I'd ever been to a computer before this was 'The Box', and I'd never really used that. The course was intensive and complex, and at the end of the course I'd done okay.

In September 1989, I was called upon to help Newcastle CID with a murder investigation. All major enquiries for the north of the county were operated from the old magistrates' court building in Water Street, Newcastle. The single men's bedrooms that used to be on the first floor had now all been given over for the use of major investigations, and all contained desks, computers and filing trays. The Newcastle Police Club, with its bar and function room, was still in use downstairs, but the court had been operating from a new building in the town centre for some time.

I'd really had enough of deaths and murders over the past few years, and had already been over at Newcastle helping out on a different murder where a young Asian man had been beaten to death and his body dumped in a stream just half a mile from the town centre. The only good thing about this latest inquiry would be that I would be back working with my old friend Whitey again. Geoff White had done really well since the days of Hanley CID. We'd kept in touch over the years and I wasn't surprised, when I heard he had been appointed as detective inspector in charge of Newcastle CID.

I'd started to have problems with my back as a result of an old injury and when I arrived at Newcastle on my first morning I was given the job of 'action man'. I would really have preferred to go out and do some proper enquiries, but I guess I wasn't up to it as I was looking towards a big operation on my back - I was given an office on the first floor of Water Street.

"Here you are, Reg," said Whitey, "beautifully furnished."

The old, pale blue four-panelled door swung open to reveal the small stark-looking room with high ceiling, which would be my workplace.

"But, Reg," I said to Whitey, "this was Des's bedroom."

"You're joking," he said, and burst out into laughter as he wandered away up the corridor.

The room had changed since the days when I would pick up a bleary-eyed Des when we were on the drug squad together and when we worked on the Carl Bridgewater murder. It had been split in half to make two rooms, and a large old-fashioned cupboard was in place behind the chair that I would sit upon for the next few months.

This murder was indeed different yet again, in that the victim was a housewife living in the area known as May Bank, only about half a mile outside Newcastle. The lady had not been seen for some time. People had become suspicious, particularly so as the husband had been seen digging the back garden and then laying a new lawn.

One thing had led to another and, consequently, the police had moved in to assist the occupant with his gardening. The lady's body was discovered buried under the new lawn, and eventually the husband admitted to being responsible for the death, but claimed severe provocation.

Whilst Whitey was in direct charge of the investigation, other more senior detectives all had a hand in it and would frequently show their faces to supervise and offer their suggestions. Whitey was still blessed with his bizarre sense of humour and would frequently play crazy tricks on me, whilst being careful not to let any of the junior or senior officers into the fact that he was still 'a bit of a nutter'.

Often whilst I was working at my desk, which faced the door, I would suddenly become aware that the door was ever so slightly, slowly creaking open, but there was no one to be seen, no hand on the door. I would have to ease myself up in the chair and look down to floor level where I would see a prone Whitey lying flat on the corridor floor with just his head poking around the gap in the open door and looking up at me like a mad person.

Such idiocy helped us both get through the long days until it was time for a beer or two, usually at the Waggon and

Horses in town, sometimes at the police club downstairs if we were running really late, and occasionally in the Bull's Head in town, which was now run by Des, who had left the police to become a licensee. Des was interested to hear that I now had his old bedroom.

Quite often we would get a visit from 'God's deputy', Detective Chief Superintendent Malcolm Bevington himself. Bev was a suave, good-looking man who had been promoted early in his service. Bev knew his job, he liked a laugh, but you always had to remember, he was 'the boss'.

I arrived at my office as usual one morning at about 8 a.m. and rummaged through my in tray. We had pretty well wound everything up now, and my part of dishing out actions and checking other bits and pieces was all but done. I settled my aching back down into the chair and started to sort out any new jobs that might need attention before the file could be completed. I looked up from my desk as the office door swung open to see 'Bev', his usual dapper resplendent self, in a grey pinstriped suit.

"Morning, Mr Pye," he said, looking down at me.

"Morning, Sir," I replied, as I eased up out of my chair.

"Anything new in, or are we all systems go?" he asked.

"I think everything's on track now, Boss. We're still waiting for something to come through about the different grass seed that was used on the lawn, but everything else looks pretty *sown up*, if you'll excuse the pun."

"Oh, spare me the humour, Mr Pye," Bev said, half-frowning, half-grinning. "Have you seen Mr White yet?"

"No, not yet, Boss, but his coat's hanging up, so he's about somewhere," I replied, hoping that Whitey really was in.

"Right, I'll go and find him," said Bev as he turned and walked off down the corridor.

I settled back down into my seat as the clicking of Bev's heels disappeared away down the corridor towards the main office. I rubbed my chin as I pondered over the reply written on a returned 'action' and then suddenly and instinctively jolted upwards and forwards halfway across my desk as I heard a shuffling sound from the large cupboard behind me. I sprawled across the desk, knocking a wire tray of papers to the floor as I looked around in horror, wondering what the hell was in my cupboard. Whitey's head peered out, his eyes wide and the furrowed brow twice as furrowed as usual.

"What the bloody hell?" I exclaimed.

"Shh!" hissed Whitey. "Has he gone? My whole job flashed before me. I've been hiding in there waiting to jump out on you, I've been there ten minutes. I was just on the verge of bursting out when I heard him come in, I've had to sit there waiting and hoping you didn't want to get anything out of this bloody cupboard whilst he was here, I nearly died of fright."

We had an extra few beers that evening to celebrate the winding up of the inquiry, and we had more than a few laughs over the cupboard incident.

All that sitting in my computer chair at Water Street pretty well finished my back off. I could hardly walk, so it was off to hospital for an operation to remove part of the offending disc. I was off work for a while, but the operation had been a success and I hadn't been back at

Stone that long before I got the call to go and see the Chief Constable, Charles Kelly.

I had put in for promotion to inspector and been on the selection boards. I'd done a stint of 'acting uniformed inspector' and 'acting detective inspector', so I was pretty certain why I was being called to see the chief and I knew that it would almost certainly be as uniformed inspector rather than detective. It was just 'where was he going to send me?' that was on my mind more than anything.

Visits to the chief's office were pretty rare – for me, just the 'vampire visit' to see Mr Rees back in 1973 and my promotion to sergeant in 1982. The office hadn't changed much since my last visit.

"I'm promoting you to uniformed inspector and sending you to…" he said.

The wait seemed interminable. *Biddulph* flashed through my mind, or even worse, was there anywhere worse?

"*Hanley*" came the chief's decision, eventually.

Great, I thought, back home at last, even though it is uniform.

It was certainly time to move on; I'd been at Stone for six years now, including all those courses and times away helping out on murders and bits of 'acting inspector' here and there. I'd loved Stone, and, despite all the deaths there had been some amazingly interesting enquiries and good results.

FIFTEEN

It was time for another trip over to the uniform stores at headquarters. The ageless Mr Ryan was still there; he measured me up for my new inspector's uniform - white shirts! All the old blue ones I had left over from my sergeant's uniform could now be used for gardening and mending the car. I was to have a smart, inspector's, flat peaked cap with its black material strip across the beck, a pair of brown leather gloves, not black ones, and a brown envelope full of chromium plated 'star pips' to go on my shoulder epaulettes, so some things hadn't changed; I'd still got to bodge holes to fix them on.

I'd got a full envelope of 'pips' and would have to fix two to each shoulder. As I'd got more than enough, I wondered if anyone might notice if I put three on each shoulder, giving me the rank of 'Chief Inspector'. I decided it probably wasn't worth the risk and made do with being an inspector.

I started with my shift of two sergeants and fifteen constables, including four WPCs, at Hanley on an early 6 a.m. shift. It was a strange, unnerving feeling as I walked down the familiar corridor on the ground floor from the inspector's office towards the parade room.

How strange this was. Could it be almost twenty-one years had passed by, when I was the one standing to attention and saying, 'Yes, Sir, no, Sir!' every time an inspector appeared?

I was aware I was being scanned by a multitude of eyes, mostly young men and women of a similar age to me when I was at Stoke in the early seventies. No doubt they were all thinking similar thoughts. What is this boss going to be like? Is he going to make our lives hell? Is he just going to be after making a name for himself?

It wasn't until they'd all left the room that I realised I'd pretty well reiterated the words that were said to me by Chief Inspector Phillips, as a cadet back in 1967, and then again as a nineteen-year-old constable by Inspector 'Wild Bill' Holdcroft all those years ago. I then set off on another journey in my career that was to last two years.

The members of the shift were a really mixed bunch, all real individuals, some had had a 'previous life' in the services or in a trade. One fairly new arrival on the shift was Simon, who had been in the navy. He was an immensely likeable young man with a sense of humour that reminded me of young PC Pye, but he was blighted by bad luck. Every job in which he was involved seemed to go wrong and turned into an 'ever expanding monster'. He had got himself tied up in knots with a theft report, where someone had stolen hundreds of old Victorian blue bricks by uprooting them from the pavement in a street just off the town centre. The blue brick inquiry seemed to be destined to follow him for the rest of his life and, despite his humour and mischief, he was clearly burdened with the thought that he would be in trouble if he didn't finalise the matter somehow or other.

I had a meeting with the superintendent one morning and he had expressed his concern saying:

"What about young Simon on your shift? Seems a nice lad, but can't seem to shift his paperwork."

"Yes, Boss," I replied, finding it difficult to get out of my CID vernacular. "He seems to have the Midas touch in reverse; everything he touches turns to shit."

"That sums it up nicely," replied the superintendent, nearly choking on his tea.

After Simon's blue bricks had been resolved, he became a new man, although the reverse Midas touch was not completely gone.

* * * *

Stoke-on-Trent is a huge urban sprawl being made up of the six original towns of Burslem, Tunstall, Fenton, Longton, Hanley and Stoke.

All these busy town centres are completely joined up by residential and industrialised areas, and to the uninitiated the whole area becomes indistinguishable as separate places; it is one concrete jungle with no green bits in between. The nearby town of Newcastle is also joined seamlessly into this mass, making the entire area appear as one gigantic city.

Hanley for many years has been regarded as the city centre and is the busiest of these towns by far; it has always been regarded as *the* shopping centre for the area and boasts a lot of the prestige stores.

Shoplifting in Hanley has, in consequence, forever been a major headache. Of course, like all other busy police areas, we were unfortunate enough to 'possess' our very own homegrown professional shoplifters, who would be 'at it' every day. Often they would find it difficult to make a living on their own turf and would have a day out somewhere farther afield where they would not be recognised immediately by any police officer or store detective with half-decent eyesight.

Reg Lownes was Stoke-on-Trent's biggest problem in this particular field and was very deserving of possessing more than just one small Christian name (albeit a very good one!). Barely a day would go by without Reg being spotted 'at it' and followed. Sometimes he would be arrested, occasionally with sufficient evidence to charge him, and sometimes he would have to be released without charge due to his guile. He was like a squirrel and would hide stolen property in the town somewhere as soon as he had pinched it, coming back later to collect.

Confusion would often reign when new recruits, who were trying to come to terms with their newly acquired police vernacular, were on duty, and the shout went over the radio, 'Reg is on the town'. This could have meant anyone!

Shoplifters came from all different walks of life from high court judges to down and out vagrants, from professional shoplifters like Reg to the elderly and absent-minded, who would hopefully always be treated compassionately, and accordingly, police officers themselves have joined the list, often with a tale of stress or some domestic upheaval. Single mothers on the breadline formed a category, but a large number were often drug addicts stealing goods to sell on and feed their habit.

As shift inspector I would have to spend quite a part of my day down in the custody suite, which adjoined the cell block. It was part of my duty to supervise what was going on with prisoners, check the paperwork was okay and that the prisoners were being treated correctly (whether they deserved it or not).

I would often by chance be present when a prisoner was brought in by an arresting officer to be 'booked in'.

As Hanley had such a shoplifting problem it had one entire shift of officers (known as shift five) whose job it was, theoretically, to deal just with shoplifters.

One afternoon a fairly elderly lady was bought in whilst I was down in the custody suite, to be booked in for shoplifting. The poor soul was completely bemused by the situation and obviously needed looking after rather than putting before a court. She had stolen a packet of Jaffa Cakes from Woolworths, which had a value of just a few pence.

Sadly, before any kind of help could be offered to her, the legal niceties had to be complied with, which entailed searching her, listing, to the very last penny, her money and any other valuables, checking her identity and all the same rigmarole that would have gone along with the arrest due to a serious bank robber.

The lady, who was very dishevelled and confused, was strangely adamant that she would not allow us to search her tatty and decaying-looking string shopping bag. However, at the custody sergeant's insistence, the contents were eventually removed and placed on the counter for listing. A silence overtook the custody suite as the young PC, who had had to arrest the lady, removed fifteen brown envelopes from the bag with a look of complete disbelief on his face as he opened each one to reveal its contents of one thousand pounds. In total the lady had £15,350 in her shopping bag.

A sad story lay behind the lady's situation and it transpired that the money was the proceeds of the sale of her house. She had kept the money with her rather than trust it to the safe keeping of a bank. She was released into care without charge, but not until a bank account had been opened and the money deposited there for her. The usual 'black police humour' followed the arrest, with someone trying to work out how many packets of Jaffa Cakes you could purchase for £15,350.

Another unusual shoplifter was a young black feller who was a heroin addict. I recall he lived in Wolverhampton and was out and about trying to steal something worthwhile to get money for his heroin. He was only about nineteen, and had made his way over to Hanley and gone into one of the exclusive jewellery shops on the town. He had somehow managed to get hold of a very valuable, heavy, chunky gent's gold bracelet, but had come under suspicion early in the game and the police had been called.

Before he knew what was happening, eager young PC Ian Crutchley had arrived in the shop and with the description that had been given made a beeline for the feller, who then panicked and, as discreetly as he could, had pulled the bracelet from his pocket and stuffed it into his mouth.

As the constable closed in on the young thief his panic level had increased so much that he had made the decision to swallow the huge bracelet. He admitted afterwards that he just didn't know how he had managed it, as the bracelet was simply massive. He choked as he got it past his throat and could feel it slowly moving down his gullet into his stomach.

The lad was moved about between police station, court and hospital, and a close watch was kept on him over the next few days in the hope that he might pass the bracelet out naturally, although the thought still brings tears to my eyes (those sharp chunky bits, ooh!).

The bracelet had decided to 'stay put' in his stomach, so later in hospital it was decided for his own safety that it would have to be removed by surgical operation, which was carried out successfully and the bracelet returned to the shop after a clean and polish.

The lad in question turned out to be a very likeable young man, who had had his life ruined by drugs. The case was a feature on the TV news and in the national newspapers at the time. I often wondered who eventually purchased the bracelet and if they knew of its travels.

My time at Hanley was strangely like a breath of fresh air. I'd loved CID work, but maybe I had got a little out of touch with all the other things that were going on and this was an opportunity to become involved again. There was, of course, a mountain of paperwork each day, and no one would have said much if I'd just stayed in my office keeping on top of that, but I really had to admit to myself that I'd missed going out on patrol as I used to do all those years ago when I was a PC. I took every opportunity to get out, either walking on the town centre or driving in the white, Ford Escort 'inspector's car'.

The morale on the shift seemed to be boosted by my attitude and maybe it was my imagination, but the long faces and morose attitudes were replaced by smiles, camaraderie, pranks and good humour. With the increase in morale came the bonus of a higher standard of work and a much bigger input. The shift would usually manage a pint together in the police bar, which was on the top floor of Hanley nick, after noons, and even sometimes after earlies at the Smithfield pub over the road.

We arranged a curry club and would all chip in to pay for the ingredients, which would be cooked once a month, whilst on nights, by the shift 'curry officer', PC Pete Nixon. The smell of curry would start to waft through the building from about 5 a.m. and we would tuck in after finishing duty at 6 a.m. We always had to put some of the curry to one side for anyone who had to work over on a job. We would take it in turns to do the dishes (me included), and the earlies shift, who took over from us, could not believe that we were eating curry at 6 a.m.

Another old drug squad friend, John Wowra, had now joined the shift when the complement of sergeants was increased to three. John mostly worked downstairs in the cell block as custody sergeant, booking the prisoners in. We often laughed about some of the drugs raids we'd been on together and couldn't believe how many of the same old faces were still being dragged in for the same old things even after all those years.

PC Phill Barnes was another character on the shift; I had known Phill almost forever. He had joined the cadets around the same time as I had and then was posted to Stoke the same as I had been. Phill now worked in the control room at Hanley on my shift.

The control room was the nerve centre for every incident. Years ago the control rooms at police stations tended to be part of the enquiry office, where members of the public came in, but for some time now they had mostly been placed in a large room completely away from the enquiry office.

There was a large foyer at Hanley Police Station where people would wait to be attended to at the enquiry desk. One busy Friday evening Phill answered a call in the control room to the effect that 'there was a *big fight* going on in the *foyer*'.

Phill, always very protective of his younger colleagues, and presuming that the fight must have involved his fellow shift members, pulled out his phone plug and raced off downstairs, bursting out into the foyer with fists clenched, and his telephone headset and mouth piece still fitted onto his balding pate with the wire and plug trailing behind him.

An elderly gent, who was standing at the counter waiting to produce his driving licence for inspection, swirled around at the sudden commotion and the sight of this wide-eyed manic demon complete with trailing wires, who for no reason at all shouted, 'What's going on?', then disappeared as quickly as he had arrived.

The call had been from the *Foyer Nightclub* in the town centre.

Charlie Martin was another PC who worked as a controller along with Phill on the shift and I had known Charlie even longer, as, although a few years older than me, we had attended the same secondary modern school. Charlie, an ex-CID man was unflappable and always knew exactly what was going on.

A civilian, Dennis, worked as a controller on the shift, and it would be the job of these three to log all incidents coming into the station onto 'The Box'. Everything had to be entered onto 'The Box' and a decision made as to what action should be taken and who to send to deal with the incident, depending on who was still available.

The sheer volume of jobs was massive. We could have as many as over one hundred incidents 'open' (being dealt with/not finalised) and if we had whittled it down to thirty, which had to be passed on to the shift following us, we had done quite well. There would often be occasions when everyone on the shift was committed on one or more jobs and I would attend and deal with incidents myself.

The variety of different incidents was phenomenal. As always throughout my police service, there were 'sudden deaths' (still called form 12s) and, as shift inspector, I had to visit most such incidents if there was any hint of anything a little unusual. Whilst on nights one time, I was requested to visit Galloway Road on the Bentilee council estate where a PC was dealing with a form 12 following a report of a horrible smell and an infestation of flies. The constable had broken into the downstairs flat and had been almost overwhelmed by an enormous swarm of flies inside. He directed me through to the downstairs toilet of the flat with both of us wearing gloves, raincoats and a towel around our heads as fly protection, despite the warm summer weather.

The smell was vomit-inducing and the barely recognisable, rotting liquefied corpse of the tenant of the flat was lying on the floor of the toilet. The man had clearly been dead for a long time and it seemed cruel that living so close to other people, it had taken so long before anyone became concerned. The remains of the body could

John Pye

actually be seen to be moving, caused by the writhing of the thousands of maggots.

On arriving home that morning, my clothes smelled so strongly that I had to remove almost everything and dump it all outside the back door. Fortunately the neighbours hadn't got up and didn't manage to catch a glimpse of me stripping off. I even emptied several flies out from my pockets. As always, such matters had to be looked into carefully and any hint of something suspicious would require CID involvement.

The most heartbreaking of incidents that I ever had to attend were those that we have all come to know as 'cot deaths'. It really didn't matter how hardened you had become through years of police work, the sight of a tiny lifeless baby would always be something that would live in your memory.

Of course such deaths were, and still are, the subject of intensive debate, and many people have dedicated their lives to uncovering some factor that could be a primary cause. Great care and detail went into investigation into cot deaths and would entail a routine sending of mattress, bedding and any other everyday items away to the forensic science laboratory in the hope of finding something that might reveal a cause.

The one factor that I found present in every home cot death that I had attended was that there were smokers living in the house. I always made a point of including this in my report.

Hanley still covered some of the same deprived areas that it had done when I worked on the CID back in the early 1980s. There were several large council estates where alcoholism and drug abuse were rife. When I had first joined, many of the deaths resulted from industrial diseases caused by the pottery or mining industries, but now this seemed to be overtaken by alcohol and drug-related deaths.

I had other duties that I had to see to, apart from the running of the shift. I was the appointed 'diseases of animals' officer for Hanley. Maybe they gave me this job when they discovered I had been at Biddulph, but fortunately at Hanley this was one job that, for a change, never seemed to create much extra work for me.

As an inspector, I was occasionally called upon to be in charge of an identification parade, which the CID were holding. It seemed fortunate that no one had heard of my past experience in this particular field. Everything was done very precisely and properly with specially printed little booklets. It looked easy, but then again the part I played now *was* easy. I just had to appear at the last minute expecting everything to be done... All that hard work trudging around and ringing up to get the stooges - that was where the work was.

I knew that the shift morale was now good when I came on for night duty one evening and discovered that on almost every door inside the station was pinned a photocopy of a photograph of me; the photograph was one that had been taken back in 1978 when I was on the drug squad, and had been included in my personal file for 'staff appraisal' purposes.

The picture was truly hilarious and showed me with shoulder length hair and a pancho moustache. I was wearing a jacket and tie, and recall that my shirt 'very tastefully' included a facsimile of human faces. I remembered that I had purchased two such shirts from a local drug dealer, who must have had a sideline in shirts. The station was in uproar at the sight of these photos and I even found one hanging in the toilets. Enquiries pointed towards Simon, who had been given the photo when the police photographic studio was having a clear-out.

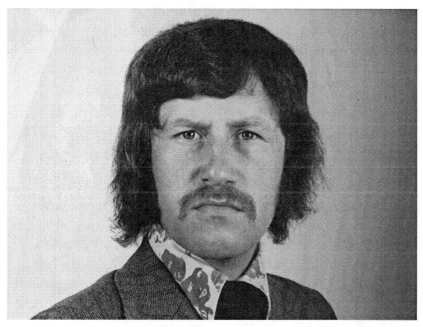

That old 'cringe making' Drug Squad photo (dig that shirt!)

It was whilst I was on duty one evening that the tale of the vampire came back to haunt me yet again. Some twenty years after it had happened I received a phone call from ATV studios telling me that their *Friday Night Live* programme was shortly to run a programme on Dracula and vampires. The lady told me that they had got together a lot of people from all walks of life who believed in vampires, professed to be one or had been attacked by one, and that they'd found out about my case and wanted me as a guest to talk about the incident.

Old Chief Constable Arthur Rees was no longer there to point me in the right direction and I was told by headquarters that I could appear on the show if I wished. However, I decided that the TV appearance would simply not be worth the huge amount of mickey-taking that would undoubtedly follow and that any chance of further promotion following the appearance would be nil, so I declined. I watched the transmission a few months later and was relieved that I had made a good decision, as it consisted of several people dressed in black capes, a couple of self-professed witches and one man who claimed to have had to drive a stake through someone's heart. I felt that I had had a lucky escape.

* * * *

There were many hair-raising car chases whilst I was at Hanley, one involving a particularly nasty drug-dealing burglar, whom I knew only too well from the past. A report came in at 2 a.m. one morning that a stolen car he was believed to be using, together with two other well known crooks, had been involved in a burglary in the nearby town of Leek; knowing that he had a girlfriend in a flat on the outskirts of Hanley town, I decided to have a look that way. As I drove along towards the house I saw that, sure enough, there was the car with its lights on outside the flat. On seeing me, the driver sped off with both back doors banging shut as he did. There then followed a manic piece of driving as he careered back and forth up various side streets and back alleys, which were barely wide enough to get a car along.

He smashed dustbins out of the way and ran over a parked moped as I followed him as best I could throughout his crazy journey, trying my utmost not to damage my police car. I could clearly see the two other heads in the back of the car being flung about as the car bounced from one wall to another. In a dangerous act of desperation he eventually tried to shake me off by screaming into an alleyway that was too narrow to get the car down and accelerating into the gap with sparks flying and door handles and wing mirrors being ripped off. I took another route as I saw him disappear through the gap, knowing that he would have to emerge on to the road that I had decided to take.

As I pulled around into Hobson Street, there he was in front of me, but not heading away from me, heading towards me and clearly intent on ramming me. The street was narrow and had parked cars either side. I had done my best to radio the situation in and could hear the radio telling me that other patrols were closing in. I was desperate to retain my record of never damaging a police car, and jammed the car into reverse and reversed away as the stolen car nosed right up to my bumper. My car whined as the revs increased the speed to around 30 mph in reverse.

I was running out of road and decided that I would have to brace for the impact, but as I slowed down, so did he. I came to a stop. He gave my front bumper a frustrated nudge then sped off, himself in reverse, as though to show me, 'I can do that as well'.

It was now roles reversed in the truest sense as I drove after him, but he hadn't quite got the hang of the high-speed reversing and as he neared the end of the street, he corrected his steering a little too much and smashed the already battered car into two parked cars, jamming it firmly in between a house and one of the cars. The driver's door sprung open and he was away like a hare, leaving his two partners in crime wedged into their handleless, battered metal box. I arrested the two without a struggle, and he was arrested shortly afterwards, hiding under the floorboards in his girlfriend's flat. The car contained the Royal Doulton figures that had been taken during the Leek burglary.

* * * *

The first Gulf War was now in full swing and some recently retired members of the military forces were being recalled to duty. They would come into the police station with their 'Recall to Duty' papers, which the enquiry office staff would have to process, and they would then be issued with a 'travel warrant' giving them free rail journeys to wherever they had to report. There weren't that many, but I told the enquiry office staff to let me know when someone did come in.

It wasn't many days before I got such a call, and promptly went to deal with the ex-sailor standing at the counter with his papers, which he handed to me. I took the papers away and photocopied them all, before completing the travel warrant and handing all the documents back. I wished him well and he went on his way whilst I Tippexed out all his details from my copies and photocopied them once again. I now had a seemingly pristine and unused set of Recall to Duty papers.

As the news started to grow about the imminent hostilities, young Simon, the ex-navy PC of blue brick fame, had made a joking comment hoping that he wasn't recalled to duty.

Simon's details were carefully and authentically typed on to the blank form and a discrete enquiry to the personnel department had provided me with his old service number.

A faked recorded delivery envelope addressed to 'The Officer In Charge, Hanley Police Station', together with an accompanying note from the superintendent, who had found the 'reverse Midas touch' so amusing and was keenly 'in on the ruse', topped the whole thing off perfectly. At the 6 a.m. duty parade the following morning, the room was packed, everyone except Simon knew, and as Sergeant John Bowers and I went through the morning's paperwork and dished out various jobs to be done and handed out mail, the moment arrived.

"Oh, one for you here, Simon," I said. "It's come from the War Office straight to the Super, he's put a note on saying he wants to see you as soon as he gets in."

I handed the bundle on and it was passed down the table to Simon, who was already a picture of puzzlement. Everyone else in the room was talking to each other and shuffling paperwork about, trying to look uninterested. Simon suddenly stood up from his chair, holding the papers in his right hand and pointing towards them with his left, his mouth was wide open, but no noise could be heard. Everyone carried on with what they were doing as though Simon didn't exist.

Eventually Simon managed a:

"But, but, but, but..."

"Someone started a moped up?" said John Bowers as he puffed on his cigarette.

"I've been called..." Simon gasped.

"Call PC Dudman!" said someone, and a titter went around the room.

"Whatever is the matter, Simon?" I quizzed in my most deceitful of voices.

"They've called me back to duty for the Gulf War," Simon finally managed to blurt out.

"Oh, dear, that's annoying," I said, "I hope they give us someone to replace you. Right! Parade's finished now everyone. See you all later on."

There was a hint of stifled laughter, which rose slightly over the rumble of the chairs being dragged as the shift all stood up and went off to their patrols and other duties.

"You stay in and get on with your reports this morning, Simon," I said, "you'll be needing to get rid of all that paperwork before you go, and remember that you've got to see the Super."

"But, Inspector, but, but..."

I left the room feeling a little guilty.

"You can't leave him too long like that, Sir," said young policewoman, Vicky, "he might string himself up."

"I know, Vicky," I said. "The Super wanted to be in on it, so we'll try to keep Simon alive until he arrives."

Fortunately the Super was early that morning and was all ears to see how the 'call-up' had gone. He had difficulty stifling his laughter as I related Simon's moped impression.

"Right, get him to come up then, before he tops himself, wouldn't look very good at headquarters if he did and they knew I was in on it."

"Okay, Sir," I replied, as I hurried off to get Simon, who I found in almost the same position still clutching the papers in his right hand.

"Right, Simon, the Super's ready to see you now," I said as a silent Simon followed me with his chin on his chest.

I knocked on the door and walked in, closely followed by a shell-shocked Simon, and I was also aware that several other shift members seemed to be lurking about in strategic positions in the corridor.

"Right then, Simon," greeted the Super, "what's all this recall to duty business?"

Simon stretched out his right hand holding the bundle of paperwork and with a gaping mouth could yet again only utter:

"But, but..."

A shuffling sound could be heard outside the boss's door, as the Super spoke to Simon.

"Do I take it then, Simon, that you don't want to go?"

"Well, no, Sir!" came back Simon's first intelligible sentence for quite some time.

"Well, Simon, I'll tell you what, don't bother, you stay here at Hanley, but no more blue brick enquiries."

"Sir, if you can sort this, I'll go down and re-lay the whole of Havelock Place Shelton with blue bricks in my spare time, but have you got the power to get around this? I mean it's from the War Office?"

"Oh, it's surprising what superintendents can do, Simon. Oh, and inspectors."

The Super's voice was beginning to crack as his eyes crinkled up. Giggles could be heard from the corridor and I had now lost it all together. A wave of recognition coupled with relief swept across Simon's face as the truth dawned upon him.

"Sir!" Simon turned directly to face me. "Permission to call you a bastard?"

"Permission granted," I replied.

"*Bastard!*" Simon shouted out in a volume probably only ever heard before in the cell block.

The giggles outside had now turned to full laughter as Simon, who was also laughing for the first time that morning, turned to the Super and spoke in a quiet voice.

"Permission to call you a bastard as well, Sir?"

"Yes, go on, Simon! You deserve it, but not so loud this time."

"Bastard... Sir!" Simon whispered respectfully.

The photograph had been avenged!

* * * *

In 1991 I became eligible for the Police Long Service and Good Conduct Medal. It was certainly a fact that I had managed the twenty-two years as a regular officer that counted as the long service, -but as for the good conduct part, -well sometimes.

I received my medal along with other good friends who had joined with me as cadets, including David Hulse and my old schoolfriend, Ian Bruckshaw; the three of us had started out on our careers on the very same day back in the winter of 1966. Also there was my buddy from Ryton,

Eric Cartwright, and my other two Ryton chums, Graham Woodward and Terry Lockett, alias the demon boot-buller.

I proudly accepted my medal from the deputy chief constable, together with the blue and white tunic ribbon to be worn on my uniform, just like the one I recalled seeing on Sergeant Haywood's uniform so many years ago at Newcastle Police Station on the day of my cadet's entrance examination. Where the hell had all those years gone?

It was around this time that, as an inspector, I was appointed as the investigating officer in an allegation made by a member of the public against the two police officers who had searched his house. The case culminated in a policewoman being sentenced at Crown court to eighteen months' imprisonment, for the theft of five hundred pounds.

This case was closely followed by another, which was concerned with corruption in another police force, and I was to spend almost two years travelling between my home in Newcastle-under-Lyme to Stafford, Burton-on-Trent and other parts of the country, including frequent train journeys down to Scotland Yard.

These two investigations were both distasteful; there was nothing very memorable or enjoyable about them. It was during the latter inquiry that I was appointed detective inspector in charge of Hanley CID and told that I would take up this post when the inquiry was finalised.

I'd completed almost twenty-seven years with the Staffordshire Police and had had the most amazing time, but the job was not the same; so many things had changed.

My back problems had reoccurred. I was now looking at a further back operation and was, therefore, not surprised when I was called to headquarters to be examined by the police surgeon. This was not a police surgeon like the one who visits police stations to take blood samples from breath test drivers, but one employed by the police to examine officers whose health is suspect and to see if they are still fit to carry out their duties.

I'd seen so many changes over the years in the job, so many different government reports into policing, from The Edmund Davies Report back in the seventies, which had given us much better pay and conditions, to the sweeping changes brought in with the introduction of the 1984 Police and Criminal Evidence Act, which had altered so many police powers and the ways in which we went about our everyday duties.

The Crown prosecution service had been introduced, and this had taken the 'final decision' whether to prosecute offenders or not, from the police.

The old, 'you are not obliged to say anything' police caution had gone, only to be replaced by an even longer version; all things that were 'burned' indelibly into my brain.

A large and costly inquiry by Sir Patrick Sheehy had suggested a wealth of changes across the board to rank structures and management in general, thankfully very little of this was implemented.

So much additional and unnecessary paperwork seemed to have crept into the job since I first started way back in 1967. All those familiar forms, each one with its own identification number, were gone and had been replaced by reams and reams of multicoloured, multipaged documents, each one having very slightly different wording and designed to be sent to a very slightly different department.

All manner of squads, units and departments had started springing up, and everybody seemed to be specialising in some small aspect of the job rather than knowing how to deal with an incident from start to finish. Dozens of new 'desk jobs' had been created to keep up with political correctness and appease minority groups.

There were some good people still there doing the job, some of them had made it to the very top.

Geoff White (Whitey) was eventually to become 'God's Deputy' himself, when he was appointed detective chief superintendent in charge of Staffordshire CID. I wonder if any junior officers had hidden from him in an office cupboard?

Whitey was eventually awarded the ultimate police decoration of 'The Queens Police Medal' and retired in 2007 - he probably wears underpants most days now!

There were a few others from around my era who were still there. Ian, my old schoolfriend whom I met on Stoke railway station so many years ago when we were a couple of giggling youngsters about to become police cadets, was to become a sergeant and, upon retiring, would take up a job as a civilian in the coroner's office at Hartshill. He must have loved those form 12s! I still bear the scar from our foggy morning's car crash.

Roger, my other old schoolfriend, who had the misfortune to be posted to Burton-on-Trent as a nineteen-year-old PC and, consequently, had been cut off from his North Staffs' mates, eventually retired, and a chance meeting with him on my last inquiry whilst at Burton one day meant that we would regularly meet again in our retirement.

John Bowers, my other old cadet mate, who kindly roped me so tightly to that stretcher twenty-six years before, would retire as a sergeant.

It was 3.30 p.m. on the afternoon of Friday, 29th September 1993, when I walked into the police surgeon's room at headquarters. He had all my medical history in front of him.

I wasn't surprised when after examining me, he said:

"I'm going to have to retire you, Inspector, how do you feel about that?"

I shrugged.

"That's life, thanks, Doc."

I shook his hand and walked out. He wouldn't have noticed a slight glisten in my eyes as I made my way back along the corridors of power over the marcasite vinyl floor tiles. They'd never had khaki-coloured lino here.

As I walked across the car park, I passed a couple of fresh faced young PCs each with a bundle of law notes under his arm, and heard one say to the other:

"What you doing tonight, Reg?"

"Don't know yet, Reg," was the reply. "Perhaps go for a beer when I've done my homework."

I looked over at them and smiled to myself. They didn't even know who I was and they had even less idea why they were both calling each other Reg...

I got into my car and drove down towards the main road, passing by the white police dog training jumps and ladders that had been a feature of the front of Staffordshire Police Headquarters forever, and smiled to myself as I recalled seeing them for the first time almost twenty-seven years before, little realising that their days were also numbered with the removal of the force's regional dog training status.

As I turned right onto the A34 towards Stafford town, I instinctively cast a thought back to my three friends who had lost their lives in that tragic road accident so many years ago when I was on a driving course. I drove slowly back towards the city, passing through Stone as I went - more memories from the past. Just a hint of a tear dampened my cheek as I cruised along, finding it quite hard to come to terms with the fact that I was no longer 'in the job' and that I wouldn't be making it back to Hanley.

I was jolted back into concentration as a patrol car zoomed past me with lights blazing and claxon blaring. Something was happening somewhere, but then again, it always was, it always would be.

As I neared home, my pager started to buzz in my pocket. I pulled onto a lay-by and read the message. It was Whitey's number…

REG… We've just had a good result on a job… George & Dragon for a pint, if you can make it… REG!

Why not?

ISBN 142517599-6

9 781425 175993